THE SOCIAL CONSTITUTION

In *The Social Constitution*, Whitney Taylor examines the conditions under which new constitutional rights become meaningful and institutionalized. Taylor introduces the concept of "embedding" constitutional law to clarify how particular visions of law come to take root both socially and legally. Constitutional embedding can occur through legal mobilization, as citizens understand the law in their own way and make legal claims – or choose not to – on the basis of that understanding, and as judges decide whether and how to respond to legal claims. These interactions ultimately construct the content and strength of the constitutional order. Taylor draws on more than a year of fieldwork across Colombia and multiple sources of data, including semi-structured interviews, original surveys, legal documents, and participation observation. This title is part of the Flip it Open Programme and may also be available Open Access. Check our website Cambridge Core for details.

WHITNEY K. TAYLOR is Assistant Professor of Political Science at San Francisco State University. Her research focuses on the intersection of rights, law, and contentious politics.

CAMBRIDGE STUDIES IN LAW AND SOCIETY

Founded in 1997, Cambridge Studies in Law and Society is a hub for leading scholarship in socio-legal studies. Located at the intersection of law, the humanities, and the social sciences, it publishes empirically innovative and theoretically sophisticated work on law's manifestations in everyday life: from discourses to practices, and from institutions to cultures. The series editors have longstanding expertise in the interdisciplinary study of law, and welcome contributions that place legal phenomena in national, comparative, or international perspective. Series authors come from a range of disciplines, including anthropology, history, law, literature, political science, and sociology.

A list of books in the series can be found at the back of this book.

CAMBRIDGE
STUDIES IN
LAW AND SOCIETY

THE SOCIAL CONSTITUTION

Embedding Social Rights Through Legal Mobilization

Whitney K. Taylor

San Francisco State University

CAMBRIDGE
UNIVERSITY PRESS

CAMBRIDGE
UNIVERSITY PRESS

Shaftesbury Road, Cambridge CB2 8EA, United Kingdom

One Liberty Plaza, 20th Floor, New York, NY 10006, USA

477 Williamstown Road, Port Melbourne, VIC 3207, Australia

314–321, 3rd Floor, Plot 3, Splendor Forum, Jasola District Centre, New Delhi – 110025, India

103 Penang Road, #05–06/07, Visioncrest Commercial, Singapore 238467

Cambridge University Press is part of Cambridge University Press & Assessment, a department of the University of Cambridge.

We share the University's mission to contribute to society through the pursuit of education, learning and research at the highest international levels of excellence.

www.cambridge.org
Information on this title: www.cambridge.org/9781009367769

DOI: 10.1017/9781009367738

First published 2023

A catalogue record for this publication is available from the British Library

A Cataloging-in-Publication data record for this book is available from the Library of Congress

ISBN 978-1-009-36776-9 Hardback

CONTENTS

FIGURES

TABLES

ACKNOWLEDGMENTS

The book you are now reading was once my PhD dissertation. It has been substantially revised and substantially improved, thanks to the comments, critiques, and advice of many, many individuals.

First and foremost, a heartfelt thank you to the wonderful people I worked with and asked questions of in both Colombia and South Africa, including Pastora and Leo, who welcomed me into their home; Zeller Álvarez and his team of student-enumerators, who made survey work fly by; "Daniela," who encouraged me to think more critically about the dualities and contradictions present in Colombian life and law; and the members of Abahlali baseMjondolo, who invited me to their neighborhoods, meetings, and funerals, and reminded me of the awesome power of people who follow their convictions. Thank you to all of the people who I formally interviewed and surveyed, as well as to all of those who chatted with me over tintos, in taxis, and while waiting in line.

I am immensely grateful for the support and encouragement of so many mentors, colleagues, and friends throughout my time in graduate school and as I began my career as an assistant professor. Thank you to my dissertation committee – Ken Roberts, Matt Evangelista, Sid Tarrow, Lisa Hilbink, and Aziz Rana – who have been, without exception, generous with their time and unwavering in their support. Ken's ability to take your loose series of thoughts and pull out something that is not only intelligible but exactly what you meant is unrivalled and has benefitted just about every comparativist at Cornell. I am grateful also for Ken's guidance in connecting my work to broader debates in comparative politics. Matt reads more carefully than anyone I have ever met – as far as I can tell, he has never missed a typo. His engagement with my work has always been thoughtful and thought-provoking. Sid's high standards pushed me to continually strive to be more precise in my claims and more rigorous in my methods. He models what it looks like to generously support colleagues and to cultivate networks across disciplines and continents. Thank you also to Lisa, who has always believed in me and who has never shied away from telling me when I could do better. Her expertise and encouragement have been invaluable. Aziz's excitement, curiosity, and ability to see the hidden linkages between events, texts, and ideas have inspired me, and discussions with him dramatically enhanced the project.

Thank you to Jamila Michener. She provided sharp, thoughtful feedback throughout the development of the project and has always been quick with a smile and supportive words. Her commitment to amplifying the voices of those who are often overlooked in political science and to unearthing the real-life consequences of what may seem like technical policy choices make her a scholar-citizen whom I hope to emulate. Thank you also to Joe Margulies, who read early drafts of chapters and has offered a clear example of what it means to be an engaged teacher, researcher, and community member.

I cannot thank my graduate school friends and colleagues enough. I was blessed with a wonderful cohort, made up of people who are both intellectually curious and genuinely nice. In particular, I am grateful to have taken classes and developed projects with David De Micheli and Michael Allen. David and Michael have been not only great friends, but also amazing teachers. Liz Acorn was the first person I met in Ithaca. Her thoughtfulness and generosity are qualities I deeply admire. She also provided a much-needed example of how to take work seriously but not get lost in the process. Janice Gallagher's enthusiasm for life and commitment to telling the stories of the people who comprise political struggles (and, more importantly, her commitment to those people and those struggles) has inspired me throughout graduate school. Our conversations across Ithaca, New Orleans, Mexico City, Medellín, and New York City have both enriched and grounded my research. I was lucky that my fieldwork in Colombia partially overlapped with Bridget Marchesi's. Her critical eye and pragmatic approach greatly improved my project. Thank you also to Martha Wilfahrt and Natalie Letsa, who offered advice and friendship, and shared tips and materials for navigating the job market and the first few years on the tenure track. Janet Smith has been a consummate cheerleader and friend, reminding me to take breaks and enjoy the best of Ithaca all year round (and later the Bay Area, though the case for enjoying the Bay all year round is a much easier one to make, of course). Emilio Lehoucq made sure that I not only worked during my fieldwork in Bogotá, but also had fun. He has read almost everything I've ever written and has provided timely, thoughtful feedback and encouragement, no matter how busy he was.

I lucked out once again with the wonderful colleagues I have at San Francisco State University. Each one reached out to me to help ease the transition from graduate school to being an assistant professor, and they all went above and beyond in their efforts to support me as a teacher, a researcher, and a person. On hikes with Wendy Salkin (and our dogs, Jackson and Birdie), I honed the arguments in this book. Her curiosity and drive to suss out the roots and the implications of each and every claim, as well as her reminders to be precise with language, certainly made this book stronger. Runs with Nicole Watts, walks with Rebecca Eissler, and beers with Chris Longenecker and Kurt Nutting helped me to stay grounded while pushing this project forward.

In 2020, I was given the opportunity to participate in the Cambridge Studies in Law and Society Early Career Book Workshop, alongside Toby Goldbach. The workshop, organized by Rachel Stern, Mark Massoud, and Jens Meierhenrich, came at just the right time and provided both the push and direction I needed to transform my dissertation into a viable book project. Along with Rachel, Mark, and Jens, Dan Brinks and Jamie Rowen offered careful guidance and excellent feedback on the project.

The project also benefitted from comments offered at conferences and workshops. I am grateful to have been able to present parts of this book at various American Political Science Association annual meetings, Law and Society Association annual meetings, Latin American Studies Association annual meetings, and the Socio-Legal Studies Association conference, as well as the Global Law and Politics Workshop (organized by Rachel Cichowksi, Dan Brinks, Jeff Staton, and Kyle Shen) and the Cultivating Networks and Innovative Scholarship in Law and Courts conference (organized by Monica Lineberger, Alyx Mark, and Abby Matthews). Comments from Karen Alter, Celeste Arrington, Dan Brinks, Jenn Earl, Chuck Epp, Diana Fu, Janice Gallagher, Mary Gallagher, Esteban Hoyos, Alex Huneeus, Filiz Kahraman, Gabi Kruks-Wisner, Ke Li, Michael McCann, Angela Páez, Wendy Salkin, Nick Smith, Kira Tait, Sid Tarrow, Lisa Vanhala, Andrea Vilán, Susan Whiting, and many others helped me develop this book into its strongest form. Lisa Vanhala, in particular, has been a tireless supporter of this project and all my research.

Luis Robayo captured a moment that perfectly encapsulates the argument you will find this book, and I am so grateful for his support in using that photograph as the cover image.

Thank you also to my family: Mom, Dad, Leah, Jackson, Filbert, and Hazelnut. Your love and support mean the world to me.

Acknowledgments sections often include a line or two suggesting that the book is for family, friends, or interlocutors. I couldn't have done it without the gracious help of everyone listed above, but this book was my dream; it's for me.

Finally, this book relies on some of the same interview and survey data that appears in previously published articles, including my 2018 *Law & Society Review* article, "Ambivalent Legal Mobilization: Perceptions of Justice and the Use of the Tutela in Colombia," my 2020 *Comparative Political Studies* article, "On the Social Construction of Legal Grievances: Evidence from Colombia and South Africa," my 2020 *Comparative Politics* article, "Constitutional Rights and Social Welfare: Exploring Claims-Making Practices in Post-Apartheid South Africa," and my forthcoming *Human Rights Quarterly* article, "Judicial Agency and the Adjudication of Social Rights." Each of these articles, however, advances a distinct argument from the core argument of the book.

Map of Colombia with Departments
Source: Wikimedia commons, Camilo Sanchez

CHAPTER ONE

INTRODUCTION

The Social Constitution

A man said to the universe:
"Sir, I exist!"
"However," replied the universe,
"The fact has not created in me
A sense of obligation."

Stephen Crane

This is a book about how new constitutional rights provisions become meaningful in everyday life, moving from parchment promises to constraining institutions. It focuses on the embedding of "social constitutionalism," by which I mean the constitutional recognition of rights to social goods, like health, housing, and social security, and the empowerment of courts to hear claims to those rights. Around the world, written constitutions have become ubiquitous. In fact, Canada, Israel, New Zealand, San Marino, Saudi Arabia, and the United Kingdom are the only states that do not have such a document.[1] Written constitutions set out the parameters of the contemporary nation-state: who belongs to the nation and who does not, the organization and commitments of the state, and the rights and duties of citizens. While the number of rights – especially social rights (see Figure 1.1) – included in constitutional texts has increased steadily over time, rights realizations in practice have lagged behind those promises, particularly when they involve already marginalized individuals and groups.

[1] These countries all have some sort of "basic law," set of customs, and/or collection of constitutional statutes rather than a single, unifying document.

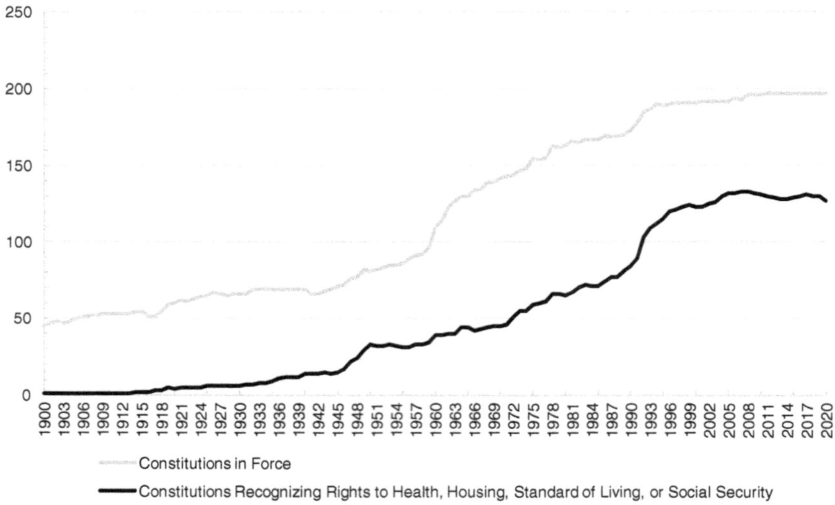

Figure 1.1 Constitutions and social rights over time (Elkins and Ginsburg 2021). Importantly, these data include unwritten or uncodified constitutions, as well as written constitutions.

The transition from an unequal society to one based on a sense of obligation regarding the needs of all citizens is not a natural or inevitable one, and powerful actors often try to thwart this process. Yet, this seemingly impossible situation has been met time and time again with obstinate contestation, with people who refuse to accept this lack of recognition, with people who imagine better futures and work toward those futures tirelessly. Though the story involves macrohistorical institutional change by way of significant revisions to the core documents that outline the parameters of the state, it begins and ends with individuals. Individuals – both those who advance rights claims and the judges who respond to them – together construct and reconstruct notions of obligation, specifically the conditions under which the state has a duty to provide for the social needs of its citizens. In this book, I present a detailed study of the Colombian experiment with social constitutionalism, uncovering how new written constitutions and constitutional rights can come to be more than simply words on paper and instead fundamentally shape both social and legal life. The adoption and embedding of social constitutionalism account for the expansion of access to social goods throughout much of the world. And in a global climate defined by democratic backsliding and backlash against progressive constitutional provisions,[2] understanding the conditions under which the justiciability of social rights becomes a taken for granted aspect of political life and a widely accepted "rule of the game" becomes even more important.

Before moving forward, however, I want to offer an example of how social constitutionalism plays out in people's lives. One Sunday afternoon in April 2017, a woman named Teresa[3] told me about her life in Agua Blanca, a densely populated district on the outskirts of Cali, Colombia. Teresa operated an informal sewing business out of her living room, and weathered as best she could the interrelated threats of violence, drugs, and economic insecurity that swirled around her. Social service provision in Agua Blanca is sorely lacking, and accessing doctors and hospitals is particularly difficult. The state's presence appears to be limited to police officers, who – according to residents of the neighborhood – punch, kick, and shoot first, asking questions later, if at all. Teresa told me about how, after she developed a problem with her trachea that made it difficult for her to breathe, she attempted but failed to attain what she deemed to be adequate medical attention. In the midst of this difficult situation, what did she do? She turned to the courts, filing a claim to the constitutional right to health through a legal procedure called the *acción de tutela*, because, as she put it, "everything happens through the tutela."[4]

Teresa's assessment is only a slight exaggeration. In fact, Colombians have filed almost eight million legal claims to their constitutional rights through tutelas since 1992, the year the tutela was introduced (see Figure 1.2). The *acción de tutela* is a legal procedure that allows individuals to make immediate claims to their "fundamental" constitutional rights before any judge in the country and does not require the service of a lawyer.[5] This has occurred in a country in which the majority of citizens routinely express little to no confidence in judges (on average just over two-thirds of Colombians, according

2 See, e.g., Bermeo (2016) and Levitsky and Ziblatt (2018).

3 A note on names: I refer to those who I interviewed in whatever way they felt most comfortable with – for most of those who I met in their professional capacity, this means using their full names; for those interviewees who I describe as "everyday Colombians" (i.e., people like Teresa who do not work in the formal legal sphere or academia), this entailed using a placeholder first name to protect their anonymity.

4 Interview conducted April 9, 2017 in Cali, Colombia. "Todo funciona a medida de tutelas."

5 This legal mechanism is comparable to the *amparo* found throughout Latin America (Brewer-Carías 2009).

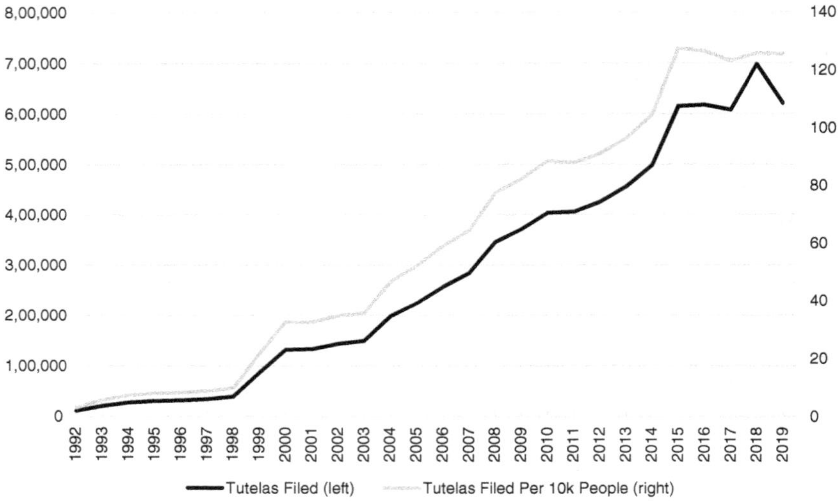

Figure 1.2 Tutela claims filed, 1992–2019.
Interview conducted April 9, 2017 in Cali, Colombia. "Todo funciona a medida de tutelas."

to surveys fielded between 1996 and 2020).[6] Even more surprisingly, actors generally not associated with constitutional rights talk, such as doctors, pharmaceutical companies, and insurance companies, openly encouraged citizens to file these claims. Far from simply being words on paper, the 1991 Constitution has come to be an important part of the social fabric of everyday life in Colombia.

How exactly did this occur? How did shifts in ideas about the law translate into substantive tools that allow citizens to make claims on the state, reshaping access to social goods in Colombia and elsewhere? More generally, how do constitutional rights provisions become embedded in social and legal life? These are the questions that this book tackles.

1.1 THE GLOBAL EMERGENCE OF SOCIAL CONSTITUTIONALISM

According to conventional wisdom, citizens pursue social welfare claims by voting, lobbying, and pressuring elected officials. The story

[6] Latinobarometro surveys show that, on average, 68.7 percent of Colombians expressed "no confidence at all" or "little confidence" in the judiciary (compared to "a lot of confidence" and "some confidence") between 1996 and 2020.

goes that judiciaries are conservative bastions of the old order, perhaps valuable for advancing elite interests, but hardly useful for defending individual or group rights to social needs like healthcare, housing, and education. Further complicating the turn to law to advance access to social welfare goods, the content of social rights is often underspecified and subject to progressive realization and available resources at both the national and international levels. Yet, against the backdrop of expanding constitutional recognition of social rights, progressive and pro-status quo actors alike have engaged the law and courts in pursuit of their social and political goals. At times, social rights protections have even come to have binding influence, fundamentally reshaping the relationship between citizens and their state.

Historical accounts trace the development of legal systems and constitutional law to the changing nature of relationships within groups. Formalized law derives from informal rules fashioned to create or maintain social relationships, and this formalized law governs not just horizontal relationships between equals but also vertical relationships between rulers and those they rule. In other words, law emerged to regulate the behavior of members of a political community, limiting the relative power of leaders through a system that exchanges protection (from internal repression and external threat) for resources in the form of taxes (e.g., Tilly 1990), and developing standards to support economic growth (e.g., North and Weingast 1989). Others argue that those in power consent to constitutional regulation in order to avoid revolutionary overthrow (e.g., Acemoglu and Robinson 2006) or as a response to specific electoral pressure (e.g., Ginsburg 2003; Hirschl 2004). None of these accounts entail a need for the state to ensure, through universal legal principles or "rights," the basic welfare of its citizens. However, over time, understandings about the appropriate relationship between state and citizen have changed.

Specifically, the fourth wave of constitutionalism (Van Cott 2000) marks a significant change in the thinking underlying the relationship between the law, the state, and the citizenry. This form of constitutionalism, which was prominent in the 1980s, 1990s, and early 2000s, includes an expansive set of rights recognition, particularly social and economic rights, and, often, broad review powers for the judiciary.[7] Scholars have variously termed this model "new," "social,"

[7] None of this is to say that the recognition of social rights or declarations of state attention to citizen needs were necessarily absent before this period.

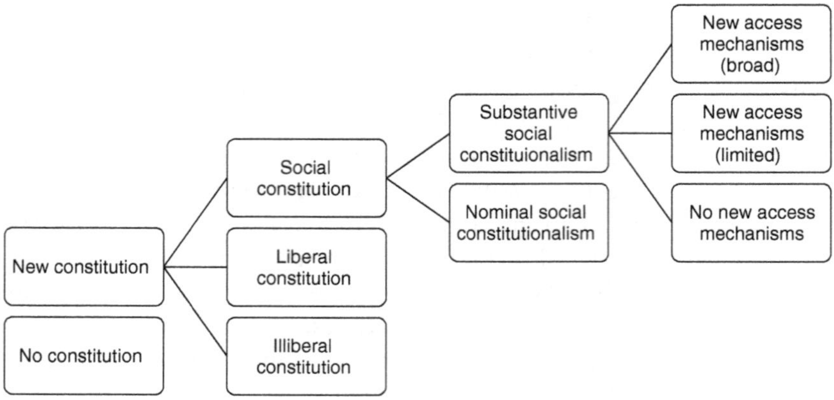

Figure 1.3 Differentiating types of constitutions and constitutionalism.

and "social rights" constitutionalism (Hilbink 2008; Angel-Cabo and Lovera 2014; Brinks and Forbath 2014; Brinks, Gauri, and Shen 2015). Throughout this book, I refer to this model of constitutionalism as "social constitutionalism."

Features of the social constitutionalist model had been around for decades – for instance, the Mexican Constitution of 1917 recognized a limited set of social rights and the International Covenant on Economic, Social, and Cultural Rights was drafted in 1966 – but these features only became commonplace in the 1980s and 1990s. In the social constitutionalist model, law is understood as an appropriate tool to address social ills, at least under certain conditions. At times, this shift in the function of constitutional law has been accompanied by the creation of mechanisms to allow citizens to claim their rights with relative ease.

Yet, this move to a more responsive vision of constitutional law was neither uniform nor inevitable. Between 1980 and 2000, seventy-nine countries – primarily in eastern Europe, Latin America, and sub-Saharan Africa – adopted new constitutions. While many of the resulting constitutions fit the social constitutionalist model, not all do. Figure 1.3 represents the set of choices related to the drafting of a constitution available in the context of a transition. In the midst of an effort to refound the state (whether substantively or simply rhetorically), the initial choice is whether or not to draft a new constitution at all. The resulting constitution – if drafted – could take a variety of forms, grouped broadly as social, liberal, or illiberal.

As described earlier, social constitutions recognize a wide range of rights that indicate state obligations to the needs of citizens and allow for the "judicialization of political disputes under the social rights rubric" (Brinks et al. 2015: 290). In contrast, liberal constitutions – the most common constitutional design choice in Europe and North America following the end of World War II – feature a circumscribed set of individual rights protections, offer few opportunities for contestation over social goods through the formal legal system, and tend to limit the ability of racial and ethnic minority groups to fully participate in political life (Ginsburg, Huq, and Versteeg 2018). Importantly, however, liberal constitutions do set out a vision of state–society relations in which the state is obligated to serve citizens' interests. The core differences lie in whose interests count and what those interests are understood to include. Illiberal constitutions even more narrowly serve to protect the interests of an elite class and refrain from setting out a view of state obligations to the broader citizenry.

Even after constitution drafters select the social constitutionalist model, they still have a variety of choices at hand. For one, they must decide whether to recognize social rights as guiding principles (sometimes described as directives for state action) or to recognize them as justiciable, as actively claimable and contestable. Figure 1.3 distinguishes between these two forms, referring to the former as "nominal" social constitutionalism and the latter as "substantive" social constitutionalism. If a constitution includes substantive social rights protections, then the resulting question is how easy or difficult is it for citizens to make claims to those rights? We can set off additional types of substantive social constitutionalism: ones that include new mechanisms that effectively reduce the barriers to accessing the judiciary and making legal claims in a broad or in a more limited sense, and one that relies on more longstanding or general mechanisms for legal claim-making. This book presents a detailed investigation of the 1991 Colombian Constitution, which is a substantive social constitution that includes newly created access mechanisms like the *acción de tutela*. While the tutela procedure was initially limited in scope, over time that scope broadened significantly.

1.2 COUNTERVAILING FORCES IN THE EARLY 1990S

In addition to there being distinct models of constitutionalism in play at this particular historical moment, rendering the adoption and embedding of social constitutionalism far from guaranteed, the dominant emergent economic model – understood variably as neoliberalism, market fundamentalism, or the Washington Consensus – seemed to imply an oppositional set of political and legal institutions to those implied by social constitutionalism. In both scholarly and popular usage, the term neoliberalism refers to "an overlapping set of arguments and premises that are not always entirely mutually consistent" (Singh Grewal and Purdy 2014: 2). Broadly, the neoliberal economic model as understood in the early 1990s emphasized a substantial reduction of the size of the state, the privatization of industries, and limits on economic and social rights protections. The Washington Consensus formally involved ten policy prescriptions (Williamson 2004), with the underlying idea being "to cut overall social spending in order to cut budget deficits, increase the targeting of spending by increasing means testing, decentralize spending and administration to regions/states/provinces or municipalities, and privatize the pension system" (Huber and Stephens 2012: 206). Thus, the prevailing beliefs about the most appropriate and effective economic arrangement during this time period seems to have directly cut against the social constitutionalist idea of how to organize the state and how (or whether) to moderate state–society relations. Further, this period of the early 1990s featured dramatic changes to the international system. The fall of the Soviet Union inspired a reordering of connections and alliances between countries. Neoliberalism, if only momentarily, was seen as one of the last models of political and economic life standing.

The dominant version of neoliberalism envisioned an important, but limited, role of law and courts in political and economic life. At a basic level, neoliberalism requires the protection of property rights and individual freedoms that would allow for participation in the economy. David Singh Grewal and Jedidiah Purdy (2014: 9) go a step further, arguing that "neoliberalism is always mediated through law," with respect to "the scope and nature of property rights (including intellectual property), the constitutional extent of the government's power to regulate, the appropriate aims and techniques of administrative agencies, and the nature of the personal liberty and equality that basic constitutional protections enshrine." While law and neoliberalism may be intimately intertwined, it is clear that social constitutionalism involves the recognition and advancement of a different kind of citizenship, a different kind of citizen–state relationship than does neoliberalism. In the neoliberal view, the law protects citizens so that they can pursue their economic interests, while social constitutionalism makes no necessary claim about the economic pursuits of citizens. In fact, under the social constitutionalist model, the law is meant to step in to protect even those, or perhaps especially those, citizens who have not succeeded economically.

In practice, however, the choice turned out not to be neoliberalism or social constitutionalism – one or the other – but how exactly these two seemingly incongruous models might come to coexist in one country. We might think of the combination of these two models as the result of an uneasy compromise between different sets of actors. Another possible interpretation is that of a bait and switch, wherein elites offer empty promises of social equality and democracy, in keeping with the overarching scripts of the time, but with no intention of making good on those promises. Yet another possibility is that of unrecognized tension between these models. This is perhaps most likely where constitution-drafting procedures are fragmented across distinct working groups. Finally, it could be that these models are not, in fact, incongruous. To the extent that both rights-based constitutionalism and neoliberalism result in the individualization of social problems and obligations, there may be less of a disjuncture between these models than originally appears. Regardless of the exact dynamics at play, what we see is that these two models did come to the fore at roughly the same historical moment, with countries at once adopting neoliberal economic policies and new constitutions that recognized social rights. Whether or not these legal visions provided any substantive protections for the individual depends on the extent to which both social constitutionalism and neoliberalism became embedded. This book tracks these processes in Colombia, and provides insights for understanding the tensions between social constitutionalism and neoliberalism elsewhere in the world.

1.3 THE ARGUMENT IN BRIEF: CONSTITUTIONAL EMBEDDING THROUGH LEGAL MOBILIZATION

The Social Constitution introduces the concept of embedding constitutional law and documents how legal mobilization can propel constitutional embedding. Turning to the concept of embedding helps us to understand how constitutional rights become "real," or how the promises written into constitutions come to have social and legal meaning, thus shaping the behavior of both everyday citizens and judicial system actors. Table 1.1 breaks down the argument of this book.

TABLE 1.1 Argument: constitutional embedding through legal mobilization

Constitutional embeddedness refers to the degree to which constitutional law shapes everyday expectations and behavior
Constitutions will meaningfully impact everyday life only to the extent that they are embedded socially and legally
Social and legal embedding can develop independently of one another, but they can also serve to reinforce one another
When the social and legal components of constitutional embedding reinforce one another, a constitution will be resistant to efforts to dislodge it
Legal mobilization can serve as a mechanism of constitutional embedding

What exactly does constitutional embedding look like? Following the adoption of new constitutions that recognized a wide set of rights, citizens gradually come to learn about these rights, and they begin to take some of the problems in their lives to the formal legal system, experimentally. Some of the time, this experimental claim-making solidifies into general patterns in claim-making, as citizens begin to view particular issues as amenable to a legal solution and as societal actors encourage further claim-making. Simultaneously, judges' beliefs about their own role and whether and how the law applies to social issues change, in part because of the way that legal claims and daily life combine to expose them to these social issues. As judges continue to decide cases, opportunities for further claim-making shift. In this way, legal mobilization can serve as a mechanism of constitutional embedding, with the iterative process of legal claim-making shaping how both everyday citizens and legal actors understand what the law is and does – or what the law ought to be and what it ought to do.

There are two distinct, but related, components of constitutional embedding: social and legal embedding. Social embedding refers to the degree to which ordinary people know about rights, talk about rights, and, at times, make legal claims to their rights.[8] Beliefs about constitutional law – whether technically accurate or inaccurate – set out

[8] It is important to note that even in the absence of robust social embedding, some social movement organizations or NGOs may engage in legal claim-making. Social embedding refers to the notion that beliefs about the possibilities of the constitution and ensuing practices are widespread throughout society.

TABLE 1.2 Observable implications of constitutional embedding

Social embedding	Legal embedding
Everyday people develop a set of beliefs about the constitution	New legal institutions, mechanisms, and actors meant to instantiate a particular vision of constitutional law are created
People start to talk about specific rights and legal tools that can be used to claim rights in casual, informal, or everyday contexts	Judges and lawyers establish, alter, and expand precedent related to that vision of law
Folks actually make legal claims to their rights	The mainstream view among active lawyers and judges (including who work at levels below the high courts) is that this vision of law is viable and appropriate

the possibility that the constitution and constitutional rights become reference points in social life. As those beliefs are contextualized within people's everyday experiences, they become less abstract and more locally meaningful. These beliefs then provide the foundation for legal claim-making, influencing which issues people see as a matter of rights, claimable through the courts, or protected by the constitution and which ones they do not. Thus, social embedding can be thought of as a subset of legal consciousness, which refers to the ways people think about and use or do not use law more broadly.

Legal embedding refers to the process by which a particular vision of constitutional law becomes the dominant understanding held by actors in the formal legal sphere. Newly developed constitutions set out rights, rules, and obligations whose enactment requires the construction of an infrastructure made up of physical settings, such as courthouses, and various people, including judges, clerks, bureaucrats, and the like. Without this infrastructure, neither the state nor citizens will be able to make claims or settle disputes under the law. These various actors, in carrying out their jobs, influence how the law comes to life, both opening up new possibilities and closing off others for different groups of people. Ultimately, when legal embedding is robust, the mainstream view among lawyers and judges will be that the new vision of constitutional law is both viable and appropriate, rather than one to be ignored or undermined. Table 1.2 summarizes the observable implications of both social and legal embedding.

Successful constitutional embedding – along either or both the social and legal dimensions – is not inherently or necessarily a positive development. It may occur unevenly across rights areas, and it does not mean that the system works for all citizens. Rather, constitutional embedding means that certain rights have been institutionalized and normalized; that they have become accepted parts of everyday life. Individual constitutional rights protections, when realized, may meet the needs of some people, but they may not adequately serve everyone. Some problems might fall outside the realm of constitutional law or be caused by structural factors that are difficult to remedy with individual legal orders. Here, we might think of an inversion of Anatole France's comments on the law's majestic equality: law offers the same promises to everyone, even if needs are not the same.[9] Further, constitutional embedding may not develop evenly across all constitutionally recognized rights. Some rights may garner more attention in society writ large than others, and some may be viewed as more binding or, on the other hand, as more aspirational by the legal community than others. Even when this variation is present, a constitution may still be deeply embedded in a particular context.

One driver of constitutional embedding is legal mobilization. Legal mobilization involves decisions by both everyday citizens (who choose whether or not to make legal claims on the basis of how they understand the law) and judges (who decide whether and how to respond to those legal claims). The iterative process of claim-making in the formal legal sphere shapes how everyday citizens and legal actors understand what the law is and does, or what the law ought to be and do. By engaging in this kind of claim-making, potential claimants, judges, and intermediaries collectively redefine: (1) the kinds of problems that social actors understand as "legal grievances," or as claimable in the formal legal sphere; and (2) judicial receptivity to particular kinds of claims, or the extent to which judges view a category of claims as appropriately falling within the realm of law. When legal and societal actors agree that particular issues fall within the domain of the law, feedback loops can form, incentivizing continued claim-making and positive judicial responses to those claims. Over time, these patterns can stabilize, resulting in the embedding of a new vision of constitutional law and the heading off of challenges to that new vision. This is exactly what

[9] France (1894) wrote: "The law, in its majestic equality, forbids the rich as well as the poor to sleep under bridges, to beg in the streets, and to steal bread."

occurred in Colombia following the drafting of its new, social constitution in 1991. Constitutional embedding in Colombia was catalyzed by claim-making using the tutela procedure, especially for claims to the right to health, that the newly created Constitutional Court affirmed. Over time, constitutional embedding expanded, though not always consistently, across rights arenas.

1.4 THE SIGNIFICANCE OF SOCIAL CONSTITUTIONALISM

The rights implicated in social constitutionalism encompass not only the most immediate provisions necessary to make participation in political and social life theoretically possible (e.g., the right to assemble or the right to vote), but also those provisions necessary to make participation in social and political life actually feasible (e.g., access to healthcare, housing, and education). Social constitutionalism may be thought of as implying formal social citizenship, to use T. H. Marshall's terms. Marshall (1950: 11) defines social citizenship as "the whole range [of rights], from the right to a modicum of economic welfare and security to the right to share to the full in the social heritage and to live the life of a civilized being according to the standards prevailing in the society."[10] Here, social citizenship is described in relation to social and economic rights. This understanding of citizenship does not necessarily entail full equality. It simply poses limits on inequality on paper.[11] Formal social citizenship suggests only equality of opportunity in social and economic realms, while substantive social citizenship might go a step further, requiring some basic level of social welfare provision, though even substantive social citizenship does not necessarily imply complete equality.

As such, legal claim-making related to social goods moves beyond traditional understandings of citizenship rights defined in narrow legal and political terms. In this book, I argue that how people use the law

[10] See also Powell's (2002) discussion of Marshall's social citizenship and subsequent works on the topic.

[11] Marshall (1950: 30) proclaimed: "National justice and a law common to all must inevitably weaken and eventually destroy class justices, and personal freedom, as a universal birthright, must drive our serfdom." However, later scholars do not necessarily share his optimism, pointing to the ways in which law often continues to benefit the already privileged at the expense of the poor, racial minorities, and others (e.g., Motta Ferraz 2011).

has changed precisely because how they understand the law and rights has shifted. Legal mobilization for social rights reflects claims to citizenship rights that include social benefits and new forms of social inclusion or incorporation. Deborah Yashar (2005: 6, emphasis in original) notes that citizenship regimes determine "*who* has political membership, *which* rights they possess, and *how* interest intermediation with the state is structured." She continues, "[a]s citizenship regimes have changed over time, so too have the publicly sanctioned players, rules of the game, and likely (but not preordained) outcomes." Most of the time, citizenship regimes have been oriented around specific civil and political rights, with only limited recognition of social citizenship rights. The recognition of social (citizenship) rights generates important shifts in the nature of the promises that the state makes to its citizens and in the opportunities available to citizens to contest the conditions of their lives. At least on paper, these commitments to address inequality and specifically the unequal access to social goods dramatically change the nature of state–society relations. Here, poverty and inequality become not simply the byproducts of economic or social relations, but evidence of the failure of the government to live up to its obligations.

Typically, social incorporation or the provision of social welfare in developing societies has occurred through one of three dominant models of state–society relations: patron-clientelism, corporatism, or the market alternative. In a setting defined by patron-clientelism, social goods are not universal rights but discretionary benefits that are selectively allocated by political authorities or brokers to individuals in exchange for political loyalty (Bratton and van de Walle 1997; Auyero 2001; Chandra 2004; Kitschelt and Wilkinson 2007; Stokes 2013). Corporatism, on the other hand, enables access to social goods through segmented linkages between states or ruling parties and organized sectors of the formal economy, particularly workers with membership in labor unions (Schmitter 1974; Collier and Collier 1979; Yashar 1999). Finally, the neoliberal or market alternative holds that the marketplace and the private sector facilitate a more just, rational, and efficient provision of social goods than the state. In this system, social goods become available to citizens on the basis of their ability to pay the market rate, with the state providing a minimal safety net for those who are incapable (e.g., due to age or disability) of meeting their needs in the marketplace (Hall and Soskice 2001; Adésínà 2009).

The social constitutionalist commitment to promoting access to social goods on the basis of an understanding of inherent human dignity marks a stark difference from these traditional models of social incorporation. Social constitutionalism is grounded in principles of universal rights, in contrast to traditional models that offer social inclusion in a formally selective, discretionary, or politically mediated fashion that excludes large numbers of citizens – in particular, those who lacked the partisan ties, organizational advocates, or market leverage required to access social benefits. Moreover, social constitutionalism assigns the courts a prominent role in processing and adjudicating claims to social goods; claims that traditionally have been channeled through political parties, legislative bodies, and state or municipal social service agencies, or simply depoliticized through their relegation to the private sphere of commodified market exchange.

Comparative social policy scholarship has tended to focus on the differences in and determinants of formal welfare policies or types of welfare states (e.g., Esping-Andersen 1990; Powell and Barrientos 2004; Lynch 2006; Pribble 2011; Huber and Stephens 2012). Another strand of scholarship has explicitly examined why developing countries have failed to construct robust social welfare protections comparable to those in western Europe (e.g., Gough et al. 2004; Haggard and Kaufman 2008; Rudra 2008; Mares and Carnes 2009; Huber and Stephens 2012; Garay 2016). Further work on developing countries has explored the role of conditional cash transfers as part of social welfare policy (Valencia Lomelí 2008; Fiszbein, Rüdiger Schady, and Ferreira 2009; Ferguson 2015). Scholars have also begun to identify informal dimensions of welfare policy (Holland 2017), the role of nonstate actors in the provision of social goods and social programs (e.g., Wood and Gough 2006; Martinez Franzoni 2008; Cammett and MacLean 2014), and the importance of shared histories and social identities for social policy development (Singh 2017; Wilfahrt 2018).

According to these accounts, with greater or lesser success, citizens pursue such channels as voting, lobbying, and otherwise pressuring elected officials to voice their preferences or make social welfare demands, or they look inward, to self-help or friends and family. In particular, existing studies of the development of social policy regimes emphasize the electoral determinants of social policy change or policy enforcement (e.g., Iversen 2005; Mares and Carnes 2009; Garay 2016; Holland 2017), the importance of the preferences of employers (e.g., Swenson 2002; Mares 2003), or the strength of the political left (e.g., Esping-Andersen 1990; Huber and Stephens 2012). The ability of the poor to influence social policy historically has been limited due to challenges to effective political mobilization, including but not limited to labor informality, diverse and even contradictory interests, and exclusionary or clientelistic political contexts (e.g., Weyland 1996; Cross 1998; Roberts 1998, 2002; Kurtz 2004; Kitschelt and Wilkinson 2007; Haggard and Kaufman 2008; Abdulai and Hickey 2016).

Considering the barriers facing the poor and marginalized, social constitutionalism and legal mobilization potentially offer citizens who are otherwise cut off from formal channels of political access the chance to express need or discontent; an opportunity that is largely unavailable for individuals in the context of other modes of social incorporation. In this view, the courts may serve the interests of the poor, perhaps more so than any other democratic institution. In the context of social constitutionalism, issues related to the provision of social goods are thrust into the legal sphere. On paper, the guarantees of social constitutionalism are universal in nature, though, like other universalistic guarantees, access to these social goods and services in practice often remains less than desired. In this context, social policy expands and contracts in part on the basis of the ability of individuals or groups to make legal claims and receive a positive response from courts. Here we see a new form of selectivity: one that differs from the selectivity inherent to clientelism, corporatism, or market-based access to social goods. In addition, the social constitutionalist model raises the question of who or what institutions will enforce the social rights claims that judiciaries may assert but cannot on their own deliver.

While social rights may appear in international law as a single, coherent idea, providing the minimum conditions necessary for a dignified life and conferring both positive and negative obligations on the state, the goods that comprise social rights relate to the market in very different ways and are claimable in very different ways. These goods can be constructed as public, private, or a mix of the two, and the extent to which the state engages in the public provision of each good may vary across time and place.[12] For instance, in the present day, most states provide for some degree of basic education and require school attendance, often through the end of secondary school. On the other hand, states vary substantially in terms of investment in large-scale public infrastructure and investment designed to provide access

[12] As Holland and Ross Schneider (2017) discuss, the extent to which the state delves into a welfare-related issue may depend in large part on whether the good falls within an "easy" form or "hard" form of social policy provision.

to other social goods. Healthcare can also be understood primarily as a private good, a market commodity accessible by individuals through private insurance plans, clinics, and hospitals, or as a mix of the two. The same can be said for housing. Generally speaking, the market alternative, clientelism, and corporatist models do not treat healthcare or housing as public goods in that some measure of formal excludability persists, which is not true of social constitutionalism. Social constitutionalism and the ensuing legal mobilization for social rights, thus, fundamentally shift the boundaries of social policy and the nature of social incorporation.

The durability and long-term consequences of this kind of expansion of access to social welfare goods as rights are largely unknown. Constitutional rights offer equal access to all citizens on paper, yet real access is determined by the ability of citizens to make claims to these goods, either as individuals or as part of a group. Thus, legal recognitions offer an indirect route to social incorporation and to social policy change; one that might reify rather than offer redress for preexisting disadvantage. In order to assess these consequences, however, we must first understand how social constitutionalism came about and developed over time – something that the subsequent chapters of this book document for the Colombian case.

1.5 EMPIRICAL APPROACH

In order to explore constitutional embedding, I turn to the case of the 1991 Colombian Constitution. In some ways, Colombia is exceptional. Unlike much of Latin America, Colombia's constitutional history throughout the nineteenth century was remarkably stable, which means that there were competing, previously institutionalized visions of law in existence as the country sought to draft a new constitution. Further, the 1991 Constitution featured a significant shift in the content of constitutional law – from liberal to social constitutionalism. And perhaps most obviously, the tutela procedure allows nearly unprecedented access to the judiciary for everyday citizens. The tutela procedure considerably reduces the cost, time, and knowledge or experience necessary to make constitutional rights claims. The relative ease of making claims and the scope of claim-making possibilities helped to push the embedding of the 1991 Constitution. The constitution came to be part of daily life, from accessing state information to gaining healthcare services. This outcome, however, was not a foregone conclusion. The tutela procedure was initially limited to civil and political rights claims. Those limits could have persisted. Judges could have stymied claim-making. Claimants could have turned away from the tutela procedure for a variety of reasons. Constitutional embedding could *not* have happened. The existence of the tutela did not guarantee embedding, and the initial design of the tutela would not suggest embedding as a particularly likely outcome.

In other ways, the case of Colombia is quite ordinary. Following a period of social and political strife, citizens mobilized, calling for significant reforms to the institutions of government and a refounding of the country based on new constitutional principles. These institutional changes took place in an international and regional environment that privileged rule of law and judicial reforms (Hammergren 2006; Santos 2006). Those reforms were enacted and developed in unexpected ways, changing as various actors – from legal and political elites to everyday citizens to insurance companies – came together to negotiate meanings and possibilities of the law. By carefully examining how visions and uses of law changed in Colombia throughout the 1990s and 2000s, we gain insight into how constitutional embedding can occur (and/or be hindered) through the process of legal mobilization, as well as the limitations of constitutional embedding.

To examine how and why constitutional embedding occurs, I spent one year in Colombia between June 2016 and May 2017. During this time, I primarily lived and worked in the cities of Bogotá, Medellín, and Cali. I conducted interviews with both "legal elites" – a term that loosely refers to lawyers, judges, law professors, and activists at nongovernmental organizations (NGOs) that include litigation within their strategies[13] – and, to a lesser extent, everyday citizens. This amounted to eighty-four interviews with ninety-two legal elites, as well as seventy-four interviews with ninety-three everyday citizens. The elite interviews were primarily conducted in the cities of Bogotá, Medellín, and Cali between June 2016 and May 2017. I also conducted a few interviews remotely after my research trip had ended. Typically, these interviews took place in judges' chambers, law offices, or on college campuses, though some took place in interviewees' homes. And typically, these interviews lasted between one and two hours. Several elite interviews involved two interviewees at a time. Often, this occurred

[13] Importantly, many activist interviewees are not elites in terms of their socioeconomic status. Even so, I use this term for the sake of convenience.

because I sought out an interview with a particular individual who then invited a colleague to join our conversation.[14]

One set of nonelite interviews was conducted in Bogotá in February and March 2017. With the help of a Colombian research firm, the Centro Nacional de Consultoría, respondents were randomly selected within three class categories or *estratos* (lower, middle, and upper). Interviews were conducted in locations chosen by the respondent, usually the respondent's home. Over the course of an hour-long semi-structured interview, respondents were asked to share their views on their neighbors and neighborhoods, on any difficulties they or their family members had in terms of topics ranging from healthcare, housing, education, social security, or pensions to minor disputes between neighbors, and, at the end of the interview, on the Colombian legal system.

I conducted the second set of nonelite interviews – twenty-four unstructured individual and group interviews with forty-three people – in Agua Blanca, Cali during April and May of 2017. These interviews took place in respondents' homes and more often than not took the form of informal conversations about justice in Agua Blanca or in Colombia. A local interlocutor connected me with each interviewee and was present for the majority of these interviews. As a result, these interviewees were primarily part of her social network and are not necessarily representative of the district as a whole. These interviews varied significantly in time, ranging from ten to fifteen minutes to well over an hour. After transcription, each set of interviews was organized, coded, and analyzed.

These interviews allowed for the probing of the orientation of the judicial establishment, as it appears on the inside (to judges and lawyers) and the outside, as well as to those who have tried to traverse those boundaries (including claimants, activists, and academics). They also allowed me to assess beliefs about the appropriate role of legal institutions in democratic society and the status of social rights (specifically to what extent they are justiciable or claimable).

I also fielded a survey, with the help of several law students from the Universidad de Antioquia, in March 2017 of 310 tutela claimants.[15]

[14] The Appendix offers a list of my elite interviews, including information about the profession of each interviewee.

[15] Zeller Álvarez of the Universidad de Antioquia coordinated this team of students. I had originally intended to take part in the fielding of these surveys; however, my presence near the courthouse proved to be something of a spectacle, making it harder for respondents to complete the survey with some degree of privacy, so I stepped away from this role.

The survey was based on a convenience sample of people waiting in line outside the Palacio de Justicia in Medellín to file a tutela claim in April 2017. As such, they reflect the views of individuals who have already decided to file a legal claim rather than the views of the general population. This survey only includes claimants – individuals who had already recognized something in their lives as problematic and who had decided to turn to the legal system to address that problem – and, as such, the respondents are not necessarily representative of the broader population.

Beyond these interviews and surveys, I analyzed both archival and legal documents. In order to assess the debates that took place at the Asamblea Nacional Constituyente (the constitution-drafting body), I turned to a collection held at the Biblioteca Luis Ángel Arango. I collected data on two types of legal cases: tutela cases (T-cases) and abstract review cases (C-cases).[16] Every Constitutional Court decision is available online, which allowed for the scraping of a random sample of tutela cases from the Constitutional Court's website and to organize that sample into a dataset.[17] I obtained information about abstract review cases from the Congreso Visible project at the Universidad de los Andes. I also consulted numerous reports issued by the ombudsman's office and the judiciary.

In addition, I participated in the two-week "Caravan for Peace, Life and Justice," organized by Colombian social leaders in November 2016, which involved visits to a variety of small and large Colombian cities, as well as rural areas that were hard-hit by the decades-long armed conflict between the Colombian government, the Fuerzas Armadas Revolucionarias de Colombia (FARC), other guerilla groups, and various paramilitary groups. Finally, I spent significant periods of time in law offices and courtrooms, community group and social movement meetings, and government agencies observing and, less frequently, participating in the events occurring around me. This participant observation, while difficult to meaningfully quantify, proved to be invaluable in helping me to better understand both the patterns I observed in legal claim-making practices as well as what I learned through the

[16] These constitutional abstract review cases are called "C-cases." Typically, C-cases result from *acciónes pública de inconstitucionalidad* (public action of unconstitutionality) – claims contesting the constitutionality of bills, executive decrees, and constitutional amendments.

[17] Thank you to Josh Meyer-Gutbrod for help with web scraping.

semi-structured interviews and survey responses. Many of these experiences do not explicitly appear again in the pages that follow, but they provided vital insight into the ways in which the broad shifts in the meaning of law that form the core focus of this project are manifest in and by lived experience.

1.6 OUTLINE OF THE BOOK

This book examines the construction and reconstruction of notions of obligation, specifically with respect to the conditions under which the state has an obligation to protect the social needs of its citizens in Colombia. Focusing on one particular site of contention over these notions of obligation – the formal legal sphere – I investigate the dynamics of legal mobilization for social claims as they relate to the activation and embedding of social constitutionalism. In the process, I address issues related to the functioning of democratic institutions and the actors that operate within them, state–society relations, social welfare provision, and institutional change. The rest of this book proceeds as follows.

Chapter 2 introduces the idea of "constitutional embedding" and describes how legal mobilization can put into motion processes that result in the embedding of social constitutionalism. Constitutional embedding occurs along two dimensions: social and legal. Where social and legal embedding reinforce one another, constitutional embedding will be particularly robust. Where they do not, constitutional embedding will be vulnerable to challenges related to the scope of the law, concerns of powerful actors, and the workload judges must navigate. Each type of challenge can derail both social and legal embeddedness, and, as a result, limit the potential for social constitutionalism to translate into gains in real access to social welfare goods. Legal mobilization can catalyze constitutional embedding, as it facilitates the social construction of legal grievances and the development of judicial receptivity to particular kind of claims, in the process shaping views about the law.

Chapter 3 provides the backdrop of constitutionalism in Colombia, demonstrating that although many sectors of society sought dramatic legal change with the 1991 Constitution, few imagined the breadth of the social changes that would come with that legal text. It tracks how substantive social constitutionalism and the creation of new access mechanisms, most importantly the tutela procedure, emerged. It closes with an introduction to early legal claim-making under the 1991 Constitution.

Chapters 4 and 5 detail the ways in which social constitutionalism became socially and legally embedded, respectively. Chapter 4 tracks how the tutela procedure came to attain a central place in Colombian life, as people were inundated with opportunities to learn about the new constitution, including through media campaigns, popular television shows, board games, and comics. Over time, the tutela became "vernacularized," and Colombians not only talked about the tutela procedure but transformed the word tutela in several different verb forms. Colombians developed a set of beliefs about the possibilities created by the new constitution, and these beliefs – whether accurate or inaccurate in relation to the constitutional text – drove claim-making using the tutela procedure, which in turn ensured the social embedding of the constitution.

Chapter 5 explores legal embedding in Colombia. It tracks why and how Colombian judges – both at the Constitutional Court level and the lower-court level – came to be receptive to the new constitutional order, especially claims through the tutela procedure, even when those claims appeared to be beyond its formal scope. The combination of repeated exposure to particular kinds of legal claims in the formal legal sphere and exposure to the problems those claims implicate in everyday life seems to drive judicial receptivity. Judges are particularly receptive to claims when they interpret them as consonant with contemporary sociolegal values.

Chapters 6–8 cover the three challenges to the stability of Colombia's social constitutionalist order: scope, power, and work. Chapter 6 examines the limits of legal legibility, or what – and whose – problems are legible to the law, and who gets left behind. The chapter looks to the community called Agua Blanca in the western part of Colombia. There, the most visible impact of the 1991 Constitution seems to be the conversion of rights promises into paperwork. While residents of Agua Blanca still use the tutela procedure, accepting the idea that filing tutela claims is what one has to do to try to gain access to services, they see the 1991 Constitution as largely irrelevant to their lives, which are instead constrained by violence and marginality.

Chapter 7 focuses on overt, political efforts to confront social constitutionalism and unravel rights protections. Following the introduction of the 1991 Constitution, established elites within the judiciary, the executive, and the legislature bristled at the changing political and legal landscape. They attempted to stymie those changes in various ways, primarily seeking to disempower the newly created Constitutional

Court and limit the newly created tutela procedure. The popularity of the Constitutional Court and the tutela procedure – and continued legal mobilization using the tutela procedure – however, meant that these efforts to dislodge social constitutionalism in Colombia failed.

Chapter 8 turns to the labor of law, or the difficulty of keeping up with the daily work that underpins this legal order. While Constitutional Court judges have garnered substantial attention, lower-court judges are tasked with the majority of the work of social constitutionalism in Colombia. They are the ones who have reviewed each of the nearly eight million tutela claims that have been filed since 1992. Many of these lower-court judges report that they feel overworked and underresourced. Material and normative pressures, thus far, have combined to ensure that these judges continue to keep up with the labor of social constitutionalism.

Chapter 9 extends the argument of this book to the case of the 1996 South African Constitution, demonstrating the usefulness of examining the contours and limits of constitutional embeddedness beyond the Colombian context. The South African case is one of partial constitutional embedding, where legal embedding significantly outpaced social embedding. While judges, lawyers, legal aid organizations, and NGOs embraced the language and tools of the new constitution, many social groups adopted rights discourse hesitantly, if at all, and still others explicitly rejected rights (Smith 2015). This comparative examination probes different ways in which constitutional embedding can occur in practice, and it helps to show how constitutional embedding is not a necessary or inevitable phenomenon.

Chapter 10 draws out the implications of this study of constitutional embedding for how citizens access social goods around the world and how scholars ought to study constitutional law and legal mobilization. Though not without important limits, the introduction of social constitutionalism to Colombia has resulted in tangible material gains for many citizens and generated new possibilities for citizens to contest the conditions of their lives.

CHAPTER TWO

CONSTITUTIONAL EMBEDDING THROUGH LEGAL MOBILIZATION

A vision of law set out in a new constitutional text is not guaranteed to filter into either social or legal discourse. In fact, constitutions can be short-lived and subject to serial replacement (Levitsky and Murillo 2013). According to Gabriel Negretto and Javier Couso (2018: 7), the eighteen countries of Latin America collectively drafted 195 constitutions between 1810 and 2015.[1] To date, comparative scholars have focused primarily on the political dynamics that allow for different forms of constitutional change, specifically the emergence of judicial review and constitutional courts. Transitions featuring elite pacts help to explain the rise of both of these institutions, as actors facing the uncertainty of electoral politics are incentivized to create checks on power, assuming that another group may someday (re)gain power (Ginsburg 2003; Hirschl 2004; Dixon and Ginsburg 2017).[2] Constitutional courts may seek to build their power by taking on increasingly larger caseloads, seeking to weigh in on important political and legal matters arguably beyond their purview (in the process pushing out alternative sites of adjudication or establishing a new judicial hierarchy), and developing "constituencies" that help to shield them from

[1] Elkins, Ginsburg, and Melton (2009) and Versteeg and Zackin (2016) show that this turnover is not abnormal – in fact, constitutions globally are amended or replaced every five years and fully replaced every nineteen years.

[2] Some scholars also note that politicians at times seek to expand judicial power out of a desire to govern effectively, rather than to constrain competitors (Nunes 2010b).

unfavorable political actors (Landau 2014).[3] These works give us a clear sense of the "high politics" of constitutionalism, but they tell us less about how constitutional law comes to impact everyday citizens or how citizens come to make constitutional rights claims.

This book explores the phenomenon of constitutional embedding, or how we move from constitutions as window dressings or parchment promises (Carey 2000) to constitutions that shape both the social and legal expectations of all citizens, not just those who view themselves as benefiting from the constitutional order.[4] I focus specifically on the embedding of social constitutionalism, a form of constitutionalism that commits the state to the protection of access to social welfare goods, like healthcare, housing, and education, and offers citizens the opportunity to make legal claims to those goods (Brinks, Gauri, and Shen 2015). Varun Gauri and Daniel Brinks (2008) study claim-making within the context of social constitutionalism, though their approach focuses on how expectations about the future encourage or discourage individual and group efforts at legal mobilization. By contrast, I examine how legal mobilization propels constitutional embedding, in the process reshaping possibilities for future claim-making.

Legal mobilization is not the only mechanism that catalyzes constitutional embedding. For instance, effective civic and legal education campaigns may also shape or solidify both social and legal understandings, in turn altering expectations about the function of constitutional law. The same goes for more diffuse social processes by which particular constitutional provisions come to be understood as fundamental to citizenship. Consider, for example, the place of the "right to bear arms" in common discourse in the United States. Litigation has not been the main driver of this discourse; instead, individuals and groups have mobilized around this right both politically and socially, through the National Rifle Association and outside of it, and, over time, for at least part of the population, the right to bear arms came to be understood as a core component of *American* citizenship and *American* nationhood.

3 Alternatively, new constitutional courts may seek to "lay low," frequently deferring to the other branches of government, rather than attempting to carve out their own space (Fowkes 2016).

4 Charles Epp (2009) similarly explores the move from bureaucratic window dressing to rights-protective policy implementation, though his focus is on changes to long standing practices, rather than on new constitutions.

My goal is not to fully catalogue all possible mechanisms of constitutional embedding. Instead, I aim to demonstrate how, under certain conditions, legal mobilization can be an efficient driver of constitutional embedding that can overcome significant challenges to the embedding process. The rest of this chapter details the concept of embedding and explains the relationship between legal mobilization and constitutional embedding.

2.1 WHAT IS "CONSTITUTIONAL EMBEDDING?"

There are robust literatures across disciplines and subfields that use some variant of the term "embeddedness." International relations and international law scholars have used the term embedding to refer to the degree to which international legal covenants and dispute resolution mechanisms are present or bolstered in domestic legal frameworks (Keohane, Moravcsik, and Slaughter 2003; Helfer 2008; Elkins, Ginsburg, and Simmons 2013; Alter 2014).[5] Embedded liberalism (Ruggie 1982) or embedded markets (Polanyi 1944) emphasize the ways in which societal ideas and expectations about the economy shape political outcomes.[6] In this book, I shift the level of analysis and use more specific terms (constitutional embedding, legal embedding, and social embedding). Rather than examining the relationship between the international and the domestic, I look to the relationship between national-level context and societal actors. I am also concerned with disentangling the formal or parchment changes in law from the informal changes in everyday practice – and the relationship between the two.

Constitutional embedding refers to the process by which a particular vision of constitution law comes to take root in everyday life.[7] It is helpful to think of constitutional embedding along two dimensions: social and legal, or how individuals and groups operating in the social sphere understand and relate to the constitution, and how those

[5] This sense of embedding international law closely reflects what I call the legal dimension of embedding.

[6] This understanding more closely maps onto what I call the social dimension of embedding.

[7] In some ways, constitutional embedding is related to the judicialization of politics (Hirschl 2008), a topic of particular concern for analysts of Latin America (Sieder, Schjolden, and Angell 2011).

working in the formal legal sphere do so.[8] Social embedding occurs when (1) everyday people develop a set of beliefs about the constitution, (2) "rights talk" enters the vernacular and does so with respect to specific rights and legal tools that can be used to claim rights, and (3) folks actually make legal claims to their rights. This vernacularized understanding of rights may or may not map on to the technical scope of the law. When we talk about an "overly litigious" society, we are talking about a situation in which some vision of law has become socially embedded. The implicit claim is that social understandings of law are wider than legal ones – in short, litigation is occurring at a high rate because of social demands rather than legal appropriateness. When some vision of constitutionalism is socially embedded, people may turn to law for a variety of reasons: out of hope, despair, resignation, cunning, or ambivalence. In this context, people share a common frame of reference, but not necessarily a common interpretation of that frame. At the individual level, the turn to law may or may not be habitual or reflect buy-in (Lovell 2012), but at the societal level, it becomes seen as normal, expected, necessary, or just part of life. When constitutionalism is not socially embedded, those who we might call – drawing on the language of Patricia Ewick and Susan Silbey (1998) – "true believers" and "savvy gamers," as well as those who have law thrust upon them (Zemans 1983), may still turn to law to make and contest claims, but the place of law is less central and less firmly established overall.

Legal embedding occurs when (1) new legal institutions, mechanisms, and actors come to make their presence known in the daily work of law, and when (2) judges establish, alter, and – especially – expand precedent related to the particular vision of constitutional law. Further, while there may still be some differences of opinion within the legal profession, (3) the mainstream view among active lawyers and judges must be that this vision of law is generally viable and appropriate (e.g., that social rights are not nonjusticiable) in order for there to be legal embedding, including those who work at levels below the high courts. Among the legal profession, skeptics may remain, though their voices will become more and more marginal within the community of lawyers who work on the issue areas in question. The extent to which legal embedding is necessary for continued legal mobilization depends

[8] Of course, there is no such thing as fully distinct spheres of life – lawyers and judges do not operate outside of broader society, and vice versa.

on the ease of access to justice. Where courts are more accessible and legal support is less necessary, buy-in from the legal establishment is less important; though, of course, whether or not judges are willing to accept new claims remains key.

In short, we might think of embeddedness as the degree to which something is no longer unusual in social or legal life, or the degree to which something has become part of what shapes social and legal expectations and behavior. Thus, social embedding is similar to a change in legal consciousness (Merry 1990; Ewick and Silbey 1998; Silbey 2005) or constitutional veneration (Levinson 1990),[9] yet it departs from these concepts in key ways. Legal consciousness studies encompass examinations of identity construction, hegemonic state control of society through the law, and the relationship between individual and group consciousness and mobilization decisions (Chua and Engel 2019). While legal consciousness refers to "the ways law is experienced and understood by ordinary citizens" (Merry 1985), the social component of constitutional embedding shifts the focus to constitutional law and rights specifically. In the context of newly promulgated constitutions, constitutional law is often described as a way to "refound" the country and emphasize new values and commitments. When people frame their grievances and rights claims in constitutional terms, they are, in effect, linking their demands to a larger political project.[10] Constitutional embedding departs from constitutional veneration in that while veneration indicates a stable positive attitude about the constitution, the concept of embedding allows a flexibility about the content of the legal vision and the tenor of citizen evaluations. Likewise, legal embedding is related to, but moves beyond, a change in institutional culture or judicial role conceptions (e.g., Hilbink 2008; Nunes 2010a). The reference point is specifically the constitution, and judges may be motivated to work within the constitutional vision for either ideological or strategic reasons.

The processes of social and legal embedding are not independent of one another. In fact, they develop recursively and together define how embedded a constitutional order is at any given moment. At the same time, constitutional embedding is not an all-or-nothing game. Uneven

[9] Sanford Levinson (1990) cites James Madison in *Federalist No. 49* when explaining constitutional veneration. Scholars working outside the US context have used a similar term, "constitutional patriotism" (Gloppen 1997).

[10] I thank Ke Li for this insight.

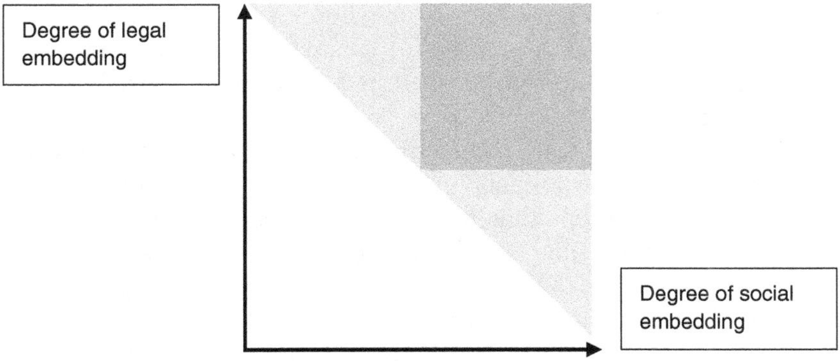

Figure 2.1 Plotting constitutional embedding.

or partial embedding is not only possible, but likely. Uneven embedding suggests that there is variation in terms of the constitutional rights that are embedded (a few versus most or all). Partial embeddedness implies relatively more social embedding than legal embedding, or vice versa. In these cases, some components of the constitutional vision, but not others, will become embedded. A context defined by embedding along only one dimension implies that the constitution is less well embedded overall than a context in which both social and legal embedding have occurred. The impact of a partially embedded constitution is likely to be diminished, though it may still shape expectations and behavior around claim-making (on the socially embedded dimension) or judicial behavior (on the legally embedded dimension). Further, both uneven and partial embedding may give way to relatively complete embedding over time, as embedding develops across rights arenas or sectors of society in a piecemeal fashion.

Plotted graphically, we might imagine the degree of social embedding on the x-axis and legal embedding on the y-axis (as shown in Figure 2.1). As you move up and to the right (into the shaded area), a constitution becomes more embedded. We would expect the greatest frequency of mobilization of law in this top right quadrant (dark gray), as the behavior of both social and legal actors reflects the belief that constitutional provisions are meaningful; that citizens can make claims to the rights listed in the constitution. At the top left, we see a high degree of legal embedding without much social embedding. This combination indicates significant changes in law and the expectations of judicial system actors, but negligible changes to societal expectations or discourses. Here, a support structure (Epp 1998) can help to ensure that legal mobilization occurs, even if claimants would not by themselves be able to pursue – or be interested in pursuing – social change through the law.

At the bottom right, we have a high degree of social, but not legal, embedding. If citizens talk about social goods as rights, but the legal system does not accept that frame (which would include both the rejection of the possibility of making claims and the rejection of claims once they are made), then we are in the world of this quadrant. This kind of disconnect could occur because of "sterilization by judicial interpretation,"[11] a term coined by Manuel José Cepeda to indicate active judicial efforts to restrict the meaning or scope of rights, or it could reflect that judges and lawyers are not necessarily opposed but nonetheless have not yet fully embraced this new legal vision. Rights talk may still serve claimants as they mobilize outside the legal sphere (McCann 1994), and the continued mobilization within the legal sphere may over time encourage judges to accept the validity of rights claims (Taylor 2020a).[12] In the bottom left quadrant (not embedded either socially or legally), we have a constitution as that is understood by societal and judicial actors alike as a set of parchment promises or as otherwise insignificant. While an unembedded or weakly embedded constitution may become more embedded over time, the longer a constitution remains unembedded, the less likely it is to ever structure social and legal expectations.

The positioning of social and legal embedding is at no point fixed, and it will likely differ substantially subnationally and across categories of difference (e.g., social or racial groups, class). State presence can vary dramatically between more central and more peripheral locales (O'Donnell 1993; Heller 2013; Kruks-Wisner 2018). Further, numerous scholars have documented how the experiences of race–class subjugated communities, for example, are defined by the coercive rather than protective or distributive capacities of the state (e.g., Soss and Weaver 2017; Rothstein 2017; Alexander 2010; see also McCann and Kahraman 2021). These social experiences and the state's orientation toward these groups will condition both components of constitutional embedding. Turning to temporal dynamics, at the moment of drafting, constitutions will not yet be embedded (for anyone). Social and legal

[11] Elite interview 68 (February 23, 2017).

[12] Judges could instead become hardened to certain claims (see Kim et al. 2021).

embedding might proceed quite quickly after the promulgation of a constitution, or these processes may stagnate.

Constitutions or constitutional orders can become dislodged in a variety of ways, including challenges related to workload, powerful interests, and the scope of the law. Each type of challenge impacts both social and legal embeddedness. Work-related challenges have to do with the new labor created by this new constitutional vision. Judges must hear new kinds of claims (sometimes an extremely large number of these claims). The workload itself may prove difficult for judges to keep up with, and the new content of claims may cause additional complications, especially if judges do not feel that they have adequate training to decide cases on these new matters. This situation presents a challenge to legal embedding to the extent that judges decide cases imperfectly, offer contradictory decisions, or otherwise undermine precedent and shared understandings of the law. When citizens have negative experiences, especially ones that do not align with social expectations of the way that rights and the law ought to function, these experiences can also undermine social embeddedness. Ideational buy-in from judges, fear of sanctions, and additional training and other measures to reduce the workload (such as the hiring of new judges) can help mitigate the potentially destabilizing impact of these challenges.

Actors both within and outside of the formal legal system may also present challenges to the embedding or stability of the new constitutional order. As the new constitutional order empowers certain actors – like judges, especially Constitutional Court justices, as well as different sectors of society – those who object to the constitutional vision or those who are relatively disempowered by it may attempt to limit or delegitimate the order. For example, actors within the executive or legislative branches may refuse to comply with court orders or they may draft legislative acts that would restrict the courts or reshape the scope of existing legal tools. These actors might also criticize the courts and their interpretation of rights in the media. To the extent that they are successful in sowing seeds of doubt about or generating disdain for the constitutional project, these can impede or even dislodge both social and legal embedding. Those empowered by this new vision of law can contest these power-related challenges, particularly if they are able to build constituencies (Landau 2014) or coalitions of support.

Finally, there are limits (though they are perhaps quite flexible at times) to the kinds of problems that are legible to the law. Some problems are easier to document and describe in ways that are compatible with legal system processes than others, for instance where there is a specific harm that is directly attributable to some identifiable actor. More diffuse problems – both in terms of their causes and effects – are more difficult to package in the language and procedures of law. Those whose problems fall into this latter category may see a yawning gap between their lives and the value of the rights they are purported to have. As they are left behind or frozen out, they may come to see law and rights as less than relevant in their lives, or at least as insufficient to remedy their problems. This perception presents a challenge to social embedding (in addition to normative concerns about equal or equitable treatment under the law or realizing the transformative potential of the new legal order). Citizens and organizations may offer creative legal arguments in favor of broader rights protections or judges may expand rights protections of their own accord in response to this challenge, but neither of these responses is guaranteed. Further, these responses present a new potential stumbling block for legal and social embedding if they exacerbate conflicts with political actors or if these efforts lead to an overexpansion of the promises of law (but not the delivery of remedies) and citizens come to view rights and law as empty promises.

Working against these challenges to the embedding of constitutional law is legal mobilization. When patterns of legal mobilization become self-reinforcing, constitutions come to be embedded both socially and legally in such a way that prevents or at least limits the dislodging of a constitutional order – a process described in detail in Section 2.2. The endpoint of constitutional embedding, however, is not the full realization of rights or a rights utopia, but the large-scale transformation of politics, such that politics are processed through the lens of constitutionalism.

2.2 LEGAL MOBILIZATION AS A MECHANISM OF CONSTITUTIONAL EMBEDDING

Patterns in legal claim-making and judicial decision-making determine the extent to which social constitutionalism remains a parchment promise and the extent to which it comes to be a defining feature of citizens' everyday lives. In this section, I draw on a constructivist perspective on legal mobilization, which helps illuminate how current interactions between claimants, intermediaries, and judges shape future possibilities for legal claim-making, by influencing both institutional rules and societal expectations (McCann 1994; Vanhala 2010; Taylor 2020a). Through this lens, the key role that legal mobilization can play in embedding constitutions becomes evident. In what follows, I first discuss the concept of legal mobilization, before detailing the social construction of legal grievances and the development of judicial receptivity. I close with a demonstration of the relationship between legal mobilization and constitutional embedding.

2.2.1 What Is Legal Mobilization?

Definitions of legal mobilization abound. For instance, Frances Zemans (1983: 700) suggests that "[l]aw is mobilized when a desire or want is translated into a demand as an assertion of rights," while Richard Lempert (1976: 173) offers that legal mobilization refers to "the process by which legal norms are invoked to regulate behavior." More recently, Lisa Vanhala (2011) has proposed that legal mobilization encompasses "any type of process by which an individual or collective actors invoke legal norms, discourse, or symbols to influence policy or behavior." Scholarship on legal mobilization has proliferated, though often in the absence of a clear operationalization of the term and not always in a coherent, additive research agenda.

When I refer to legal mobilization, I mean the explicit, self-conscious use of law involving a formal institutional mechanism (Lehoucq and Taylor 2020: 168).[13] In other words, legal mobilization corresponds to claim-making practices in the formal legal sphere, whether individual (Zemans 1983) or collective in nature (Burstein 1991). Legal mobilization implicates an internal process (of defining a grievance or a struggle in terms of legal language or symbols) and an external process (of sharing that understanding with outside actors). The actions encompassed by the term legal mobilization then include administrative procedures, quasi-judicial procedures (such as those complaints processed by human rights or gender commissions and ombudsman's offices), and legal procedures (litigation). The focus on legal claims made in the context of formal institutions rather than any number of activities potentially related to law – such as bargaining in the shadow of the law (Mnookin and Kornhauser 1979) or using the discourse of rights in everyday settings to frame problems as legal in nature – facilitates

[13] See Lehoucq and Taylor (2020) for an in-depth consideration of the concept of legal mobilization and closely related concepts, like legal consciousness and legal framing.

careful comparison across contexts, assuring that the comparisons involve like units. Further, rights talk may or may not coincide with legal claim-making, and a conceptualization of legal mobilization that distinguishes between the two allows for the probing of whether or not they occur together.

Legal mobilization is a form of political participation. Legal claims in the aggregate (if not always individually) reflect disagreements about the proper distribution of resources and about the proper way or ways in which societal actors ought to interact, thus they imply political demands (see, e.g., Zemans 1983; Marshall 1998; Gallagher 2006, 2017; Gallagher and Yang 2017; Taylor 2018; Kim et al. 2021), as well as particular understandings of the rights of citizens and obligations of states. Legal mobilization can involve a wide array of agents acting in apparently independent ways without overt political motive. These agents may not view themselves as mobilizing law, but collectively they are part of the mobilization of law, and that mobilization has consequences for politics, for who gets what, when, and how (Lasswell 1936).

2.2.2 How Can Legal Mobilization Serve to Embed Constitutionalism?

By looking to the process of legal mobilization, we can make sense of the shift between an initial period of experimental claim-making that comes in the wake of the creation of new, progressive constitutions – a time in which understandings about rights, the law, and state obligations held by both potential claimants and judges are unsettled – and later, more established patterns of claim-making and judicial decision-making.[14] This shift involves (1) the social construction of specific issues as legal grievances and (2) the development of judicial receptivity to particular kinds of claims through a reinterpretation of the meaning and scope of fundamental constitutional rights. Under certain circumstances, the combination of these processes can result in a positive feedback loop, with one catalyzing the other. If potential

[14] My analysis formally begins after a constitution has been created. This practical choice – one must establish the bounds of a research project somewhere – should not be taken as a claim that what comes before or how there comes to be a new constitution is independent from what comes next. As Lisa Vanhala (2010), Rachel Cichowski (2007), and others clearly show, civil society mobilization prior to legal rights recognitions can have significant downstream effects. Chapter 3 details the development of constitutional law in Colombia prior to the 1991 Constitution, as well as the social and political context around the 1991 constituent assembly.

claimants come to view an issue as a legal grievance, they are more likely to engage in legal claim-making around that issue. Those efforts as legal claim-making can prompt judicial receptivity, especially when judges are also exposed to the underlying issue in their everyday lives. Where legal claim-making is met with judicial receptivity, this both confirms the sense that the issue is a legal grievance and prompts further claim-making, resulting in a positive feedback loop. Thus, patterns of legal claim-making (especially claims regarding the right to health, as shown in Chapters 4 and 5) can become solidified over time, which is exactly what occurred in Colombia. At times, however, this pattern will be interrupted, leading to partial embedding or the dislodging of an embedded constitution.

The four panels in Figure 2.2 provide a stylized illustration of the four possible end points of constitutional embedding through legal mobilization: no embedding (Panel 1), two variants of partial embedding (Panels 2 and 3), and embedding (Panel 4). Panel 1 depicts what happens when neither the social constitution of legal grievances nor the development of judicial receptivity to particular kinds of claims occur: following the introduction of a new constitution, some folks may engage in experimental claim-making, but this claim-making will stagnate, with no positive feedback dynamics developing. Under these conditions, constitutional embedding will not occur. Panel 2 shows that the social construction of legal grievances may occur without the concurrent development of judicial receptivity. Here, citizens' understandings of the law and their problems will change, but their claims will be stymied in the courts: social embedding, but not legal embedding will occur, rendering constitutional embedding partial. Panel 3 shows the inverse, legal embedding without social embedding. In this case, judges may be receptive to particular kinds of claims, but few claims will be brought before them. Once again, partial embedding results. Panel 4 tracks the full process of constitutional embedding, where the social construction of legal grievances and development of judicial receptivity feed into and reinforce one another, propelling sustained legal mobilization and both social and legal embedding.

While the Colombian case follows the self-reinforcing logic shown in Panel 4 of Figure 2.2 – where both social and legal embedding occur – this pattern will not always result. If initial, experimental legal claim-making is met with little receptivity on the part of judges or broader society, the constitutional vision may quickly fade from everyday life, such that ultimately it is merely words on paper. Citizens may push for rights

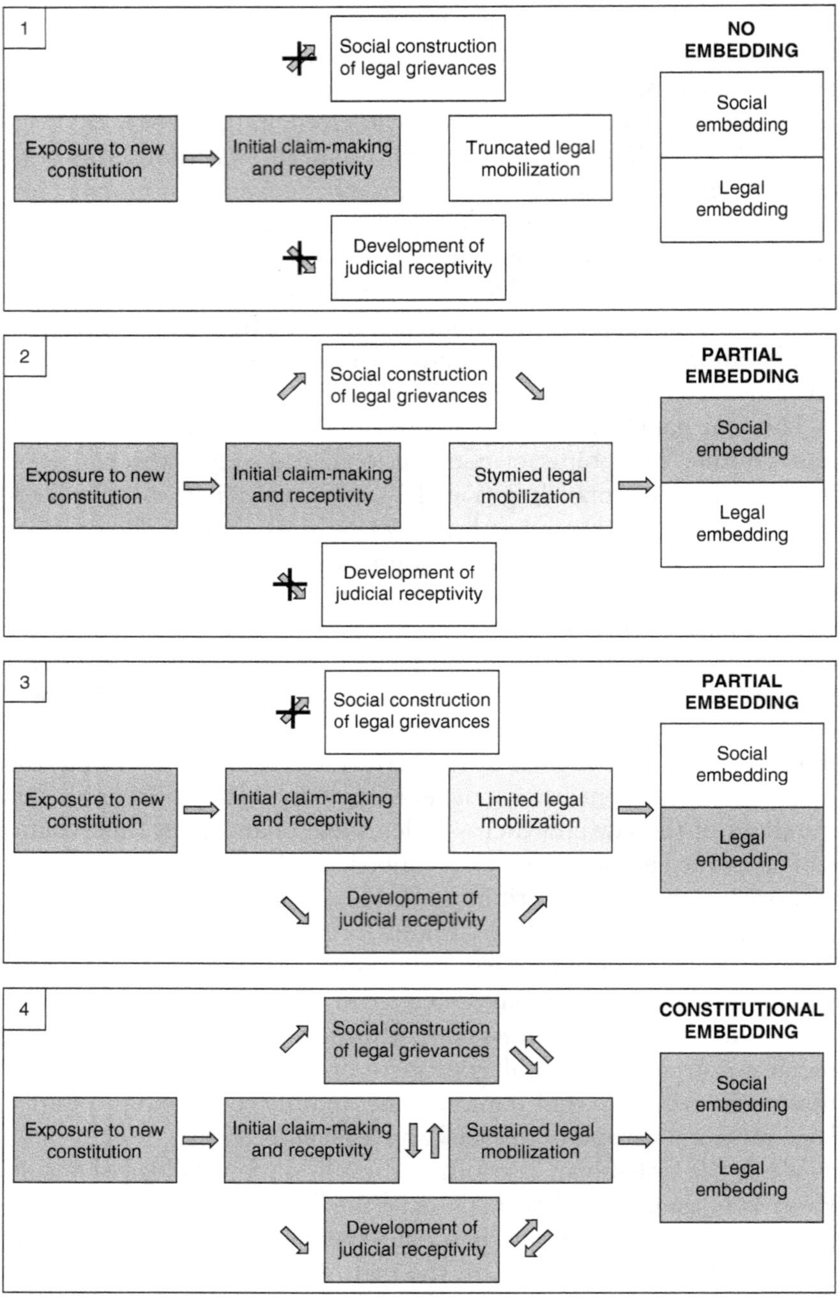

Figure 2.2 The process of constitutional embedding.

protections by way of other strategies or they may not. Middle-ground outcomes, in which constitutions are neither fully embedded nor largely irrelevant to legal or social life, are also possible. Where social and legal visions of the constitution do not overlap, we may see partial embedding. Here, positive feedback loops do not form. Social embedding without legal embedding may still propel citizens to advance legal claims, and legal embedding without social embedding may lead to judges issuing rights-protective decisions for the limited claims that come before them. This partial embedding will be less stable and more prone to fragmentation than combined instances of legal and social embedding.

Further, under the right conditions, legal mobilization can even lead to negative feedback effects and the dislodging of a constitutional order. Social embedding – especially when driven by state-sponsored outreach efforts – can raise expectations among claimants about both the way the legal system will work and the effect their claim-making efforts will have. When citizens are encouraged to file claims and those claims are summarily dismissed or met by judges who hold a conflicting understanding of the law, legal mobilization may undermine the embeddedness of constitutional law. If a regime has sought to use constitutional law and rights rhetoric for legitimation purposes and set up incentives for judges to limit rights protections (Whiting 2017, forthcoming; Kim et al. 2021), citizens may develop what Mary Gallagher (2006) calls "informed disenchantment" or what Marc Hertogh (2018) describes as "legal alienation." Here, the experienced disconnect (between visions of law held by potential claimants and visions of law enacted by legal actors) cuts against embeddedness, showcasing the contradictions and tensions of law rather than its promises.

This majority of this book focuses on the "positive" case of successful constitutional embedding in Colombia, exploring how this one particular outcome developed and the moments at which embedding seemed less likely and less possible.[15] Chapter 9 presents a short case study of constitutional embedding in South Africa, where the 1996 Constitution came to be embedded firmly along the legal dimension without similar depth of embedding along the social dimension.

[15] As mentioned in Chapter 1, positive here simply refers to the state of constitutional embedding: that a constitution has been embedded. Successful constitutional embedding may or may not yield normatively positive outcomes; that is a separate question.

Before turning to the case studies in these later chapters, the rest of this chapter explores the social construction of legal grievances and the development of judicial receptivity – processes set into motion by legal mobilization that can then drive constitutional embedding. The chapter closes with an explanation of how these two processes interact with one another.

2.2.2.1 The Social Construction of Legal Grievances

In order to understand how certain issues come to be understood as potentially claimable in the formal legal system and how these understandings solidify into patterns over time, we must look to (1) the transformation of beliefs about rights and law, as well as (2) the role of societal actors in framing everyday problems as legal in nature. I describe this process as the "social construction of legal grievances,"[16] a term that emphasizes the ideational and interactive elements of this process.[17]

The ways that citizens learn about their rights as new, progressive constitutions are debated, drafted, and implemented are important for understanding the transformation of beliefs about rights and law. This transformation is likely to be a slow process. The institutional changes implied by the adoption of new constitutions are meaningful only insofar as citizens actually engage them. Stated differently, opportunity for mobilization emerges not when rights are codified, but when (at least some) citizens gain awareness of these rights and believe that they can make claims to them. What is important is not only the accumulation of accurate knowledge about the Bill of Rights or the legal process, but more specifically the development of a set of beliefs about the nature of rights and the purpose of the legal system, as well as the understanding that claims to those goods or services can or should be advanced in legal forums.

Many different sets of actors – including some who are traditionally associated with the legal system and some who are not – will be involved in this process. I highlight how societal actors – a catch-all term referring to those actors not employed in or by the formal legal

[16] The "social construction of legal grievances" may be defined as both a direct and an indirect symbolic effect of legal mobilization, to use César Rodríguez Garavito's terms (2011).

[17] This feature of my account fits in neatly with Chris Hilson's (2010) call to bring grievances back into the study of legal mobilization, as well as Erica Simmons' (2014; 2016) and Janice Gallagher's (2022) entreaties to consider the meaning behind specific grievances.

system, including pharmaceutical and insurance companies, advocacy networks, NGOs, and community organizations – impact views on which issues are ripe for legal claim-making and which are not. Societal actors play an integral role in legal mobilization, not only materially supporting claimants in their efforts to seek redress but also actively contributing to the social construction of grievances by helping to frame certain issues as legal grievances. In other words, societal actors encourage potential claimants to view a specific problem through the lens of the law and to make claims in the formal legal system rather than doing nothing or advancing a claim in some other setting.

Many investigations of mobilization either assume that grievances are based on "underlying activity" (following Casper and Posner 1974) or are simply ever present (following McCarthy and Zald 1977). Other accounts typically fail to articulate a stance on where grievances come from and how actors recognize something as a grievance. A constructivist approach, in contrast, acknowledges that grievances, and especially legal grievances, develop through social interaction, rather than appearing unmediated as a result of material conditions (see also Simmons 2016). As activists, lawyers, judges, and government officials participate in the framing of an issue as legal in nature (by advancing such a frame, accepting it, or failing to contest it), this legal frame may spread and come to be incorporated diffusely into everyday understandings of the issue in question (McCann 1994; Pedriana 2006; Vanhala 2016, 2018a, 2018b).

There is also a more direct process by which NGOs, legal aid services, and other actors reach out to individuals who have a particular problem and argue that their problem is a legal one, which should be addressed in the formal legal sphere. This kind of action is most clear in strategic litigation campaigns, but it is potentially much broader than that. In fact, in the case of health rights claims in Colombia, insurance companies that were targeted in legal claims ultimately came to encourage legal claim-making in this direct fashion, as the legal cases counterintuitively offered these companies the possibility of financial gain rather than sanction. Another variant of this process involves NGOs and legal aid services convincing potential claimants to actually pursue litigation, vouching that there is a viable argument and reasonable chance of winning. Through these processes, potential claimants come to view issues that previously they were willing (or resigned) to ignore or to deal with in other ways as legal issues or as legal grievances. Here, the material reality of people's lives does not change, but their understanding of that reality does.

Only by examining beliefs and repeated interaction between potential claimants, judges, and societal actors can we understand the social construction of legal grievances. These beliefs are constructed and reconstructed through a dynamic and interactive process in which various actors contest the boundaries of what issues are considered to be legal in nature. These societal actors influence the social construction of legal grievances, which then feeds into patterns of legal claim-making. Beliefs about rights and the law, thus, impact claim-making beyond rights knowledge or rights consciousness. But the social construction of legal grievances is only one of the factors feeding into continued legal mobilization; how judges respond to claims is also important.

2.2.2.2 The Development of Judicial Receptivity

In order to understand how judicial receptivity to particular kinds of claims emerges and solidifies over time, we must look to (1) the relationship between judicial agency and shifts in institutional rules, as well as (2) the impact of societal actors and daily life on how judges understand the nature of the problems that come before them in the form of legal claims (Taylor 2020a, 2023). The exercise of judicial agency can entail the creation of new rules, tests, and standards regarding rights protections. When this possibility of the exercise of judicial agency combines with the public exposure of judges to problems, judicial receptivity to particular kinds of rights claims can result, leading to the embedding (or not) of a particular constitutional order.

In short, judicial agency refers to actions undertaken by judges as they fulfill their judicial functions: they decide cases, and in doing so, they interpret law that is often ambiguous. Further, they must make decisions in their nonneutral social environments, and these decisions have political consequences. As such, judges ought to be conceptualized as situated political actors. Judges make choices about which cases to hear and how to decide the cases they do hear, and these choices have potentially long-lasting and unforeseen consequences. Perhaps most importantly, judges make these choices in specific social contexts.

By looking to role conceptions, attitudes, and strategic incentives, existing scholarship on judicial decision-making seeks to explain the kinds of choices judges make. Importantly, though, with each decision a judge takes, they *could have chosen otherwise*. If a judge (1) holds progressive attitudes about rights, (2) envisions their role as one that protects the rights of citizens, and/or (3) sees an opportunity to expand the power of the courts, they may issue a rights-protective decision in a given case. Still, the judge has leeway in how to delimit the decision and what legal foundation to rely on, among other things. They must offer reasons for their decisions, but there may be many potential reasons for any particular decision. And, of course, judges may instead view their roles narrowly, have rights-restrictive views, and/or face incentives to deny rights claims – and they may issue their rights-restrictive decisions in a variety of different ways.

Judges can shape opportunities for legal mobilization by changing understandings about and uses of preexisting institutional arrangements, through the contingent exercise of judicial agency. This exercise of judicial agency is likely to be particularly influential in the moments during and following constitutional transition, where understandings of rights, state obligation, and the role of judges are unsettled. Contingent choices made by judges during these periods will have outsized effects on questions of justiciability and can serve to either institutionalize and embed constitutional models or erode them.

Importantly, judicial receptivity is not static and it does not fall solely within the domain of judges; instead, it is dynamic and the consequence of repeated interactions between judges, claimants, and societal actors over time. Existing studies have identified two pathways through which societal actors can influence judicial receptivity to particular claims: changes in argumentation about points of legal interpretation and changes in personnel. With respect to argumentation about legal interpretation, Amanda Hollis-Brusky (2015), Ezequiel González-Ocantos (2016), and Tommaso Pavone (2022), in studies of the Federalist Society in the United States, transitional justice in Latin America, and domestic use of European law in European Union countries, respectively, show how civil society organizations can play a pedagogical role, introducing and supporting new arguments about rights or interpretation to sympathetic judges.[18] They further demonstrate that societal actors may focus on personnel changes, advocating for the replacement of opposed judges and for the nomination of favored judges.

I identify an additional pathway at play in the context of the development of social constitutionalism: public exposure to problems. This

[18] These studies show how societal actors can play this pedagogical role outside of the filing of amicus briefs. Many scholars have demonstrated the potential impact of arguments presented in such briefs as well (see Cichowski 2007, among others).

pathway involves a joint public and legal process, where an issue becomes visible to judges in their lived experience outside the courtroom as well as legible to judges as legal in nature. Judges may come to believe that this legal problem is not being dealt with well or sufficiently in the context of the legal system. They then may become more open to new legal approaches to the issue. The exposure mechanism differs from the argumentation mechanism in that judges are not swayed by new legal arguments. Instead, the persistence and/or increase of claims related to a specific grievance cumulatively inform judges about an issue, making them comfortable with the scope of the issue, making them more aware of the issue's salience, and making them identify with claimants. This can spark a consideration or reconsideration about the correct legal response to that issue – and therefore those claims. Although Malcolm Feeley and Edward Rubin (1998: 160) examine judicial policy-making rather than legal mobilization, they identify a similar process at play in their analysis of the judicial response to reprehensible prison conditions in the United States, suggesting that "these conditions had existed for a century, of course; what changed suddenly, in 1965, was the judiciary's perceptions of them." Here, continued claim-making (and thus continued exposure) ultimately prompted a change in judicial receptivity.

Breaking this process down, an initial confluence of exposure in daily life outside the legal system and exposure within the legal system plays an important role in the development of judicial receptivity, inspiring judges to connect an issue that they have perhaps seen on television or in their everyday lives with the format, scope, and tools of the law. Repeated exposure to similar cases within the formal legal system can have several concrete effects. As Julio Ríos-Figueroa (2016: 29) outlines, where there is a "continuous flow of cases [judges] will not only get more and more varied information, but will also be more able to express their jurisprudential preferences under more favorable circumstances." By contrast, if there are only a handful of cases on a particular topic over a longer period of time, judges will have less flexibility in their decision-making, as they are bound by the facts of the cases before them and may be forced to decide cases in unfavorable political environments. The mere existence of many cases does not necessarily mean that judges will seek to resolve those cases in novel ways. In fact, repeated exposure alone could result in a hardening of judges' views (Kim et al. 2021). This is where an additional factor comes into play: assessments of the nature of the issue and how it comports with sociolegal values.[19] When judges view the issue as oppositional to contemporary sociolegal values, such as country-specific understandings of dignity, exposure can result in judicial receptivity, as judges come to see the issue not only as one that could be resolved in the formal legal sphere, but also as one that *needs* to be resolved.[20]

Judges' beliefs about rights and the state, which are conditioned by their personal experiences, as well as by interactions with claimants and actors outside of the formal legal sphere, are key to understanding patterns in legal mobilization. These beliefs and interactions shape the contours of judicial receptivity, encouraging judges to issue rights-protective decisions in certain kinds of cases and not others. Further, by issuing decisions on legal claims, judges alter opportunities for mobilization. Especially when they (or other actors) publicize these decisions and the reasons underlying them, judges also influence social understandings of which issues are legal in nature – in other words, judicial receptivity also influences the social construction of legal grievances. When social and legal visions of the new constitution overlap, positive feedback loops can form, with the social construction of legal grievances and the development of judicial receptivity bolstering each other, which in turn incentivizes sustained legal mobilization and serves to propel constitutional embedding.

2.3 CONCLUSION

This book examines how constitutional rights become "real," or how the promises written into constitutions come to have social and legal meaning, and thus shape the behavior of both everyday citizens and judicial system actors. Key to this process is the development of both the social and legal dimensions of constitutional embedding through legal

[19] I use "sociolegal" intentionally, because social and legal values will not always align – for example, the South African Constitutional Court's decision against the death penalty despite widespread support for it – and at times legal values may be interpreted through the lens of social values, leading courts "to defer to popularly elected branches of government when litigated claims challenge deeply held religious beliefs or traditions" (Wilson and Gianella-Malca, 2019: 154).

[20] Charli Carpenter (2007: 663) notes that on top of "permissive factors" (issue attributes, visibility, graftability), strategic considerations affect whether or not activists take up specific issues. These particular strategic factors are not likely to come into play for judges, as the constraints judges face are fundamentally different from those faced by activists. Like Carpenter, though, I view exposure/visibility as a permissive rather than a sufficient condition.

mobilization. When these two dimensions of embedding reinforce each other – as judges, lawyers, everyday citizens, and various other societal actors come to share the same vision of the possibilities and limits of constitution law – a constitutional order will be difficult to dislodge.

Legal mobilization can drive the construction of this shared vision. Following the adoption of new constitutions that recognized a wide set of rights, citizens gradually come to learn about these rights, and they begin to take some of the problems in their lives to the formal legal system, experimentally. Some of the time,[21] this experimental claim-making solidifies into general patterns in claim-making, as citizen come to view particular issues as legal grievances and as societal actors – ranging from NGOs engaged in rights-based activism to insurance companies that sought to offload costs – encourage further claim-making. Simultaneously, judges' beliefs about their role and the applicability of the law to social issues change, in part because of the way that legal claims and daily life combine to expose them to these problems. As judges continue to decide cases, the terrain of opportunity for further claim-making shifts.

Where sustained legal claim-making on a particular issue (following the identification of the issue as legal grievances) prompts judicial receptivity by exposing judges to that issue, positive feedback loops form and legal mobilization becomes self-reinforcing. Receptivity then inspires further claim-making. This is especially true when judges signaled the kinds of arguments or claims they were most likely to evaluate favorably by staging pedagogical interventions or offering "cues" (Baird 2007) to potential claimants, in the process spreading information to potential claimants about the kinds of arguments or claims likely to be accepted. Thus, the process of legal mobilization can serve as a mechanism of constitutional embedding, with the iterative process of claim-making in the formal legal sphere shaping how both everyday citizens and legal actors understand what the law is and does – or what the law ought to be and what it ought to do.

Wholesale constitutional embedding is not a preordained outcome; nor will it necessarily result from legal mobilization. Constitutional

[21] Importantly, the goal of this book is not to predict when exactly individuals will turn to law and when they will not. Nor is the goal to explain why any one individual turns to law while others do not. Instead, I seek to identify and explore broad social patterns related to legal claim-making and how they relate to the stability of the constitutional order.

embedding develops over time. It can occur steadily or in fits and starts, and once the process is started, it can develop unevenly or partially. Uneven embedding describes constitutional orders where some rights or provisions come to be meaningful while others lag. Partial embedding refers to the occurrence of a greater degree of legal embedding than social embedding, or vice versa. Partially embedded constitutional orders are more likely to be derailed than constitutional orders defined by both social and legal embedding. Subsequent chapters explore how social constitutionalism came to be embedded both socially and legally in Colombia and how challenges to that embedding were overcome.

CHAPTER THREE

EXPECTATIONS AND TRANSFORMATIONS OF COLOMBIAN CONSTITUTIONAL LAW

The façade of the Palacio de Justicia in Bogotá, which is home to Colombia's apex courts, reads: "Colombianos, las armas os han dado independencia. Las leyes os darán libertad" ("Colombians, guns have given you independence. Laws will give you freedom"). This quote is attributed to Francisco de Paula Santander, the famous Colombian military and political leader who was known as "the man of the laws." Left unspecified by Santander was the nature of that freedom promised by law.

Colombia's constitutional history indicates deep disagreements about the kinds of freedoms that can or ought to be enshrined in law. This chapter offers an overview of Colombian constitutionalism, focusing on the forces that led to the drafting of the 1991 Constitution. Following decades of social and political crises, Colombian social movement leaders demanded fundamental changes to the country and its legal system, though they did not rally around a particular constitutional vision. Instead, that vision came together piece by piece as the country's most diverse constituent assembly met and debated the content of the new 1991 Constitution. Drawing on a wide range of sources, this constituent assembly ultimately proposed a constitution that would recognize not only civil and political rights, but also social, economic, cultural, and even environmental rights. What's more, they also created a new legal procedure called the tutela that would allow Colombians to make claims to their newly codified rights.

The members of the constituent assembly did not imagine the scope of the changes to Colombian life that would come with the implementation of this new constitution. Prior moves in the direction of legally defined social commitments had never become embedded, as they were unable to endure changing political winds. How exactly social constitutionalism came to be embedded in Colombia is the subject of Chapters 3 and 4. In the rest of this chapter, however, I turn to the constitutional developments that preceded the adoption of social constitutionalism. I close with a description of the resulting constitutional text and general trends in the practice of legal claim-making in the context of social constitutionalism in Colombia.

3.1 EARLY COLOMBIAN CONSTITUTIONAL HISTORY

In 1821, delegates at the Congress of Cúcuta drafted Colombia's first national constitution, following years of regional constitutional orders.[1] This constitution is alternately known as the Constitution of 1821, the Constitution of Cúcuta, or the Constitution of Gran Colombia. A commonly told story features the independence-fighter and then vice-president Francisco de Paula Santander opening this constitutional text and laying it out over a sword, stating: "The swords of the liberators must now be subject to the laws of the republic."[2] This constitution marks the beginning of the intersection of national politics and constitutional law in Colombia.[3]

From 1821 to 1886, the country had seven constitutions, each marking intermediate points in conflicts between conservative and liberal political actors, where the victorious side drafted a guiding document in an attempt to consolidate its power.[4] None of these constitutions survived for more than twenty-three years. The longest lasting of these, the 1863 Constitution, which was also known as the Constitution of Rionegro, was implemented by a Liberal government. The 1863 Constitution featured a sizable Bill of Rights for the time and introduced a federal governing arrangement. Víctor Hugo dismissed

1 See, for instance, the Constitution of Socorro of 1810 and the Constitution of Cundinamarca of 1811.

2 See *El Tiempo* (March 29, 1992). President Simón Bolívar y Palacios was out of the country during this time, continuing to fight battles of independence against Spain throughout Latin America.

3 For more on the early history of constitutionalism in Colombia, see Restrepo Piedrahita (1993).

4 These constitutions include went into force in 1821, 1832, 1843, 1853, 1858, 1863, and 1886.

this constitution as being "a constitution fit for angels," rather than one fit for Colombia (Cepeda 2004: 532).[5]

Following yet another internal armed conflict, which culminated in the Battle of Humareda, Rafael Núñez came to power. In that moment, he is said to have declared: "The Constitution of 1863 has died."[6] A constituent assembly comprised primarily of Conservatives drafted a new constitution in 1886; one that affirmed the power of the Catholic Church, defined a centralized state, and rolled back many of the liberal reforms of the 1863 Constitution. The 1886 Constitution also set out a broader role for the judicial branch than outlined in previous constitutions. Namely, it bought about the possibility of judicial review in Colombia. In this system, the Supreme Court had the power to examine the constitutionality of legislative bills, though only under a limited set of circumstances.

A 1910 reform introduced the "public act of unconstitutionality," which allowed citizens to challenge the constitutionality of any law before the Supreme Court (Cepeda 2004: 538).[7] The reform in 1910 is just one of seventy-four reforms to the Constitution in its 105-year existence. These reforms – which created "practically a new constitution"[8] – began to "introduce a series of guarantees, particularly with the reform of 1936, which brought social rights into the Constitution … [including the idea of] the social function of property and the first land reform law in Colombia."[9] The 1936 reforms, which included substantial changes in matters of agriculture, education, and taxes, and allowed the state to play a more active role in the economy, came at the initiative of Liberal President Alfonso López Pumarejo. Hernando

[5] Juan Carlos Henao (2013), former magistrate of the Constitutional Court and rector of the Universidad Externado del Colombia, points out that historians have challenged whether or not Hugo actually said this, and importantly notes that whether or not the quote is true, the constitution in fact "expressed the intellectual aspirations and convictions of people of flesh and blood, not angels, people who believed in freedom of conscience, in the free development of the personality, of the balance of powers, of freedom of expression and information."

[6] Or more colorfully, as Henao (2013) attests, "La Constitución de Rionegro ha dejado de existir, sus páginas manchadas han sido quemadas entre las llamas de la Humareda." (The Constitution of Rionegro (1863) has ceased to exist. Its pages have been burned in the flames of Humareda.)

[7] For more on the 1910 reforms (as well as a general discussion of the development of administrative control in Colombia) see Malagón (2012).

[8] Elite interview 20 (September 6, 2016).

[9] Elite interview 30 (September 20, 2016).

Herrera traces the ideas behind these reform efforts to "the influence of the German [Weimar] Constitution and the Mexican Constitution of Querétaro [of 1917]."[10] Julieta Lemaitre also points to broader regional trends, arguing that the Liberal efforts "to push through modernizing constitutional reforms … [echo] the wider Latin American aspiration to modernity and development in the 1950s and 1960s. The 1936 reforms are part of social reforms all over the world, which include the New Deal." In her view, "[t]hese [we]re Western trends, and not particularly Colombian."[11]

As Julio Ortiz, who served as a justice on the Supreme Court, described it, these reforms could be understood as a "restricted social constitutionalism."[12] However, they were quickly undermined. For one, they did not impact judicial decisions.[13] In other words, these rights were not claimed in the legal sphere, and judges did not expand the scope of these rights through decisions. Judges, in fact, seemed to play the opposite role, leading Manuel José Cepeda to conclude that "it was a case of sterilization by judicial interpretation."[14] In addition, conservative elites opposed to President López Pumarejo attempted to initiate a constituent assembly to remove the legal foundation for these reforms. While these elites were unsuccessful in their efforts to once again reform the constitution, they did manage to roll back the reforms in the legislature.[15] Further, Gustavo Gallón, the founder of the Colombian Commission of Jurists, argues that "not only did [the reform of 1936] not become a reality, but it also gave rise to a very strong reaction on the part of the landowning sectors and was later translated into the violence of the '50s and the [violence] which we have lived until today."[16] Thus, while the 1936 reforms can be thought of as "constitutional antecedents" to the 1991 Constitution, as Hernando Herrera put it,[17] these reforms never became embedded in either a legal or social sense.

[10] Elite interview 39 (September 27, 2016).

[11] Elite interview 20 (September 6, 2016).

[12] Elite interview 33 (September 22, 2016).

[13] Elite interview 22 (September 8, 2016).

[14] Elite interview 68 (February 23, 2017).

[15] Elite interviews 20 (September 6, 2016), 27 (September 16, 2016), and 31 (September 21, 2016).

[16] Elite interview 58 (November 4, 2016). "No solamente no se hizo realidad, sino que dio lugar a una reacción muy fuerte de parte de los sectores terratenientes y se traduce después en la violencia de los años 50 y en ultimas en la que hemos vivido hasta hoy."

[17] Elite interview 39 (September 27, 2016).

Subsequent reforms in the 1950s recognized the right of women to vote (1954) and instituted a power-sharing agreement between the Conservative and Liberal parties called the National Front (1957). This power-sharing agreement was meant to stymie the continued expression of bipartisan violence, which had been a reoccurring feature of Colombian politics since the late nineteenth century. The 1957 reform also brought into effect a system of "co-option" on the Supreme Court, which meant that the Court would nominate new justices internally, as long as political balance was maintained between the two major parties (Cepeda 2004: 540). Amendments in 1968 paved the way for a transition out of the National Front, in addition to modifying congressional rules on a variety of matters. The National Front came to an official end in 1974, when both the major parties ran competitive candidates for president.

3.2 ENDEMIC VIOLENCE AND CONSTITUTIONAL CRISES

The inadequacies of Colombian state institutions became abundantly clear in the late 1970s and 1980s, as violence between the state, guerrilla groups, paramilitaries, and drug cartels continued, multiple attempted constitutional reforms flopped, and the country remained under an almost constant state of siege. Violence perpetrated by guerrilla groups endured, as did violence by the state and paramilitaries in the name of combating the guerrillas. This violence often took the form of human rights violations against ordinary citizens.[18] Throughout this period, the infamous Medellín drug cartel grew in strength and prominence, wreaking havoc across the country through car bombings and other violent tactics, oriented at both state and nonstate actors. The judiciary especially became the target of cartel violence, as a result of the possibility of extradition to the United States for drug-related offenses. This led to the creation of *jueces sin rostro* ("faceless judges") in the early 1990s: an effort to hide the identity of judges such that they would be able to decide cases without being subject to threats and homicide attempts.

Further, in 1985, the M-19, an urban guerrilla group, stormed the Palacio de Justicia, home to the Supreme Court and the Council of

[18] See Palacios (2006) and Tate (2007) for additional information on the recent history of violence in Colombia.

State, taking the sitting Supreme Court justices as well as hundreds of others hostage. The standoff ended twenty-eight hours later, following what has been described as an "excessive and disproportionate" military raid.[19] In the end, more than a hundred people, including twelve Supreme Court justices, died, and about dozen guerrillas were disappeared. According to Julieta Lemaitre (2009: 66), the violence at the Palacio de Justicia became "a symbol of the reality of the war and the impossibility of peace" to the general public. Solidifying this perception of the impossibility of peace was the near-continual state of siege, which expanded presidential powers but also indicated an inability of the government to respond to the challenges it faced. Mauricio García Villegas (2001) found that between 1970 and 1991, the Colombian government declared a state of siege more than 80 percent of the time, creating what he calls a "constitutional dictatorship."[20]

This violent context did not inspire faith in the ability of the state, including the judiciary, to respond effectively to citizen needs. Economic inequality and insecurity further exacerbated citizen mistrust in the state. As Donna Van Cott (2000: 49) notes, "economic dislocations made more apparent the extreme concentration of wealth, productive resources, and positions of authority in the hands of a small elite, and the extent to which this elite ruled in its own economic interest." Efforts to address any of these concerns seemed futile.

Two Liberal presidents – Alfonso López Michelsen and Julio César Turbay Ayala – unsuccessfully attempted to initiate constitutional reforms in 1978 and 1981, respectively.[21] The Supreme Court blocked both reforms on procedural grounds. In the case of the López Michelsen reforms, the Court argued that constitutional reform fell within the duties of the Congress, and that Congress could not delegate these duties. With the Turbay reforms, which had received congressional approval, the Court pointed to other procedural problems. In 1987, the Supreme Court announced that future plebiscites would be prohibited. Plebiscites had in the past, for example in 1957, led to constitutional reforms. John Martz (1997: 248) notes that "by early 1988 the topic

[19] See Cosoy (2015) for the BBC. Cosoy cites historian David Bushnell, who suggests that the military may have acted on its own, rather than waiting for the orders of President Belisario Betancur.

[20] See also Antonio Barreto (2011).

[21] One Conservative president, Belisario Betancur, was able to implement a proposed constitutional reform, which decentralized the Colombian state, creating local political participation mechanisms, and allowed for the direct election of mayors.

[of constitutional reform] was the single hottest political issue in the media." That year, President Virgilio Barco proposed a plebiscite on the issue of plebiscites. In an interview, Fernando Cepeda, Minister of Justice under President Barco, described this proposal by referring to the saying, "*en derecho, las cosas son rehacen como se hacen*, [or] in matters of law, you un-make laws the way you make them."[22] The plebiscite was blocked by Congress, and other efforts by the Barco government to advance constitutional reform were stymied yet again by the Supreme Court and the threat of cartel violence (Van Cott 2000).

In addition, three presidential candidates were assassinated between 1989 and 1990, including a young, popular Liberal senator by the name of Luis Carlos Galán.[23] As Van Cott (2000: 53) states, Galán's death "seemed to symbolize the deaths of hundreds of judges, politicians, journalists, and common citizens." Inspired especially by Galán's death, but also by the general climate of seemingly unending violence, students throughout the country protested, calling for constitutional reform. Alejandra Barrios, one of the leaders of the student movement recalls their motivation:

> This series of events caused us to mobilize for the right to live, for the right to die of old age … What we saw was no future, there was no way out. Impossibilities of negotiation, impossibilities of institutional changes. When we created the student movement, we were looking for a social pact. We understood the constitution not as a charter of rights or a legal agreement, but, in truth, as a new social pact … It was not so much about the content of the constitution as the chance to say, "This country has to find another way besides war."[24]

[22] Elite interview 5 (August 8, 2016).

[23] Candidates Bernardo Jaramillo Ossa (Unión Patriótica) and Carlos Pizarro Leongómez (M-19) were both killed in 1990. Another prominent member of the Unión Patriótica, Jaime Pardo Leal, was assassinated in 1987.

[24] Elite interview 46 (October 19, 2016). "Esta serie de eventos hizo que nos movilizáramos por el derecho de vivir, por el derecho a morir de viejos, ni siquiera hablamos de nuestros hijos o de nuestros papas. Era que se estaba rescatando el derecho a morir de viejos, porque además estábamos en un contexto de niños sicarios. Lo que uno veía era un no futuro, era una sin salida. Imposibilidades de negociación, imposibilidades de cambios institucionales. Cuando fuimos al movimiento estudiantil, en ultimas estábamos buscando era volver a hacer un pacto social, entendíamos la constitución no como una carta de derechos no como un acuerdo jurídico, sino de verdad, como un nuevo acuerdo social: donde tomáramos la decisión de no matarnos, no era tanto en si mismo el contenido de la constitución. Era la posibilidad de volvernos a sentarnos y decir: este país tiene que encontrar otra salida a la guerra."

In 1989, the students organized a silent march to the Plaza de Bolívar: the site of the Palacio de Justicia and a frequent culminating point for protest marches in Bogotá. The following year, the movement asked voters to fill out an additional, seventh ballot (*séptima papeleta*) in support of the creation of a constituent assembly. Though the Barco government supported such an effort, the possibility of an official plebiscite and constitutional reform had to pass through the Supreme Court, which had blocked several previous reform efforts. Surprisingly, the Court accepted the Barco government's arguments that the *séptima papeleta* represented the will of the people and that the president's state of siege powers allowed him to convoke a constitutional assembly, as the country was in crisis. Voters overwhelmingly approved the proposed assembly.[25] At this point, there seemed to be agreement that, in this time of crisis, some kind of legal change was in order. The type of change, however, was by no means predetermined.

3.3 THE ASAMBLEA NACIONAL CONSTITUYENTE AND THE SOCIAL CONSTITUTION

On December 9, 1990, Colombian voters elected seventy members to the constituent assembly,[26] including twenty-five members of the Liberal Party, nineteen of the demobilized Marxist guerrilla group Movimiento 19 de Abril (Movement of April 19, or M-19), eleven from a newly formed political party called the Movimiento de Salvación Nacional (Movement for National Salvation, or MSN), nine from the Conservative Party, and two each from the Movimiento Unión Cristiana (the Christian Union Movement, an evangelical group), the Unión Patriótica (Patriotic Union, a leftist political party affiliated with demobilized members of the FARC as well as the Communist Party), and indigenous movements. Fernando Carrillo Flórez, one of the leaders of the student movement, was elected from the Liberal Party list. The government appointed four additional members, two from the demobilized Ejercito Popular de Liberación (Popular Liberation Army), one from the Partido Revolucionario de Trabajadores (Workers Revolutionary Party), and one from El Movimiento Armado

[25] See Dugas (2001b) and Lemaitre (2009) for more detailed accounts of the student movement.

[26] For more detail on the workings of the constituent assembly, see Van Cott (2000).

Quintín Lame (The Armed Movement of Quintín Lame, a recently demobilized indigenous guerrilla group). Álvaro Gómez Hurtado of the MSN, Antonio Navarro Wolff of the M-19, and Horacio Serpa Uribe of the Liberal Party shared the presidency of the constituent assembly.[27] Juan Carlos Esguerra, a constituent from the MSN list, notes the importance of this (ideological) diversity[28] in the composition of the assembly: "The one main difference between [the 1991] Constitution and all the others before … is the fact that it was drafted a group of Colombians that were representing the entire republic, that were directly elected by the people, and they were a very small but comprehensive and full picture of Colombia."[29] This was the group of people who would determine which legal changes would take place – at least on paper.

The constituents divided themselves into five commissions, with each member deciding which of the commissions to participate in. All proposals put forward by the commissions had to be approved during two plenary debates. David Landau (2014: 89) argues that members of the constituent assembly "view[ed] solutions to the grave problems that the country was facing in 1991 in terms of judges and law" in large part due to the historical involvement of the Supreme Court "in a broad range of political disputes." Even within the context of this legal focus, the constituents had a wide range of viable options from which to choose as they drafted a new constitution. When we take a close look at the ideational considerations of the constituents, we see that the adoption of social constitutionalism was neither inevitable nor necessarily expected by the actors involved in the constitutional debates. The constituents evaluated many approaches to constitutional law, and, perhaps more importantly, they did not always anticipate the consequences of the choices they made as they drafted a new constitution.

Those who were involved in the Constitutional Assembly uniformly recollected a commitment to exploring different legal traditions that could be adapted to better fit the Colombian context. Manual José Cepeda describes the preparation that he and the other advisors to

[27] See Banco de la República (n.d.) for more information on each of the constituents.

[28] Only four women participated in the assembly: Helena Herrán de Montoya (Partido Liberal), María Mercedes Carranza Coronado (M-19), María Teresa Garcés Lloreda (M-19), and Aída Abella Esquivel (Unión Patriótica).

[29] Elite interview 35 (September 23, 2016).

President Gaviria undertook before the constituent assembly in the following way:

> [E]very Saturday morning we had a discussion on comparative constitutional law with the president. From 9:00 am to 12:00 or 1:00 pm, we discussed how different problems were approached in different countries, problems that were relevant for Colombia. And we didn't look only at the text of the constitution but [also] at the decisions rendered by the respective courts.[30]

Hernando Herrera, who worked as an assistant during the assembly, explains that the "primary function [of the assistants] was investigative, looking at comparative law and what happened in other countries," especially with respect to "how certain institutions in Colombia could work better."[31] In assessing the resulting constitution, Herrera estimates that, in terms of rights protections, "one could say that about 25 percent come from Germany, 15 percent from Mexico, another 15 percent from Spain, 10 percent from North America, and the rest from Colombia." He further recalled that "a fundamental element was the jurisprudence of the high courts of the United States, Germany, Mexico, and Spain."[32] Diana Fajardo, who also served as an assistant at the assembly and who later became a Constitutional Court justice, confirms this comparative approach within the assembly, and points specifically to the constitutions of Spain, France, and the United States as having inspired different parts of the resulting 1991 Colombian Constitution.[33]

For many constituents, the goal of this comparative inquiry was to determine the best way to modernize Colombia's constitution. Constituent Jaime Ortiz (1991), drawing on the French constitutional theorist

[30] Elite interview 68 (February 23, 2017).

[31] Elite interview 39 (September 27, 2016). "Nosotros teníamos una triple función, una función primero investigativa para efectos de buscar a nivel de derecho comparado cómo funcionaban algunas estructuras institucionales que Colombia podía mejorar o que no había en Colombia."

[32] Elite interview 39 (September 27, 2016). "Uno puede decir que tiene en esa parte de derechos, que tiene diría que un 25% alemán, un 15% mexicano, otro 15% español, un 10% norteamericano y el resto si, digamos, lo que dio la tierrita. Pero digamos que es como el ADN de la constitución. Un elemento fundamental, importantísimo, fue la jurisprudencia o las sentencias producidas por las cortes de los Estados Unidos, de Alemania, de México y de España."

[33] Elite interview 42 (September 28, 2016).

Georges Burdeau, defined the modern constitution as the proper guide for the 1991 assembly:

> The modern constitution draws the contours, not of the existing order, but of the future. They indicate the place of the individual, the family, [and] the intermediary groups, define the rules to govern economic activity, the role of limits of property, indicate to the state the activities to be undertake and the needs to be met. They specify the extent and nature of the help [a citizen] can expect from the society as well as [his or her] duties within it. This idea of the future society that the text lays out is nothing other than the "idea of right" that power must be dedicated to realizing.[34]

In addition, constituents referenced international law, including the Universal Declaration of Human Rights, in their draft proposals.

The Spanish legal tradition was particularly influential. As Rodolfo Arango – who also served as an assistant during the Constitutional Assembly – put it, the "the German and Spanish Constitutional Courts were the motor of constitutional development in the post-war period … but Spanish law – due to language – was perhaps most influential [on Colombian law]."[35] Arango points specifically to Spanish author Eduardo García de Enterría as key in developing the ideas that constitutions could have normative form and immediate, direct application, rather than serving as programmatic guides.[36] Mario Cajas adds that "Manuel Aragón Reyes and other Spaniards had some influence on the constitution … [The constituents] were looking at the Spanish model of *estado social de derecho*, and, in fact, the definition [of *estado social de derecho*] is the same" in the constitutions of both countries.[37] Still

[34] In fact, though the concept of the *estado social de derecho* is often associated with social constitutionalism, the idea that the state is limited both by social concerns and the rule of law does not imply a robust recognition of social rights per se.

[35] Elite interview 16 (August 25, 2016). "Mientras el tribunal constitucional alemán y español fueron el motor desarrollo de la constitucional de la pos-guerra … Pero realmente el derecho español por la lengua, tal vez fue el más influyente." Arango later served as a conjuez and a clerk at the Constitutional Court. He also ran for the Senate in 2014. He is currently a philosophy professor at the Universidad de los Andes.

[36] Elite interview 16 (August 25, 2016).

[37] Elite interview 27 (September 16, 2016). "Lo que sí sé es que Manuel Aragón Reyes y otros españoles tuvieron alguna influencia en esa constitución, no sé si directamente ellos o a través de constituyentes que se sirvieron de ellos pero sí sé que estaban mirando al modelo español de estado social de derecho de hecho, la definición es igual."

others point to Manuel García Pelayo – a prominent Spanish jurist and expert in comparative constitutional law – in tracing the connection between German, Spanish, and Latin American legal thought.

One might imagine that pressure from below included concrete ideational directives for how to change the existing constitutional order. In fact, this was not the case. Citizens did not necessarily advance a specific ideology or legal agenda other than change from the existing constitutional foundation. Julieta Lemaitre (2009: 74) holds that:

> Colombian legalism, the inheritance of Santander ("el hombre de las leyes"), had been attacked and questioned by the right and the left since the middle of the twentieth century … For the right, this legalism signaled the inability to understand the urgency of the defense of life and property. For the left, liberal rights were an illusion; they were the masked face of oppression. As such, both positions despised the foundational legalism [of Colombia].

As a result, social groups across the political spectrum felt the need for legal reform. Several guerrilla groups, including the M-19 and El Movimiento Armado Quintín Lame, demobilized around this time and were granted the opportunity to participate in the constituent assembly directly as constituents. In addition to these political actors who sought changes to the existing legal infrastructure, students formed a student movement for constitutional reform. As Rodolfo Arango explains, "the student movement opened the door for constitutional change that had not been possible before."[38] However, this pressure focused on the need for constitutional change toward equality, democracy, and peace without necessarily going into details.[39] It would be a stretch to relate this directly to social pressure for change and any specific model of government responsiveness.

Importantly, as Eduardo Cifuentes recalls, the constituent assembly took place in the context of several other constitution-drafting experiences in Latin America. He explicitly references the Brazilian constitution of 1988:

> [T]hese constitutions generally introduced a very broad charter of fundamental rights … and the new Latin American constitutions recognized

[38] Elite interview 16 (August 25, 2016). "Entonces los hechos de violencia llevaron una movilización estudiantil. Y se abrió la puerta a un cambio constitucional que no había sido posible antes."

[39] Elite interview 46 (October 19, 2016).

> of economic, social, cultural rights as well as collective rights, together with fundamental rights. This was not an innovation of the 1991 constituent assembly, but it follows the current trend that was then in fashion in Latin America.[40]

This context provided a set of examples of other states in the region exploring social constitutionalism, in whole or in part. Still, the Colombian constituents often went further in terms of rights recognitions and the development of mechanisms or institutions meant to promote and protect rights than their neighbors. For instance, the 1993 Peruvian Constitution did not include the right to housing or shelter, and the 1988 Brazilian constitutional reform did not involve the creation of an entirely new court to hear rights claims (though it did include the creation of a new constitutional chamber within the existing Supreme Court).

While ideas related to social constitutionalism were being experimented with in neighboring countries, constituents still made choices about whether and how to implement these ideas in the Colombian context. Rather than expanding these ideas, they could just as easily have adopted more restrictive versions, such as expressly nonjusticiable social rights, a position that had been favored by many experts on human rights law. Some members of the constituent assembly, like Alberto Zalamea Costa, cautioned against overinclusiveness in listing rights. Zalamea argued that a "list of the thousand and one rights is not necessary, but [instead, we need] the enumeration of the essential ones plus the rights that, for certain reasons, have been more violated in Colombia."[41] For Zalamea, the rights to life, equality before the law, free association, and the prohibition of torture were these key rights.

Further, Colombia had long been a holdout relative to the rest of Latin American legal development, most clearly in their late adoption of a mechanism similar to the *amparo* (a writ of protection for constitutional rights).[42] Mexico adopted the mechanism in 1857, and

40 Elite interview 1 (July 26, 2016). "Estas constituciones políticas generalmente introducen una muy amplia carta de derechos fundamentales ... y las nuevas constituciones Latinoamericanas hace su ingreso de derechos económicos, sociales, culturales y también los derechos colectivos, juntos con los derechos fundamentales. De modo que no se trataba de ninguna innovación del constituyente de '91, sino que segué la corriente que entonces estaba en boga en América Latina."

41 Tramite de Proyectos, Comisión Primera, "Derechos y Deberes Humanos" (March 7, 1991).

42 For more on the development of the amparo and its legacy in the region, see Brewer-Carías (2009).

Guatemala (1879), El Salvador (1886), and Honduras (1894) followed suit soon after. In the early twentieth century, Nicaragua (1911), Brazil (*mandado de securança*, 1934), Panama (1941), and Costa Rica (1946) adopted similar mechanisms. Next came Venezuela (1961), Bolivia, Paraguay, Ecuador (1967), Peru (1976), and Chile (*recurso de protección*, 1976). Colombia adopted the *acción de tutela* a full fifteen years after Chile and 134 years after Mexico. In other words, it was by no means obvious, in historical perspective, that Colombia would adopt regionally or internationally trending ideas about constitutional law at any particular point in time.

One can easily imagine the constituent assembly instead embracing a new vision of liberal constitutionalism, revising the rules governing the Congress and its duties (which it did in part), and stopping there. Considering Colombia's historically conservative political sphere, as well as the interests of still-powerful elite families, and the violence that ensued after the previous attempt at social reform in 1936, the drafting of a liberal constitution seems to have been highly plausible. While the 1991 constituent assembly was more representative than any previous constituent assembly in Colombia, more than 41 percent of delegates came from the Liberal and the Conservative parties, and more than 15 percent came from the MSN, whose delegates were, for the most part, political and legal elites themselves. The assembly did include many "nontraditional" members, including delegates from demobilized guerrilla groups, but traditional political elites still maintained a majority.

Instead of doubling down on liberal constitutionalism, however, the constituent assembly embraced a robust social rights discourse and empowered new institutions, like the Constitutional Court and the Defensoría del Pueblo (akin to an ombudsman's office), to defend these rights. This choice to embrace a newer form of constitutionalism came about as a result of the belief among the liberal and progressive members of the constituent assembly in the value of reforming and modernizing. For instance, Helena Herrán de Montoya used the following slogan in her campaign to be elected to the assembly: "Vote for me. As a constituent, I am going to reform Colombian political customs, and I am going to give you the possibility of guaranteeing rights that will serve us all."[43] She later reflected on

[43] "Voten por mí, que voy a ser constituyente y voy a reformar las costumbres políticas colombianas y les voy a dar a ustedes la posibilidad de garantizar unos derechos que a todos nos van a server" (Restrepo-Yepes, Bocanument-Arbeláez, and Rojas-Betancur 2014: 18).

her time at the assembly, stating that, "we began to study other constitutions, to look at other alternatives to see how Colombian customs could be modernized through a new Constitution ... [We] were told that we had to modernize the country by introducing fundamental rights, human rights."[44]

Conservative constituents did not necessarily agree on the importance of "modernizing" the Constitution as such. However, only twenty constituents came from lists created by conservative groups, and not everyone on the Movimiento Salvación Nacional list was ideologically conservative. Juan Carlos Esguerra explained to me that:

> Even though I have always been a member of the Liberal Party, I was approached by Álvaro Gómez, who was the leader of the Movimiento Salvación Nacional, and he himself was a very representative conservative in Colombia, but he said, "I want to organize a group of people who include different tendencies and different political representations," and so he made a list in which we were [both] Liberals and Conservatives.[45]

Thus, the group of constituents who sought to draft a more modern constitution, moving away from liberal constitutionalism, was sufficiently strong to outweigh those who favored relative stasis in terms of constitutional rights protections.

In May 1991, the First Commission – the one tasked with determining the list of rights that should be included in the Constitution – put forward a proposal that favored the broad inclusion of all generations of rights.[46] The proposal held:

> There is no doubt that the fundamental axis of democracy lies in recognizing a set of guarantees for the citizens and people of Colombia that not only dignify the content of life, but also progressively favor the formulation of new freedoms ... It has been understood that human rights form an inseparable whole, without divisions or fundamental differences between the different generations, into which they can be subdivided doctrinally.[47]
>
> ...

[44] "[E]mpezamos a estudiar otras constituciones, a mirar otras alternativas para ver cómo se lograban modernizar las costumbres colombianas a través de una nueva Constitución (Restrepo-Yepes et al. 2014: 18) ... a la gente se le decía que había que modernizar el país, introducir los derechos fundamentales, los derechos humanos" (Restrepo-Yepes et al. 2014: 25).

[45] Elite interview 35 (September 23, 2016).

[46] Tramite de Proyectos, Comisión Primera, "Carta de Derechos, Deberes, Garantías y Libertades" (May 22, 1991).

[47] "No cabe duda que el eje primordial de la democracia radica en reconocerle a los ciudadanos y personas que habitan en Colombia, un conjunto de garantías que no solo

> In terms of rights and freedoms, our constitution cannot sacrifice the exact expression of the guaranteed rights for brevity, nor risk possible misunderstandings that could derive from imprecise definitions.[48]
>
> Hence, instead of a simple list of rights, such as the one in force [in the Constitution of 1886], a Charter of Rights, Duties, Guarantees and Freedoms is proposed, in which the citizen can know exactly the rights and freedoms guaranteed by the State and the legal order that expresses them, with the greatest possible precision.[49]

Although it was Diego Uribe Vargas, from the Liberal Party list, who presented this proposal, members from all of the various parties to the assembly signed it, even Alberto Zalamea, who had previously expressed a preference for a more limited list of rights.[50] After discussing this proposal, and debating which rights should be "considered fundamental," the constituents voted on the text of each right in June 1991.

Ultimately, the assembly agreed to organize the list of rights into five chapters in a section of the Constitution titled "Concerning Rights, Guarantees, and Duties," which would follow the section on fundamental principles. Social rights were not particularly divisive, receiving a high percentage of votes (e.g., fifty-eight of seventy for health, fifty-eight for housing, and fifty-two for education, compared to forty-three for the rights of children and forty-seven for the right to strike). And fifty-six constituents approved the text of Article 86, which describes the tutela procedure.[51] Table 3.1 shows each of the five

dignifiquen el contenido de la vida, sino que favorezcan progresivamente la formulación de las nuevas libertades que la evolución contemporánea han ido poniendo en evidencia. Se ha entendido que en la actualidad los derechos humanos formen conjunto inseparable, sin poder establecer escisiones o diferencias fundamentales entre las distintas generaciones, en que doctrinariamente se pueden subdividir."

48 "Sin embargo, en materia de derechos y libertades nuestra Carta no puede sacrificar por la brevedad, la expresión exacta de los derechos garantizados, ni arriesgar los posibles equívocos que se pudiesen derivar de definiciones imprecisas."

49 "De ahí que, en lugar de un simple título de derechos, tal como el que está vigente, se proponga una Carta de derechos, deberes, garantías y libertades, en la cual el ciudadano pueda conocer con exactitud sus prerrogativas, y con la mayor precisión posible los derechos y libertades que garantizan el Estado y el orden jurídico que los expresan."

50 The full list of signatories is: Jaime Ortiz, Francisco Rojas, Raimundo Emiliani, Misael Pastrana, Jaime Arias, Álvaro Leyva, Marcos Chalita, Augusto Ramírez Ocampo, Horacio Serpa, Otty Patiño, Alberto Zalamea, Aída Abella, María Mercedes Carranza, Diego Uribe Vargas, Juan Carlos Esguerra, German Toro, and Darío Mejía.

51 "Informe de la Sesión Plenaria del día de 29 de Junio de 1991."

TABLE 3.1 Rights, guarantees, and duties in the 1991 Colombian Constitution

Title I: Concerning Fundamental Principles	
Title II: Concerning Rights, Guarantees, and Duties	
Chapter 1: Concerning Fundamental Rights	Articles 11–41
Chapter 2: Concerning Social, Economic, and Cultural Rights	Articles 42–77
Chapter 3: Concerning Collective Rights and the Environment	Articles 78–82
Chapter 4: Concerning the Protection and Application of Rights	Articles 83–94
Chapter 5: Concerning Duties and Obligation	Article 95

chapters that articulate these rights, guarantees, and duties, as well as the articles that fall within each chapter. The Constitution was promulgated on July 4, 1991, and the newly created Constitutional Court began to hear cases the following year.

3.4 CLAIM-MAKING UNDER SOCIAL CONSTITUTIONALISM

Nothing about public discourse prior to the creation of the constituent assembly or the debates within it suggested any particular patterns in claim-making that would follow, except perhaps that claim-making related to civil and political rights should outpace claim-making related to social, economic, and cultural rights. The initial design of the tutela indicated that there would be an opportunity for claim-making for civil and political rights and not social rights. The idea underlying the tutela was that it would help to make the 1991 Constitution "real" to Colombian citizens and help to "give teeth to constitutional rights."[52] Juan Carlos Esguerra uniquely proposed the *acción de tutela* instead of the more regionally common *amparo* procedure to protect the newly enshrined constitutional rights. Esguerra likens the tutela to the hero of the short story, radio, film, and television franchise *Boston Blackie*. Boston Blackie was considered a "friend to those who have no friend." Esguerra recalls that "the tutela was intended to be the remedy for

[52] Elite interview 16 (August 25, 2016). "[L]a tutela … le da dientes a los derechos."

those rights who have no remedy at all, so that it would … complete a panorama of a law system that had lots of remedies."[53] Article 86 of the Constitution outlines the tutela procedure:

> Article 86. Every person has the right to file a writ of protection before a judge, at any time or place, through a preferential and summary proceeding, for himself/herself or by whomever acts in his/her name for the immediate protection of his/her fundamental constitutional rights when that person fears the latter may be violated by the action or omission of any public authority.
>
> The protection will consist of all order issued by a judge enjoining others to act or refrain from acting. The order, which must be complied with immediately, may be challenged before a superior court judge, and in any case the latter may send it to the Constitutional Court for possible revision.
>
> This action will be available only when the affected party does not dispose of another means of judicial defense, except when it is used as a temporary device to avoid irreversible harm. In no case can more than 10 days elapse between filing the writ of protection and its resolution.
>
> The law will establish the cases in which the writ of protection may be filed against private individuals entrusted with providing a public service or whose conduct may affect seriously and directly the collective interest or in respect of whom the applicant may find himself/herself in a state of subordination or vulnerability.

The unexpected development with the tutela was its rapidly expanding scope. It was used not only for the civil and political rights that fall within the "fundamental rights" chapter of the 1991 Constitution, but also for social rights claims. Citizens pushed the bounds of the tutela, and judges endorsed this expansion. Between 2003 and 2019 (the period for which disaggregated data are available), the right to petition[54] and

[53] Elite interview 35 (September 23, 2016). Esguerra proposed a new legal mechanism – the tutela – instead of the adoption and importation of the Mexican amparo. In his proposal, he argued: "In short, establishing the *amparo*, within the Mexican tradition, would be to unhinge the Colombian system and expose it to a series of conflicts of jurisdiction." Comisión Primera, "Proyecto de Artículo Constitucional que Consagra la Acción de Tutela para la Protección de los Derechos Constitucionales" (May 8, 1991).

[54] Article 23 defines the right to petition: "Every person has the right to present petitions to the authorities for the general or private interest and to secure their prompt resolution. The legislative body may regulate the presentation of petitions to private organizations in order to guarantee fundamental rights."

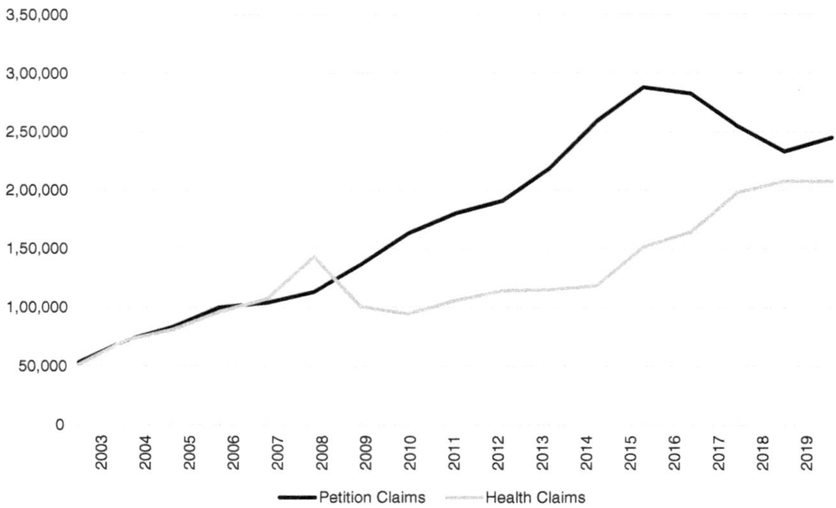

Figure 3.1 The most commonly invoked rights in tutela claims, 2003–2019.
Source: Author's elaboration using data from the Defensoría del Pueblo (2003–2020).

the right to health[55] were the most commonly invoked rights in tutela claims, as shown in Figure 3.1. In 2003, both types of claims were made around 50,000 times. Though health claims outpaced petition claims in 2008 (by about 30,000), after that year petition claims grew at a faster clip than health claims. In 2019, Colombians filed just shy of 245,000 petition claims and about 207,000 health claims. This story is not limited to claim-making regarding the right to health and the right to petition, however. Each year, Colombians file thousands of

[55] Article 49 details the right to health: "Public health and environmental protection are public services for which the state is responsible. All individuals are guaranteed access to services that promote, protect, and rehabilitate public health. It is the responsibility of the state to organize, direct, and regulate the delivery of health services and of environmental protection to the population in accordance with the principles of efficiency, universality, and cooperation, and to establish policies for the provision of health services by private entities and to exercise supervision and control over them. In the area of public health, the state will establish the jurisdiction of the nation, territorial entities, and individuals, and determine the shares of their responsibilities within the limits and under the conditions determined by law. Public health services will be organized in a decentralized manner, in accordance with levels of responsibility and with the participation of the community. The law will determine the limits within which basic care for all the people will be free of charge and mandatory. Every person has the obligation to attend to the integral care of his/her health and that of his/her community."

tutelas that invoke other rights, including, for example, the right to water (1,097 claims in 2019), the right to work (8,472 claims in 2019), and the right to due process (76,447 claims in 2019).

According to reports by the Defensoría del Pueblo issued between 2012 and 2019, specific healthcare providers, the courts, and the Unidad para la Atención y Reparación Integral a las Víctimas (UARIV) – the national organization meant to oversee the implementation of the 2011 Victims' Law (Law 1448), providing aid and assistance to those impacted by the internal armed conflict – have been subjected to the most tutelas each year out of all public and private entities. Claims against the courts have routinely amounted to about 5 percent of all tutelas filed each year during this period. Data from 2019 show that, in filing their claims against the courts, many Colombians held that their due process rights (76.9 percent), their right to access to justice (19.4 percent), or their right to petition (6.9 percent) had been violated.[56]

In 2012, the first year of the UARIV's existence, 7 percent of all tutelas (or nearly 30,000) were directed at that agency. This statistic increased to a high of 31.1 percent in 2016 and dropped consistently after that. In 2019, 10.6 percent of all tutelas named the UARIV. This number partially obscures the prevalence of victim-related tutela claims in Colombia's biggest cities. In 2019, almost one-third of all tutelas directed at the UARIV in 2019 were filed in Medellín and almost one-quarter in Bogotá. Most of these claims (79 percent) formally invoked the right to petition, with the underlying goal being to attain the aid and reparation measures promised to those who are recognized as victims of the armed conflict.

Tutelas against healthcare providers primarily involve right to health claims (84.8 percent in 2019), as perhaps is obvious. Some of the time, however, the tutela claims invoked other rights, including the *mínimo vital*,[57] the right to petition, and the right to life. While some healthcare providers were the subject of just a few thousand claims, others were named in large percentages of all tutela claims. In 1999, the state-run social security agency, the Institute for Social Security, was the subject of 85.7 percent of all health claims and 16.1 percent of all tutela claims, statistics that fell steadily through the early 2000s. Nueva EPS (health) and Colpensiones (pensions) ultimately replaced the Institute for Social Security. Nueva EPS has been

[56] Defensoría del Pueblo (2019).

[57] This is essentially a right to subsistence. See discussion in Chapter 5 for more detail.

the subject of between 2.5 percent and 4.3 percent of all tutela claims each year since 2011. Colpensiones was named in 17.1 percent of all tutela claims in 2012, regardless of the right invoked. This percentage decreased through 2019, when Colpensiones was the subject of a mere 3.9 percent of all tutela claims. Over time, private healthcare entities came to be named in a substantial percentage of tutela claims as well.

What does this claim-making look like on the ground? As noted in Article 86, Colombians can bring tutela claims before any judge in the country ("at any time or place"). Their claims can be made orally or in writing. One judge explained to me that if you want to file a tutela, "you can go before a judge, sit next to him and tell him what happened, and the judge writes [out your claim] on the computer. That happens, it actually happens … I have seen them and I have processed verbal tutela claims. It does not happen in most cases but it does happen."[58] More frequently, however, claimants stand in line outside courthouses, like the one shown in Figure 3.2, waiting to hand their typed or handwritten paperwork to a secretary whose primary job is to collect tutela claims. Judges then review these claims, assessing whether or not a rights violation may have occurred, regardless of whether or not the individual characterized the problem as one related to constitutional rights. This first instance of review must be completed within ten days. Further, ordinary courts are required to prioritize tutelas over other types of legal claims. As such, the tutela procedure offers individuals the chance to make claims without paying legal fees or enduring the time-intensive process of traditional litigation. Still, filing a tutela claim is not costless – individuals must travel to the courthouse during business hours and often wait in long lines to submit their paperwork. These time and resource costs pale in comparison to the costs of filing other kinds of legal claims, but they are not negligible for those of relatively little means.

All tutelas are eventually sent to the Constitutional Court for possible review, though given the sheer quantity of tutela claims, the Court only formally reviews a small fraction of cases. At the Constitutional Court, the tutelas are first catalogued by law students from across the country,

[58] Elite interview 80 (April 18, 2017). "La acción de tutela puede interponerse de manera verbal, puedes ir ante un juez sentarte al lado de él y contarle lo que pasó, el juez escribe en la computadora. Eso pasa, en realidad ocurre. Yo la he visto y he tramitado tutelas verbales. Ocurre no en los de más de los casos, pero ocurre."

Figure 3.2 People waiting in line to file tutela claims in Medellín, Colombia. Source: Author's photograph.

who serve as interns. During August 2016, Hernán Correa, who was then working as a clerk and law professor, but who was later selected to serve as a justice of the Court, gave me a tour of the courthouse and introduced me to the interns tasked with cataloguing tutela claims.[59] There were six interns assigned to each justice's office, and these interns processed tutelas by the bag (see Figure 3.3). Atop each bag sat a Post-it labeled with a date and a number – the number refers to the whether the bag is the first, second, or fifteenth for that date (see Figure 3.4). That August, they received about 300 tutelas per day per office. With six interns working, that meant that each one had to read though fifty tutelas every day. The interns would type up the name of the claimant and the defendant, whether the claimant falls within a protected group, and a variety of other basic facts of the case. If the interns recommended the case for revision, they also included the lines of argument put forth

[59] Elite interview 10 (August 19, 2016).

Figure 3.3 Interns cataloguing tutela claims at the Constitutional Court.
Source: Author's photograph.

Figure 3.4 Catalogued tutela claims at the Constitutional Court.
Source: Author's photograph.

by the first- and second-instance judge. One former intern described her time working at the Court to me as follows:

> You work about a twelve-hour day, taking breaks to talk or mess around, of course, but the work is repetitive, especially in that so many of the cases had to do with health claims and prison conditions [This was in 2004.] Further, many of the lower-court judges simply copy and paste sections of other tutela decisions, even forgetting to change the name of the claimant. For this reason and others, bad decisions by the lower courts were quite common.[60]

The Constitutional Court justices rotate who is on tutela duty for the week. The on-duty justice decides which of the claims flagged by their interns to formally review. Fidelity to existing jurisprudence and proper legal reasoning are understood to drive the revision process, but the decision about whether or not to review a tutela is ultimately subject to the discretion of the justices of the Constitutional Court, specifically whichever justices are on duty that week.

3.5 CONCLUSION

This chapter documents the contours of Colombian constitutional history, up through the country's adoption of social constitutionalism in 1991. The adoption of substantive social constitutionalism – with its recognition of not only civil and political rights but also social, economic, and cultural rights, alongside the creation of new legal institutions and procedures to give citizens opportunities to make claims to those rights – was not a foregone conclusion. Liberal constitutionalism remained a common constitutional model around the world, and some members of Colombia's constituent assembly expressed a preference for that kind of model. The social constitutionalist view, favored by constituents who sought to "modernize" the Colombian state and Colombian constitutional law, won out.

The mere adoption of social constitutionalism did not guarantee that it would become embedded or institutionalized, especially considering that this adoption occurred at a time of profound social and political crisis. Examples of constitutional false starts and neutralization by political reactions or "sterilization by judicial interpretation" abound both globally and in Colombia's past. What happened in Colombia,

[60] Fieldnotes (March 30, 2017).

however, was that citizens began to routinely make claims to their constitutionally recognized rights using the newly created tutela procedure. The right to petition (a right that was initially categorized as "fundamental") and the right to health (one that was not) came to be the most commonly invoked rights in tutela claims, even though, by design, the tutela was meant only to be used to claim fundamental rights. These claims are reviewed at the Constitutional Court, first by interns and eventually by the justices.

How exactly did this happen? Why did citizens embrace the tutela, using it to claim not just civil and political rights but also social, economic, and cultural rights? How did judges – both at the Constitutional Court and the lower courts – respond to these new rights claims? These are the subjects of the next two chapters. Chapter 4 tackles social embedding, while Chapter 5 looks to legal embedding.

CHAPTER FOUR

SOCIAL EMBEDDING

Now that we have this tool, I "tutela" everything.[1]

Álvaro, 57, Bogotá

This chapter examines how the 1991 Constitution came to be embedded in Colombian society, focusing on the social component of constitutional embedding. Social embedding refers to the process by which constitutional rights talk becomes part of everyday discourse and experience. How can we know when a constitution has become socially embedded? When constitutions are socially embedded, constitutional rights and legal tools become part of (1) common knowledge and (2) language, and citizens actively make (3) legal claims to constitutionally recognized rights. Embedding occurs along a continuum. A single piece of evidence of embedding by itself will be suggestive at most, but we can confidently make relative statements about changes in embedding over time and across space. Just because embedding has begun – or just because embedding has become evident – does not mean that it will endure. Unless and until this embedding becomes part of a self-reinforcing process, it might simply reflect the momentary acceptance of a constitutional order; one that could be dislodged relatively easily.[2]

Following the spread of information about the new constitution, Colombian citizens experimented with the filing of tutela claims on the basis of newly codified constitutional rights, namely social rights. Over time, these experiences with legal mobilization resulted in a key

[1] Bogotá interview 22. "Cuando tenemos esa herramienta entonces entutelo por todo."

[2] I take up this question of dislodging in Chapters 6–8.

shift in understanding (some of) the problems in their lives as specifically legal in nature; what I describe as the "social construction of legal grievances" (Taylor 2020a). Simultaneously, the development of judicial receptivity occurred, as judges came to view these same grievances as issues that should be resolved in the formal legal sphere (a process detailed in Chapter 5). These two processes – the social construction of legal grievances and the development of judicial receptivity – reinforced one another, creating a feedback loop and ensuring both the social and legal embedding of the 1991 Constitution and therefore social constitutionalism in Colombia.

The rest of this chapter proceeds as follows. I first demonstrate that the social embedding of 1991 Constitution has, in fact, occurred. After that, I show how legal mobilization has served as a mechanism of social embedding through a close examination of the social construction of legal grievances, in the process demonstrating that this process has been particularly striking with respect to the right to health. The tutela itself has become a feature of Colombian daily life, particularly in its connection to other features of the 1991 Constitution, like the newly enshrined social rights. In this way, social constitutionalism was embedded socially in Colombia. Social embedding has occurred to such an extent that citizens continue to file claims to their new constitutional rights, especially the right to health, despite ambivalence about the effectiveness of the tutela mechanism.

4.1 SOCIAL EMBEDDING: THE COMMONPLACE OF THE TUTELA

The embedding of a constitutional text becomes discernible as relevant terms (in this case, e.g., "tutela") and images enter – and remain present in – the realm of the common knowledge and the vernacular of the population of interest (in this case, everyday Colombians). Once these terms and figures cease to be understood as purely legal or technical in nature, or once they become part of everyday life, social embedding has begun. During the 1990s, the tutela became ubiquitous in Colombia, appearing across media platforms and making its way into the quotidian expressions and expectations of citizens. It was not just that the tutela became ubiquitous in the abstract. Instead, citizens explicitly connected the tutela to rights that were newly codified by the 1991 Constitution. In this section, I detail how the tutela moved beyond the confines of the formal legal sphere to take hold in the everyday lives of

Colombians, before demonstrating the close connection of the tutela and newly codified constitutional rights.

In the early 1990s, the Colombian government engaged in a multi-pronged educational campaign. This educational campaign featured a television program, smaller advertising spots, board games, and comic books, in addition to mandatory teaching in schools, all of which was geared toward spreading information about the new constitution and the tutela procedure. Regional-level bodies in some, but not all, departments (states) have also held outreach programs, from the early 1990s to the present day. The national government even commissioned the translation of the 1991 Constitution into braille, in addition to the primary indigenous languages spoken in the country.[3] In an interview, Andrés Gómez, who was part of these educational campaigns, commented that "when the constitution came out, there was a constitutional pedagogy process, and that process lasted about three years."[4] After that, various councils and ministries oversaw these pedagogical efforts. Gómez explained that these early efforts "were eminently circumstantial and were not designed as a public policy per se, but were developed by the official on duty."[5] In what follows, I highlight two of the more coordinated pedagogical efforts – the television program, *La tutela factor humano*, and the board game, Tutela y Juega ("Tutela and Play") – that together provide a window into the government's constitutional education strategy.

Manuel José Cepeda, who served as an advisor to President César Gaviria during the constitution-drafting and implementation process (and later became a Constitutional Court justice), described the television program to me in an interview in February 2017. He explained, "*La tutela factor humano* was like a soap opera."[6] The program – which was at times hosted by famous Colombians like the comedian, activist, journalist, and politician Jaime Garzón – featured representations of

[3] By 1994, the Ministry of Justice and the Department of Anthropology at the Universidad de los Andes had translated the constitution into seven indigenous languages: Guambiana, Ikun, Kamentsa, Inga, Kubeo, Wayuunaiki, and Nasa Yuwe.

[4] Elite interview 179 (March 4, 2021). "Cuando salió la constitución hubo un proceso de pedagogía constitucional y ese proceso de pedagogía duró como tres años."

[5] Elite interview 179 (March 4, 2021). "Entonces todos los desarrollos anteriores que hubo digamos de pedagogía constitucional, eran eminentemente circunstanciales y no eran diseñados como una política pública per se, sino que eran elaborados bajo la mirada de digamos del funcionario de turno."

[6] Elite interview 68 (February 23, 2017).

real tutela claims that had already been decided. In total, seventy-two episodes of *La tutela factor humano* played over the government-owned television network, *Audiovisuales*. The program was originally intended to air for only a year, but it ended up being extended for a second year, before being replaced in the Thursday night lineup by *Full House* (El Tiempo 1995).

Sandra Bernal, one of the show's producers, during an interview in 2021, shared that "the objective of the program was to show the benefits of the tutela,"[7] specifically "the human story behind the tutela."[8] Bernal further reflected on the process by which she and her colleagues chose cases for the show. She would go the Constitutional Court and sift through claims, looking for cases that were "visually attractive." She continued, "so, what does visually attractive mean? It was something that was like a story, that could be told visually on television, that was rich [in details]."[9] I asked Bernal to say more about the tutela claims she remember selecting for the show. She replied:

> One case that stood out to me was a case in Fusagasugá [a town about 50 kilometers southwest of Bogotá] that involved a woman who found a baby in a garbage can. So, the lady welcomed the baby, she raised her as if she were her daughter. Later, the Colombian Institute of Family Welfare told her that the girl, well, she had to hand her over, that the girl was not legally hers. But then she filed a tutela claim, asking that they recognize that she had already cared for the girl, and that the girl did not really know who she was. She was a girl who was abandoned, a girl who in a very bad state of health when she was found.[10]

[7] Elite interview 180 (April 12, 2021). "El objetivo del programa era mostrar los beneficios de la tutela."

[8] Elite interview 180 (April 12, 2021). "[L]a parte humana, la parte detrás de eso de la tutela."

[9] Elite interview 180 (April 12, 2021). "Como te digo yo empecé ahí como asistente de producción y después ya como productora, tenía que ir a la corte constitucional, mirar las tutelas, mirar un caso que fuera atractivo visualmente. Somos para televisión, llevar unos casos, yo los llevaba. Había unas personas que ayudaban a seleccionar esos casos, me decían: 'Sí, Sandra este está interesante, este no está tan interesante pues para televisión' … Entonces, visualmente atractivo ¿Qué era? Era una cosa que fuera como una historia que se pudiera contar visualmente en televisión, que fuera rica."

[10] Elite interview 180 (April 12, 2021). "Bueno, a ver, de los que me acuerde que me impactó mucho fue un caso en Fusagasugá de una señora que encontró una bebé en una caneca de basura. Entonces pues la señora acogió a la bebé, la crio como si fuera su hija. Después el Instituto Colombiano de Bienestar Familiar le dijo que esa niña pues había que entregarla, que esa niña no era pues legalmente de ella. Pero entonces pues ella puso una tutela, diciendo pues que le reconocieran que esa niña

In the end, the Constitutional Court found in favor of the adoptive mother.

Beyond looking for a clear and compelling human story behind the legal claim, Bernal explained that she was looking for cases that had already been decided by the Court. At times, she and other members of the production team spoke with Constitutional Court justices, including José Gregorio Hernández, to get a more complete sense of what had happened in particular cases. These visually appealing, fully settled cases would help to educate the general public as to the scope of their constitutional rights.

A typical episode proceeded as follows. Over melodramatic music, the introduction to the show would offer a reminder to the audience:

> Many correctly say that the constitutional recognition of a series of rights does not by itself guarantee their effectiveness, but it is the first step to achieve that objective and to ensure that Colombians not only feel that the constitution rules over them, but that they also feel it protects them and belongs to them – *La tutela factor humano*.[11]

The audience would then learn about the claimant's background and hear a short, simple discussion of the problem they faced. As the episodes progressed, the audience would meet others who were affected by the same problem. Later on, the results of the tutela claim would be summarized in a voiceover. The narrator would read out the Constitutional Court's decision, listing the constitutional rights implicated and explaining how the decision relates to lower-court decisions. The show would then end with the following statement:

> With this tutela claim, a whole community benefited. We will see you next Thursday at 7:30 on Channel A, so that we can see another "human factor" that motivated a Colombian to file a tutela claim.[12]

pues como ya ella la había cuidado, no se sabía realmente de quién era. Era una niña que estaba abandonada, una niña que llegó muy mal."

11 *La tutela factor humano* episode. "Muchos dirán con razón que la definición constitucional de una serie de derechos no garantiza por sí sola su efectividad, pero es el primer paso para alcanzar ese objetivo y para lograr que los colombianos no solo sientan que la constitución los manda, sino que los protege y les pertenece. La tutela factor humano."

12 *La tutela factor humano* episode. "Con esta acción de tutela sea beneficiado toda una comunidad. Los esperamos el próximo jueves a las siete y 30 por el canal A, para que veamos otro Factor Humano que motivó a un colombiano a interponer una acción de tutela."

Edwin Cruz Rodríguez, in a discussion of his relationship to the show, held that *La tutela factor humano* was a show that documented how:

> A long-haired student "entutelaba" [literally, tutela-ed] his school for violating his right to free development of personality by trying to force him to cut his hair, [and] a pregnant teenager did the same to avoid being expelled. The tutela was offered to us not only as a safeguard of rights, but also as an important engine of social and cultural change.[13]

Using an accessible narrative form, the television show educated citizens about the tutela mechanism and constitutional rights.

This television program was only one part of the Gaviria administration's constitutional education outreach. In a similar effort, Andrés Gómez developed the board game, Tutela y Juega, with support from the United Nations and the Colombian national government. In an interview in 2021, Gómez told me about his efforts to create and share the game. The country's Ministry of Education ultimately bought and distributed 10,000 copies of the game, and Gómez and others held workshops in schools after the country to introduce students to the game. Figures 4.1 and 4.2 show Gómez at these workshops in Cauca, a department in the southwestern part of the country. National newspapers, including *El Tiempo* and *El Espectador*, as well as regional papers, including *El Pais* (Cali), *El Colombiano* (Medellín), and *La Patria* (Manizales), covered the release of the game in January 1994.[14] In addition to running news articles about the game, *El Tiempo* also ran comic strips that referenced the game.

Tutela y Juega features cards that outline real-world examples and asks players to choose from a list of options on how best to respond. For example, one card that is meant to expose players to the ability to make tutela claims regarding the right to health reads:

> An employee of a company had a spinal injury several years ago that could leave her incapacitated for life. The solution was to operate on

[13] "Un estudiante de pelo largo 'entutelaba' su colegio por vulnerar su derecho al libre desarrollo de la personalidad al pretender obligarle a cortarse el pelo, una adolescente en estado de embarazo hacía lo mismo para evitar ser expulsada: la tutela se nos ofrecía no sólo como una salvaguarda de derechos, sino también como un importante motor de cambio social y cultural" (Cruz Rodríguez 2013). Cruz Rodríguez is a political scientist at the Universidad Nacional de Colombia.

[14] Photocopies on file with author.

Figure 4.1 Andrés Gómez explaining how to play Tutela y Juega.
Source: Photograph provided by Andrés Gómez (Gómez R., Andrés. (2014) Foto tomada a niños indígenas Paeces, con servidores públicos en la Gobernación del Cauca, en actividad lúdica a través de la implementacion del Juego "Tutela y Juega." Presidencia de la República, PNUD).

Figure 4.2 Andrés Gómez (back row, center) after a workshop on Tutela y Juega.
Source: Photograph provided by Andrés Gómez. (Gómez R., Andrés. (2014) Foto tomada a niños indígenas Guambianos, con servidores públicos en la Gobernación del Cauca, en actividad lúdica a través de la implementacion del Juego "Tutela y Juega." Presidencia de la República, PNUD).

her; however, social security would not cover the operation. What can she do?

A. File a tutela
B. Continue to file petitions
C. Go to a homeopathic doctor[15]

The correct answer, of course, is A.

The primary goals of the game were to teach children about the tutela mechanism and how to use it. As part of his remarks introducing Tutela y Juega to the country, President César Gaviria said: "We are determined that constitutional rights will become part of everyday language, that new citizens will be actively linked to democracy, that they will use the instruments that the Constitution endowed them, in short, that they will not see the State as a distant entity and unattainable, but as an ally of their hopes and expectations."[16] Speaking more specifically about the board game, he said he hoped that in "Colombian homes, schools, and universities, we can have more children playing Tutela, claiming life, instead of spending their free time playing 'Cops and Robbers' or 'Cat and Mouse,' where there are always those who kill and those who die."[17] Here, we get a glimpse of the aspirational political goals behind the 1991 Constitution, with a vision of benevolent law and order replacing a history of violence.

During our interview, Gómez pointed to two examples of times that young people had learned about the tutela through Tutela y Juega and had gone on to successfully file tutela claims. The first example garnered national attention, with a story running in *El Tiempo* in October

[15] Read to me by Gómez during our interview. Elite interview 179 (March 4, 2021). "Una empleada de una empresa tenía hace varios años una lesión de la columna que la podía dejar incapacitada de por vida, la solución era operarla, sin embargo, no le daban turno en el seguro social. ¿Qué puede hacer? Entonces había tres opciones … A: Interponer una acción de tutela. B: Seguir presentando peticiones. C: Ir donde un médico naturista."

[16] "Estamos empeñados en que los derechos constitucionales hagan parte del lenguaje cotidiano, que los nuevos ciudadanos se vinculen a la democracia de manera activa, que utilicen los instrumentos de que los dotó 1a Constitución, en fin, que no vean a1 Estado como un ente alejado e inalcanzable, sino como un aliado de sus ilusiones y expectativas" (Gaviria 1993: 3).

[17] "[P]ara que en el mayor número de hogares colombianos, de colegios y de escuelas podamos tener más niños jugando a la tutela, reivindicando la vida, en vez de dedicar su tiempo libre a jugar a 'ladrones y policías' o al 'gato y al ratón' donde siempre hay quienes matan y quienes mueren" (Gaviria 1993: 4).

1994. Mayulay Villegas Vásquez, a twelve-year-old girl living in San José del Sur, a neighborhood to the southeast of the city of Santa Marta on the Atlantic coast of Colombia, had received Tutela y Juega as a gift from her father. After playing the game, she filed a claim against Telesantamarta and Gases del Caribe, a claim that ultimately led to the neighborhood gaining access to telephone, gas, and other public services.[18] The second example involved Gómez teaching a course on constitutional law in Armenia, a city in the western part of Colombia. A student in that class raised her hand and told Gómez that she had played Tutela y Juega as a child. She explained that she had successfully filed a tutela claim regarding a landfill that leaked contamination runoff into a river near her home. Gómez concluded this story by telling me that "the game did fulfill an important objective, which was to educate citizens in the institution, I say institution because the tutela has become an institution."[19]

While it is difficult to quantify exactly how many Colombians learned about the tutela through these government-sponsored constitutional education initiatives, my interviews with everyday Colombians offer suggestive evidence that the initiatives did have lasting impacts. One interviewee even explained that he learned about the ability to use this legal mechanism to make rights claims from a program he had seen on television:

> My mom's husband, for example, suffers from epilepsy so he has to be on medication … [and] it had been impossible for him to get those medications … [but] I heard on television that one can place a tutela claim. I know that if you send in a tutela claim, if you file it, they have – I do not know if it is a time of five or seven days to answer you – [but] they should answer you. It is assumed that with [a positive decision] that they are going to deliver those medicines … but no, they kept telling him "No, not right now." So, he went back and filed another tutela claim … Immediately, the judge gave the order for the medications, and they were [ultimately] delivered.[20]

[18] See *El Tiempo* (October 8, 1994).

[19] Elite interview 179 (March 4, 2021). "Entonces el juego sí cumplió un objetivo importante que era educar a los ciudadanos en la institución, yo digo institución porque la tutela se ha convertido en una institución."

[20] Bogotá interview 7. "El esposo de mi mama por ejemplo el sufre de epilepsia entonces él tiene que estar en tratamientos con eso y … ha sido imposible que le den esos medicamentos … Yo he escuchado en la televisión que si a uno no le dan un derecho esto puede colocar un derecho de tutela, una acción de tutela, entonces

This example shows how exposure to the tutela and the 1991 Constitution through public education campaigns on television can translate into legal mobilization.

Additionally, we can observe evidence of the vernacularization of the term "tutela." Everyday Colombians, who I interviewed in 2017 in Bogotá, Medellín, and a marginal neighborhood on the outskirts of Cali called Agua Blanca, used the following verbs when discussing their use of the tutela: *interponer*, *poner*, *colocar*, *presentar*, *mandar*, *montar*, *hacer*, and *usar*. The phrase "___ una/la tutela" has become widely used. Further, some shortened this construction to "*tutelar*," "*entutelar*," or "*estar tutelando*." For instance:

- "The tutela has already lost its efficiency. They are supposed to comply based on one tutela ruling, but not now. I think they found a way to evade those tutela decisions … the lawyers of the companies, because I believe they can appeal the decisions of tutelas, I believe that they can 'tutela' [*entutelar*] a tutela again."[21]
- The tutela is a tool that "benefits and helps one, it's a tool that makes those responsible for what one is 'tutela-ing' [*está tutelando*] respond to what one is asking for."[22]
- "Now that we have this tool, I 'tutela' [*entutelo*] everything– because the upstairs neighbor celebrates birthdays every fifteen days, if the insurance company does not provide me with a service, I 'tutela' [*entutelo*] them, if the power goes out in my neighborhood, I file a tutela. So, in these ways, the word 'tutela' became part of the background."[23]

fue como eso. Sé que se envía una carta a modo de derecho de tutela, la radicas, ellos tienen no sé si es un tiempo de 5 o 7 días en contestarte, te deben contestar. Se supone que con algo afirmativo o bueno de que te van a entregar esos medicamentos en el caso de él y te los deben dar, pero en el no, ha hecho eso, le dicen que no hay en el momento, el vuelve y pone otra tutela … Inmediatamente le daban su orden para que fuera por sus medicamentos y se los entregaban."

21 Bogotá interview 1. "Ya perdió su eficiencia … Pues se supone que deberían cumplir en base de un fallo de tutela, pero ahora no, creo que se encontraron la forma de evadir esos fallos de tutela … los abogados de las empresas porque creo que ahora los fallos de las tutelas se pueden apelar, creo que a una tutela la pueden entutelar nuevamente."

22 Bogotá interview 6. "[La tutela es una herramienta] que beneficia y le ayuda a uno, es una herramienta que hace que los responsables de lo que uno está tutelando le respondan por lo que uno está pidiendo."

23 Bogotá interview 22. "Cuando tenemos esa herramienta entonces entutelo por todo, porque el vecino de arriba celebra cumpleaños cada 15 días, si la entidad

- "I have a child whose right to education was being violated ... They told me that the tutela was the ideal tool to protect [*hacer tutelar*] this right ... I got a response [to my tutela claim] in an agile and effective way, because I 'tutela-ed' [*tuteló*] a right that had been violated for my son."[24]

These examples illustrate some of the ways that the term "tutela" has transformed and entered colloquial Colombian discourse. "Tutela" is not simply a formal, technical legal term (like "writ of protection" or "writ of certiorari" are in American English), but one that has become part of everyday speech and everyday life.

The understandings that folks express about the tutela and their constitutional rights may or may not all be technically accurate. Gabriel Roldán, a judge in Medellín, shared the following story with me in an interview:

> People even at the lowest levels ask about tutela. Look, for example, in my house we had domestic workers for many years and one of the last ones said to me "Don Gabriel, can you help me to file a tutela?" And I asked, "for what?" And she said, "displacement." I asked, "why displacement? You are not displaced." And she said, "my neighbors are not displaced, and they have also won tutela claims as displaced persons."[25]

He went on to say that he had explained that this was not how the tutela was supposed to work. If the 1991 Constitution and the tutela procedure were not embedded, we would not expect to hear references to them at all, whether accurate or inaccurate – and certainly not from people who have no formal legal training or education. Misunderstandings are perhaps even more informative than the parroting of correct information for social embedding. Misunderstandings reflect how

prestadora de salud no me da el servicio, la entutelo, si en mi barrio se va mucho la luz entonces, monto una tutela. Y entonces se nos volvió que la palabra tutela, se volvió tan paisaje."

24 Medellín interview 5. "Yo tengo un hijo menor de edad el cual le estaban vulnerando el derecho a la educación ... Me dijeron que la herramienta idónea para hacer tutelar de este derecho de mi hijo era la tutela ... Obtuve respuesta de manera ágil y efectiva, pues se me tuteló derecho que tenía vulnerado para mi hijo."

25 Elite interview 74 (March 22, 2017). "La gente hasta de los más bajos niveles le pregunta a uno por la tutela. Mire por ejemplo en mi casa tuvimos por muchos años empleadas de servicio doméstico y una de las ultimas me decía 'Don Gabriel ¿usted me ayuda para presentar una tutela?' y yo '¿para qué?' Y dice 'porque de desplazada' y '¿Por qué de desplazada si usted no es desplazada?' y dice 'mis vecinas no son desplazadas y también han ganado tutelas como desplazadas.'"

information has been refracted through social interaction, through word of mouth and vernacularization. These kinds of misunderstandings provide another glimpse into just how pervasive and normal references to legal mobilization for rights through the tutela procedure have become – and just how socially embedded the 1991 Constitution has become.

4.2 LEGAL MOBILIZATION AND SOCIAL EMBEDDING

The vision of the 1991 Constitution as one that offers potentially meaningful rights protections through tutela claims entered everyday discourse in the early 1990s. But would it remain there? Beyond simply knowing about the tutela, citizens also had to embrace it, to use it to make claims to the rights enshrined in the constitution. Colombian citizens have turned to the tutela to make rights claims in greater and greater numbers in the decades following the implementation of the 1991 Constitution. Julieta Lemaitre, who was, at the time of our interview, a law professor at the Universidad de los Andes (later she became a judge in the Special Jurisdiction for Peace), noted how unexpected the rise of the tutela was, stating that "I don't think in 1991 anybody could have seen the importance of tutela, but by 1994, 1995, certainly, people were starting to get it. By the end of the decade, it was clear that it was important, the only game in town."[26] Juan Sebastián Tisnés, a judge working in Medellín, echoed this view that citizens came to view the tutela as integral to their ability to obtain a wide variety of goods, services, and protections:

> [W]e want to resolve everything through the tutela, right? ... For example, if you dismiss me as your worker, instead of going to labor court, I file a tutela claim ... The health [claims], if they delivered the medications, you would not have to file a tutela, or if they delivered the drugs to you, you would not have to file a tutela. I think it is both that everything is resolved by way of the tutela or we believe that everything is resolved by way of the tutela, and because state entities do not apply that Article II of the constitution [that stipulates that the state has the duty to "serve the community, promote the general welfare, guaranteeing the effectiveness of the principles, rights, and duties stipulated by the Constitution"].[27]

[26] Elite interview 20 (September 6, 2016). Other interviewees echoed this notion.

[27] Elite interview 72 (March 15, 2017). "Todo lo queremos resolver por tutela ¿cierto? ... Por ejemplo tú me despides a mi como tu trabajador y yo en vez de ir a la Justica

Another judge working in Medellín, Gabriel Roldán, shared a similar view: "today I think that no Colombian imagines life without the tutela. It's that simple. It would be hard to imagine what Colombian society would be like without this mechanism."[28]

During interviews, everyday Colombians confirmed this sense that the tutela had become fundamental to citizens. For example, one interviewee pointed to the key role of the tutela in transforming what is written in the Constitution into substance: "I think it is important to know what [the tutela] is, to know that it is a right that is in the Constitution that, in fact, allows us to fight for the rights we all have. The tutela allows us to assert what is constitutionally written."[29] Yet, this adoption of the tutela has not translated evenly into claim-making across issue areas.

The combination of right to petition and right to health tutelas comprised the majority (between 63 and 76 percent) of tutela claims filed between 2003 and 2019.[30] The right to petition – which allows citizens to make "respectful" requests of the government, often for information – is exactly the kind of claim that the tutela was originally designed to facilitate. What ensured the deep embedding of the tutela in general and the 1991 Constitution in particular into Colombian social life, however, was claim-making regarding the right to health – a newly codified right, and one that arguably falls outside of the scope of the tutela, at least as it is described in text of the Constitution. Juan Carlos Esguerra, the delegate behind the tutela proposal at the constituent assembly, explained to me that:

> At the beginning, if you would look at the Constitution, the first answer would be tutela is not for social rights. Because for tutela is constructed for the fundamental rights and fundamental rights are chapter number

Laboral interpongo la tutela … De los de salud, si tu entregaras los medicamentos no tendrías que interponer tutela, o si a ti entregaran los medicamentos no tendrías que interponer tutela entonces creo que son las dos que todo es resuelto por vía de tutela o creemos que todo se resuelve por vía de tutela, y porque las entidades del estado no aplican ese artículo dos de la constitución política."

28 Elite interview 74 (March 10, 2017). "Hoy creo que ningún colombiano se imagina sin la tutela, es así de sencillo, sería difícil imaginar cómo sería la sociedad colombiana sin este mecanismo."

29 Bogotá interview 35. "Creo que es importante saber lo que es [la acción de tutela], conocer que es un derecho que está en la Constitución, pues que hecho nos permite luchar por los derechos que todos tenemos. Una acción de tutela nos permite hacer valer lo que constitucionalmente está escrito."

30 Disaggregated data are not available before 2003.

> one and the social rights are chapter number two … So, the tutela is [technically] not for them.[31]

Yet, in 2019, of more than 620,000 tutelas filed, 207,368 invoked the right to health. How did that happen? In this rest of this chapter, I explore the social construction of legal grievances in the Colombian context, paying particular attention to how constitutional law, the tutela, and healthcare came to be understood as fundamentally intertwined. This process – along with the development of judicial receptivity to particular kinds of claims (a topic explored in Chapter 5) – resulted in a feedback loop, spurring continued legal mobilization and embedding the 1991 Colombian Constitution.

The formal rules that regulate the tutela procedure help to mitigate the need for a traditional support structure for claim-making (Wilson 2009). Even so, actors not employed in or by the formal legal system, including pharmaceutical and insurance companies, advocacy networks, NGOs, and community organizations, were fundamental to changing ideas about the tutela and the right to health. In the case of health claims, actors not usually associated with the legal system, such as insurance and pharmaceutical companies, helped to cement the understanding that access to healthcare is a fundamentally legal issue among claimants. Concretely, citizens came to think of filing tutela claims when they were denied access to medicines, surgeries, or procedures.

By examining patterns of tutela claims rather than taking an individual case as the unit of analysis, I reveal two key incentive structures in the realm of health rights claims. First, individual citizens found practical incentives to file tutela claims. Second, insurance and pharmaceutical companies found monetary incentives to encourage the use of the tutela procedure. The combination of these incentive structures spurred changes in beliefs about how law could and should be used in the realm of healthcare.

In terms of incentives for citizens, the massive yet uneven expansion of the healthcare system that began with Law 100 of 1993 generated many potential grievances, as citizens gained access in theory (if not in practice) to more and more services and developed a greater sense of entitlement to those services.[32] Between 1995 and 2011, the

[31] Elite interview 35 (September 23, 2016).

[32] The Law 100 reforms were based on the Chilean healthcare system.

percentage of the Colombian population included in the healthcare system expanded from 25 percent to 90 percent, increasing further to 95 percent by 2016 (Lamprea 2015: 61; Lamprea and García 2016). This expansion resulted in substantially increased levels of coverage, but that coverage did not necessarily translate into real access to healthcare services for newly covered individuals. Over time, individual citizens came to understand the filing of tutelas as what one must do to receive healthcare services, and the relatively low cost of the tutela procedure allowed many citizens to file claims.

The incentive structure for insurance companies worked as follows. The companies could reasonably expect to reduce the number of people seeking access to medications, services, and procedures by initially denying that access and encouraging the filing of tutela claims.[33] Even when those medications, services, and procedures were covered in the benefits plan, the companies could reasonably expect that not everyone would follow through with tutela claims: some might pay out-of-pocket and others might simply move on without whatever it was that they had sought.

What's move, in certain circumstances, the state would help to pay for medicines and procedures out of an established fund called the Fondo de Solidaridad y Garantía, relieving the insurance company of that duty, but only after the filing of a tutela (Lamprea 2015). The idea behind this fund was to ensure that individuals would not be inhibited from accessing the medicines or procedures they needed simply because of a gap in coverage. Yet, the system was particularly susceptible to fraud and manipulation by actors in the health sphere who could deny access to a medical service that should have been covered and suggest that the patient file a tutela, as noted above. Importantly, this opportunity for manipulation was not necessarily one that would have been predictable when the fund was created (during the Law 100 reform of 1993). In 1993, it was not yet clear that the judges would be so receptive to health claims.

While some insurance companies have better reputations than others (and some seem to perform better than their reputations would suggest), the general understanding among everyday Colombians is that the healthcare sphere is characterized by mismanagement, understaffing,

[33] Interviews with former clerks (elite interviews 2 and 4, both conducted August 4, 2016).

fraud, and corruption. It is unclear exactly how frequently this kind of fraudulent and negligent activity occurs (though news reports suggest it has not necessarily been uncommon[34]), but it is less important for my account that this behavior was, in fact, pervasive than that it is *viewed as* pervasive and that the behavior of insurance companies was interpreted as encouraging the use of the tutela in the realm of health.

Everaldo Lamprea (2015) has documented financial ties between pharmaceutical companies and patients' organizations engaged in the filing of tutela claims with the hopes of expanding the scope of covered medications. These kinds of connections can be interpreted as a manipulation of the tutela process, but they also reflect the convergence of interests between patients who need specific medications and companies that would like to increase access to and the purchasing of those same drugs. Regardless of the interpretation, there is a pathway through which pharmaceutical companies encourage the use of the tutela for the protection of the right to health.

Alejandro Gaviria, the minister of health from 2012 to 2018, summarized the factors that influenced the increased use of the tutela for health claims as follows:

> People started to see in the tutela a way to expand the benefits plan one by one. For patients very sick with cancer, the basic plan did not include the medication they needed, so they would go before a judge … I believe that this is the first dimension. And the basic plan was never updated [early on]. The tutela was a way to update [the plan] and [get it to] include [the medicines you needed]. I believe that there is a second point that has to do with collective learning. Society and, above all, lawyers learned that this was the way to do things. And then there were agents among the pharmaceutical industry who began to see in the tutela a way to incorporate the latest innovations into the health system and [in the process] capture public resources.[35]

As a result, the tutela and the healthcare system came to be inextricably linked in people's minds. This was one consequence of the social embedding of the 1991 Constitution.

Thus far, I have inferred this connection between the tutela and healthcare based on behavior (that citizens routinely make health rights claims with the tutela). My interviews from across the country provide illustrative evidence that at least some everyday Colombians

[34] See, e.g., El Espectador (2012) and El Tiempo (2012).

[35] Elite interview 56 (November 2, 2016).

do, in fact, view the two as interlinked. For example, one interviewee summarized, "unfortunately, in Colombia, in order to access health services, you have to file tutelas."[36] Two other interviewees offered detailed examples of the role of the tutela in the healthcare system. One reported:

> I have a relative who is very sick. I had to file tutela actions that said the health clinic would not do the [necessary] surgery or give the [necessary] medication. Sometimes they comply, and they attend to the patient. Many times, no … [In these situations,] you have to get an order of contempt or file another tutela or go to the media. The [first] tutela is not enough.[37]

A second, drawing on personal experience, noted:

> My sister has a very complicated medical problem and has to take medications … They are covered in the [public health benefits plan], but they are not generic … She had to file a tutela claim for the [insurance company] to cover them, and [now] they're covering them. There are cases in which, unfortunately, if you think about it, it should not be a tutela claim. There should be an established process for each thing, but the tutela has become the thing that one has to use to gain access to citizenship services.[38]

The tutela is understood as the effective entry point into the healthcare system (as well as the access point for other citizenship goods). Responding to this perception in 2007, the Constitutional Court issued a decision noting that the tutela cannot be a required part of the process of obtaining healthcare (C-950/07). That the Court felt the need

[36] Bogotá interview 9. "Desafortunadamente en Colombia para acceder a algunos servicios de salud hay que poner tutelas."

[37] Agua Blanca interview 18 (April 15, 2017). "La acción de tutela con la salud, pues por los menos yo tengo un familiar grave en la clínica … Me toca que colocar una acción de tutela donde dice no quieren atender, no quieren hacer la cirugía o no quieren dar el medicamento. A veces la acatan y pues atienden la paciente. Muchas veces, no … Un orden de desacato u otra vez otra orden de tutela o a los medios de comunicación … para atender al paciente. [¿La tutela no es suficiente?] No."

[38] Bogotá interview 44. "Por ejemplo mi hermana tiene un problema medico muy complicado y tiene que tomar medicamentos … Están dentro del POS pero no son genéricos … y ella tuvo que instaurar una acción de tutela para que la EPS se los cubriera y se los está cubriendo. Hay casos en los cuales lamentablemente si lo piensa uno bien pues no debería ser una acción de tutela. Debería haber un proceso establecido para cada cosa, pero se ha convertido la acción de tutela en que para el servicio al ciudadano uno tiene que establecer una acción de tutela."

to issue such a declaration indicates the prevalence of the view that the tutela was a necessary part of accessing healthcare. Because of the way the healthcare system became judicialized, problems related to access to health came to be viewed as legal grievances.

My argument is not that these insurance and pharmaceutical companies explicitly call on individuals to file tutela claims in every case (though sometimes that does happen), but that a generalized linkage of healthcare and the tutela has emerged: the combination of incentives for insurance and pharmaceutical companies and incentives for individuals have reinforced the understanding of health as a legal issue. These incentives are particularly influential considering the unique features of the tutela, such as the low cost and quick response rate. The understanding that one must file a legal claim in order to have access to health services would be less likely to prompt litigation in a setting where litigation is costly and time-consuming.

4.3 CLAIM-MAKING DESPITE AMBIVALENCE

Colombian citizens continue to file tutela claims despite ambivalence, uncertainty, and even skepticism about both the process of filing a claim and the likely outcome. This is further evidence that the 1991 Constitution has become embedded in Colombian society. If Colombians were simply responding to cost–benefit analyses of whether or not to file tutela claims or to engage constitutional rights, we would have reason to doubt that the 1991 Constitution was truly socially embedded. Embedding indicates moving beyond means–ends calculations regarding legal tools to understanding them as common sense. In this section, I draw primarily on interviews conducted with everyday Colombians – fifty in-depth interviews with residents of Bogotá in February and March 2017, and twenty-four unstructured individual and group interviews with forty-three people in Agua Blanca, Cali during April and May of 2017 – and a survey of 310 people waiting in line outside the Palacio de Justicia in Medellín to file a tutela claim in April 2017.[39]

Almost everyone in the Bogotá sample evaluated the legal system negatively, regardless of social class. One poor respondent stated simply, "it would be better to say that Colombian law does not exist,"[40] and a wealthy respondent likewise noted, "justice here in Colombia

[39] For more on data collection, see Chapter 1 and the Appendix.
[40] Bogotá interview 29. "Mejor dicho la ley colombiana no existe."

does not function; there are no laws."[41] Isolating the differences of rights on paper and how the law functions in everyday life, one interviewee noted that "in some ways, one is sold the image that things have tended to improve [with the 1991 Constitution], but one does not see that change."[42] Another poor woman concluded, "realistically, people of few resources have not been the beneficiaries of any constitution,"[43] questioning the idea that the law anywhere helps the poor. By and large, assessments of the judiciary's inefficacy do not appear to vary along class lines.

Interviewees in Agua Blanca reported similar views on the large gap between rights and laws as they are written in the Constitution and in the codes and how they work in practice. As one respondent described, the major problem facing the legal system is that "there is the absence of the application of the laws as they are. Here we have laws, but they are not applied as they are [or as they should be]," and that the same applies to rights.[44] This perception contrasts with that of other residents who tended to state things like "there is no law" or "the law does not exist."[45] These views are not necessarily incommensurate, as the former is a statement of objective fact (there are technically laws in Colombia) while the latter offers a subjective, experiential view (residents rarely experience the law outside of delegitimizing factors such as violence and corruption). Another resident explicitly referenced the differences between the constitutional text and everyday life: "It is one thing what the Constitution says and another what happens … the rights, every day they are violated. All of them are violated."[46]

Few respondents in Bogotá gave any suggestion that they viewed their constitutional rights as effective tools in and of themselves. Instead, interviewees appeared to have more confidence in the idea that rights could have real consequences for their everyday lives only through the

41 Bogotá interview 6. "La justicia acá en Colombia no sirve; no hay leyes."

42 Bogotá interview 11. "En cierto modo a uno le venden la imagen de que tienden a mejorar [con la Constitución del 91] pero uno no ve ese cambio."

43 Bogotá interview 39. "Pues realmente digamos que las personas de bajos recursos no han estado muy beneficiados, digamos que con ninguna constitución."

44 Agua Blanca interview 6. "Falta aplicar las leyes como son. Aquí hay leyes, pero no se aplican como son."

45 Various Agua Blanca interviews. "No hay ley. La ley no existe."

46 Agua Blanca interview 5. "Una cosa lo que dice la Constitución y otra cosa lo que hacen … los derechos, todos los días los violan. Todos los violan."

use of the tutela procedure. One middle-class respondent, for example, pointed to the key role of the tutela in transforming what is written in the Constitution into substance: "I think it is important to know what [the tutela] is, to know that it is a right that is in the Constitution that, in fact, allows us to fight for the rights we all have. The tutela allows us to assert what is constitutionally written."[47] A well-off respondent similarly reported that he saw the tutela as "an excellent mechanism to access and assert my rights."[48] Across classes, interviewees shared views that suggested skepticism about the value of their rights, especially in the absence of the tutela.

Survey respondents reported very similar views. Nearly 70 percent stated that they were unconfident or very unconfident that the judiciary treated all citizens equally. Only 19 out of 310 respondents said they were confident in the judiciary, and zero respondents reported that they were very confident. Thus, respondents reported little confidence in encountering a fair judiciary. Twenty percent of respondents pointed to the view that the state should protect their rights as the primary reason for filing a tutela claim, which could be interpreted as minimal support for the idea that their constitutional rights are "real" or claimable. The nature of the survey does not allow for the same level of nuance that emerges in responses to open-ended interview questions; however, the survey yields evidence that the evaluations of the general population carry through to individuals who use the legal system. Here, claimants do not appear to be fundamentally different from nonclaimants in their assessments of the state and the judiciary.

Given this general lack of faith in the state, the judiciary, and rights, perhaps citizens view the tutela as distinct from the rest of the state's legal apparatus, as an effective tool in an ineffective system. During a group interview in Agua Blanca, members of one family (living in extreme poverty, even for Agua Blanca) explained that "we have filed many legal claims, and they do not care [or respond]," no matter what type of claim, whether to obtain access to government

47 Bogotá interview 35. "Creo que es importante saber lo que es [la acción de tutela], conocer que es un derecho que está en la Constitución, que pues que de hecho nos permite luchar por los derechos que todos tenemos. Una acción de tutela nos permite hacer valer lo que constitucionalmente está escrito."

48 Bogotá interview 32. "[La acción de tutela es] un excelente mecanismo para poder acceder y hacer valer mis derechos."

services or to report the excessive use of force by the police.[49] Another woman living in the neighborhood described the process of filing a tutela claim for the right to health as follows:

> You do not need a lawyer, but when you go to the Palace of Justice, there is a man in front who does everything for 10,000 or 15,000 COP [at the time about US$3–5] – a processor. And you say, "Good morning, what happened is … [I would like] to place a tutela," and the man processes it for you. You have to have a copy of your ID and wait in line … and after a few days, you get the response. If you do not pay a processor here, nothing happens.[50]

Ultimately, the judge found in favor of this woman's right to health claim; however, in the decision, he declared that she should have access to diapers and creams, not the twenty-four-hour nurse she had requested. In Agua Blanca, citizens rarely, if ever, reported believing that the tutela was effective in protecting their rights.

In the Bogotá sample, however, views on the tutela procedure were mixed. One middle-class respondent described the tutela in the following way:

> [The tutela] gave the ordinary citizen the possibility to enforce their rights or show difficulties in the fulfillment of some fundamental right … Before the tutela, there was nothing one could do. It was necessary to wait for a politician to be elected, and if he cared about that community, wait for him to intervene in some way. Not now. Now, an individual, a single person, can file a complaint with the tutela.[51]

An upper-class interviewee similarly considered that "[the tutela] helps, it is a tool that makes those who are responsible respond to what one is

[49] Agua Blanca interview 1. "Ponemos una cantidad de demandas y ellos no les importa."

[50] Agua Blanca interview 6. "No necesitas un abogado, pero vas al frente del Palacio de Justicia y hay un señor en frente que hace todo por 10 o 15 mil – un tramitador. Y tú dices buenas señor, lo que pasa es … para colocar una tutela y el señor tramite. [Tienes que tener una] fotocopia de la cédula y [esperar en] la fila … y después unos días, la respuesta. Si usted no paga un tramitador aquí, no hacen nada."

[51] Bogotá interview 9. "[L]e dio la posibilidad al ciudadano común de hacer cumplir o de mostrar que hay dificultades en el cumplimiento de algún derecho fundamental … antes de la acción de tutela no había nada que hacer, tocaba esperar a que un político se eligiera y que le importara esa comunidad para que interviniera de alguna manera, ahora no. Ahora un individuo, una sola persona, con una acción de tutela puede poner una denuncia."

asking for."[52] Further, a middle-class respondent said, "[the tutela] is the only thing that works – we use it because it works."[53] On the other hand, some respondents critiqued the way the tutela procedure functions in practice. As one member of the lower class noted, "the tutela is good, but what happens is that they do not comply … the people do not comply."[54] Others argued that too many tutelas have been filed, that judges are overburdened by tutelas, and that sometimes people abuse the procedure. An lower-class interviewee noted, "lately, the courts are so full of tutelas … Already [the tutela] lost its efficiency."[55] One member of the upper class spoke specifically about the overuse of the tutela, stating, "[p]eople abuse the tutela a lot and it takes up a lot of time to resolve [the tutela claims]," stressing an already overtaxed legal system.[56] Finally, some respondents simply held negative views on the tutela. As one lower-class respondent remarked, "[the idea of the tutela is] to assert our rights, but that does not work … that is a lie, it does nothing for you."[57] Similarly, a middle-class woman noted that filing a tutela "seems to me a waste of time and above all fills the courts … the perception I have is that it is of no use."[58] Thus, while respondents in Bogotá generally agreed that the justice system as a whole leaves much to be desired, perspectives on the effectiveness of the tutela procedure were more varied.

Interestingly, the view that the tutela is likely to be effective is not a necessary condition for the filing of tutela claims. This disconnect was especially clear in the interviews conducted by several research assistants from the Universidad de Antioquia with the Medellín survey respondents about two weeks after the survey had been conducted

[52] Bogotá interview 6. "[La tutela] le ayuda a uno, es una herramienta que hace que los responsables de lo que uno está tutelando le respondan por lo que uno está pidiendo."

[53] Bogotá interview 44. "[La tutela] es lo único que funciona – lo usamos porque es lo que funciona."

[54] Bogotá interview 13. "[La acción de tutela es] buena, [pero] lo que pasa es que no se cumplen … la gente no cumple."

[55] Bogotá interview 1. "Últimamente como que las acciones tutela como los juzgados están tan llenos de ella … Ya perdió su eficiencia."

[56] Bogotá interview 33. "La gente abusa mucho y eso quita mucho tiempo también para poder resolver las cosas."

[57] Bogotá interview 29. "[La idea de la tutela es] hacer valer nuestros derechos, pero eso para que, eso nunca sirve para nada … eso es mentira, eso no hace nada por uno."

[58] Bogotá interview 18. "Me parece una pérdida de tiempo y un desgaste y sobre todo llenar más allá esos juzgados … la percepción que yo tengo es que no sirve para nada."

(when the first decision to their tutela claim should have been issued). These interviews – with only minor discrepancies – followed one of two scripts: positive and upbeat, with no or only minor complaints about the process, or negative but resigned. One respondent, Liliana, shared her positive analysis with one of my research assistants:[59]

Could you tell me about your experience filing a tutela? Why did you decide to file a claim?
I needed to resolve a health problem with the insurance company.[60]
What was the process like?
I went where they receive tutela claims, stood in line, and handed it in.[61]
What was the result?
Well, they responded quickly and decided in my favor.[62]
What do you think of the results?
Good, because when one appeals for a right, and if they respond in favor, I think that's excellent.[63]
What did you like about the process and what did you not like?
[I liked] that the process was quick, but standing in line was very tedious and the time one waits there to hand in the tutela is very long.[64]
Would you use the tutela again (in the future)?
Yes, as long as one needs it, because you really have to watch over your rights and make the authorities comply.[65]

Another respondent, Rosita – who had already filed four tutela claims – held a decidedly more negative view of the tutela procedure:[66]

Could you tell me about your experience filing a tutela? Why did you decide to file a claim?
I filed a tutela claim, because I had a problem with a surgery I wanted.[67]

59 Medellín interview 7.
60 "La necesidad de que me resolvieran un problema que tenía de salud en la EPS."
61 "Yo fui allá donde reciben las tutelas hice la fila y la entregué."
62 "Pues allá me respondieron rápido y me la dieron a favor."
63 "Bien, porque cuando uno apela por un derecho y pues si se lo responden a favor de uno, me parece que eso es excelente."
64 "Que la respuesta fue rápida, pero hacer filas eso siempre fue muy tedioso y es muy largo el tiempo que uno espera allá para poder entregar la tutela."
65 "Si, siempre y cuando la necesite porque uno de verdad tiene que velar por sus derechos y hacer que las autoridades pues lo hagan cumplir."
66 Medellín interview 6.
67 "Mira yo creo que la acción tutela porque tenía problema con una cirugía que me quería hacer."

What was the process like?

It's traumatic, because you have to wait in many lines, but it didn't help me much.[68]

What was the result?

Nothing. The bypass surgery has still not been done yet.[69]

What do you think of the results?

Well, they're bad, because I didn't get what I want.[70]

What did you like about the process and what did you not like?

I like that there's the possibility of filing a tutela, but if one doesn't get what one is proposed, then really, I'm not happy with that.[71]

Would you use the tutela again (in the future)?

I don't know. I would have to, because there are no other options, but it doesn't work either really.[72]

What immediately stands out is that Liliana evaluated the experience positively after receiving a decision in her favor, while Rosita evaluated the experience negatively after receiving a negative response. One striking commonality, however, is that both women said that they would use the tutela again: Liliana enthusiastically and Rosita reluctantly. Others with whom we followed up echoed Rosita, saying that even though they were not satisfied with the tutela process, they might "have to" file a tutela claim again, "because there are no other options."[73]

Colombians have accepted the tutela and their ability to make claims to newly codified rights (like the right to health) under the 1991 Constitution, despite mixed views about the usefulness of the tutela. The use of the tutela to make rights claims may or may not result in material changes, but no other options exist, except for doing nothing. If the problem is deemed to be important enough, doing nothing may not be considered a viable option.[74] In this way, the 1991 Constitution

68 "Ese es más traumático porque hay que hacer muchas filas, pero no me sirvió mucho de menos."

69 "Nada, porque la cirugía para el bypass no me la han hecho todavía nada."

70 "No pues malo, porque no se ha logrado lo que yo quiero."

71 "Me gustó porque existe la posibilidad de colocar la tutela, pero si uno no logra lo que se está proponiendo entonces no, realmente no estoy contenta con eso."

72 "Hay yo no sé tocaría porque no hay como otras posibilidades, pero no como sirve demasiado verdad."

73 Medellín interview 12. See also Medellín interview 4.

74 What differentiates those who do not act from those who do is an open question and should be the subject of future research. Generally speaking, mobilization – both social and legal – occurs at rates lower than might be warranted by possible

came to be socially embedded and understood as a fundamental part of Colombian life.

4.4 CONCLUSION

Social embedding reflects the degree to which a constitution impacts daily social life. Outside of judges' chambers, lawyers' offices, and law school classrooms, how meaningful are constitutional rights promises? Do citizens talk about and use legal mechanisms to make claims to their rights? Do citizens even know about and believe in the possibility of making such claims?

This chapter detailed the process of the social embedding of the 1991 Colombian Constitution. In a relatively short period of time, citizens came to adopt core features of the 1991 Constitution into their everyday discourse and practices, most notably the tutela procedure. The process of social embedding began with government outreach and educational campaigns, as well as the spread of information through the media. Eventually, knowledge of tutela and social rights came to take on a life of its own. Legal mobilization served as a mechanism of social embedding, as citizens repeatedly filed tutela claims regarding new constitutional rights, even when they were not necessarily convinced of its effectiveness. Filing tutela claims came to be seen as "what one has to do" (Taylor 2018), despite official declarations on the contrary. And, as a result, the Constitution of 1991 became embedded socially – as part of what is considered "normal," "ordinary," or "everyday" at the social level.

I next turn to the process of legal embedding, or how the 1991 Constitution came to shape the expectations and behaviors of actors within the formal legal sphere. A context of social embedding without legal embedding is likely to spur claim-making initially, but if judges, lawyers, and other representatives of the state dismiss these claims as misguided, inappropriate, or unreasonable, that lack of legal embedding will begin to undermine social embedding. Chapter 5 not only details how legal embedding occurred in Colombia, but also how it reinforced social embedding. That both components of constitutional embedding occurred together ensured that the 1991 Colombian Constitution could withstand myriad future challenges and endure as a key feature organizing both social and legal life.

grievances or "justiciable events" (e.g., McCarthy and Zald 1977; Felstiner, Abel, and Sarat, 1980; Genn 1999).

CHAPTER FIVE

LEGAL EMBEDDING

The Constitutional Court wanted to ensure that the Constitution permeated the entire judicial arena. In other words, all the judges of the country, the civil judges, the labor and criminal judges, the Supreme Court, all apply the Constitution.[1]

Justice Eduardo Cifuentes

This chapter turns to the Colombian legal community and examines how the 1991 Constitution influences judicial decision-making in Colombia. Legal embedding refers to the process by which particular understandings of new constitutional rights or other legal provisions come to inform the actions of judges and lawyers. Thus, legal embedding conceptually fits within constructivist approaches to judicial behavior, which understand judicial decisions to be "influenced by the institutionalization of 'sticky' ideas about the law and appropriate professional conduct in courts' routine practices," as described by Ezequiel González-Ocantos (2014: 482). He further explains that judges' social and professional contexts can influence their "cognitive frameworks mak[ing] certain patterns of action unthinkable, certain legal solutions unknown, certain jurisprudential innovations too risky, and certain practices part of unquestioned routines" (2014: 482) Lisa Hilbink (2007: 34, emphasis in original) similarly highlights the importance of both "institutional *structure*, [or] the formal rules that determine

[1] Elite interview 1 (July 26, 2016). "La Corte Constitucional quiere que busca que la Constitución permeé en toda la habita judicial. O sea que todos los jueces del país, los jueces civiles, los jueces laborales, penales, la Corte Suprema, todos aplican la Constitución."

the relationship of judges to each other and to the other branches of the state, and thereby offer incentives and disincentives for different kinds of behavior," and "institutional *ideology*, [or] the understanding of the social role of the institution into which judges are socialized, the content of which is maintained through formal sanctions and informal norms within the institution," for explaining judicial behavior. These factors condition whatever ideological preferences judges might have or strategic pressures they might face. Importantly, legal embedding occurs in these cognitive frameworks, institutional structures, and institutional ideologies.

What does legal embedding look like in Colombia? Following the introduction of the 1991 Constitution, the new Constitutional Court and the justices that comprised it set out a new vision of constitutional law; one that was informed, but not determined, by the drafters of the constitution. These justices also reacted to citizens' claims and the problems they came across time and time again both within the legal system and outside of it. Like with social embedding, we see a key role of legal mobilization in legal embedding. As citizens continued to bring claims to a wide variety of constitutional rights (including newly enshrined rights) using the tutela procedure, justice and clerks at the Constitutional Court began to think about the tutela and the possibilities of constitutional law in more expansive ways. They were inundated with new social rights claims and some of these social rights problems came to be visible to justices in their lived experience outside the courtroom as well as legible to them as *legal* in nature. Justices came to see these problems as properly legal, as ones that fall within the scope of the new constitutional vision. They then became more open to developing new legal approaches to the issue. In other words, this process made everyday problems "real" to the law.

The rise and persistence of claims related to a specific grievance (in this case, the right to health and other social rights) cumulatively informed judges about these issues, making them more comfortable with the scope of social rights and more aware of the salience of social rights. Ultimately, they even began to identify with claimants.[2] A confluence of exposure to social rights challenges in daily life (i.e., life outside of courthouses) and exposure within the legal system played

[2] For other arguments that focus on how judges' awareness of and responsiveness to an issue may shift over time, see Feeley and Rubin (1998), Hilbink (2014), Petrova (2018), Ríos-Figueroa (2016), and Kim et al. (2021).

an important role in the development of judicial receptivity, inspiring judges to connect an issue that they have perhaps seen on television or in their everyday lives with the format, scope, and tools of law. Justices then allowed new kinds of claims to be made, viewing new grievances as issues that should be resolved in the formal legal sphere – specifically those related to social rights. Over time, this view came to be one that was held not just by individual justices or the Constitutional Court, but one that had spread throughout the judiciary. Citizens continued to make legal claims to these new social rights using the tutela, especially as the social embedding of the 1991 Constitution deepened. As will become evident, this legal mobilization helped to generate judicial receptivity and shape the legal embedding of the Constitution.

The rest of this chapter proceeds as follows. I first set out evidence that legal embedding of the 1991 Constitution has, in fact, taken place in Colombia. After that, I draw on semi-structured interviews with "legal elites" (including lawyers, judges, and law professors) and a close reading of tutela decisions to show how legal mobilization has served as a mechanism of legal embedding through an examination of early tutela decisions (especially those regarding social rights) and changes in tutela jurisprudence over time. The tutela and social rights have become core to Colombian constitutional law, not simply because of their inclusion in the 1991 Constitution, but through the repeated interactions of judges and claimants, through the social construction of legal grievances (the subject of Chapter 4) and the development of judicial receptivity to particular kinds of claims (described in this chapter). Together, these processes – specifically as they related to the tutela procedure and social rights – ensured the legal embedding of the constitution. In Section 5.3, I discuss why judges became especially accepting of health rights claims, creating an area of unevenness in constitutional embedding. Finally, I detail how legal embedding has occurred beyond the Constitutional Court and throughout the judicial system.

5.1 SIGNS OF LEGAL EMBEDDING

How might we know that legal embedding has occurred? In contrast to social embedding, which hinges on societal-level trends, legal embedding involves the acceptance of this legal vision and tools in the formal legal sphere – meaning that we need to look to judicial institutions and actors for evidence of this kind of embedding. In the case of a new constitution and a new constitutional vision, we might first consider the extent to which institutions, mechanisms, and actors that previously had not been part of the legal infrastructure have come to make their presence known in the daily work of law. If there is a new Constitutional Court or a new constitutional chamber in an existing high court, does it hear cases? More importantly, does it hear politically relevant cases? Has it come to assert itself over "ordinary" courts? If there is a new legal mechanism, a tool with which to make legal claims, are citizens able to use it? If new actors have been empowered to oversee the constitution, do they take this role seriously? Do they work to propagate and defend the new constitutional order, or do they defer to traditional views on law? The presence of these institutions, mechanisms, and actors is not enough to ensure that legal embedding will occur, but without their emergence, legal embedding is unlikely.

Second, by examining judicial actors more closely, we can observe further signs of legal embedding. When judges establish, alter, and expand precedent related to this new constitutional vision, they are taking steps to ensure that this vision will continue to impact the way things are done, the way that cases are decided, even after their tenure is over. For instance, when judges adopt tests, standards, and doctrines by which to decide cases related to new constitutional rights, those rights become more robustly integrated into legal thinking and legal practice than they were when they were simply rights provisions listed in the constitution. These tests, standards, and doctrines help to shape not only judges' perceptions of rights, but also those of litigators and claimants. As time passes and new cohorts of judges rise through the ranks of the judiciary, a new set of judicial actors will come to have the most leverage on the development of constitutional law. However, when legal embedding has occurred, judges who previously held ideological views inconsistent with the new constitutional vision have come to adopt positions closer to the Constitutional Court's (or Constitutional Chamber's) upon being appointed to higher-level courts. They come to see their role as one conditioned by this vision and the routines of their court, as detailed by González-Ocantos (2014) and Hilbink (2007) earlier.

Third, although high court judges will be more able to impact precedent than lower-court judges, the beliefs and behaviors of lower-court judges and members of the broader legal profession are also informative. To the extent that lower-level judges (particularly those who do not specialize in constitutional law) do not challenge or disregard, but instead follow interpretations of the issues that fall within the scope of the new legal vision (e.g., the justiciability of social rights), we may conclude that legal embedding has occurred. The same is true of litigators. In other words, when the broader legal profession acts as if it is constrained by the new constitutional order, we see evidence of legal embedding.[3] This remains true even if, at the individual level, there is variation in beliefs about the most viable and appropriate interpretation of constitutional law. We might also look to shifts in law school curricula, namely the inclusion of constitutional law coursework, and in the number firms and lawyers working on constitutional law for evidence of legal embedding. I turn now to legal embedding in the Colombian case.

5.2 LEGAL EMBEDDING: JUDICIAL RECEPTIVITY TO TUTELA CLAIMS

Before considering early Colombian Constitutional Court decisions regarding the tutela and how these decisions contributed to the embedding of the 1991 Constitution, it is important to note the structure of the Court and the actors who exactly comprised the early Court. In 1992, seven justices served on what became known as the "Transitional Court." Of these seven, four had previously served on other Colombian high courts: José Gregorio Hernández, Fabio Morón, and Jaime Sanín on the Supreme Court, and Simón Rodríguez on the Council of State. The other three had been academics: Ciro Angarita, Eduardo Cifuentes, and Alejandro Martínez. The three academic justices had also been associated with a commitment to human rights and an expansive view on the role of the judiciary.[4] Of these justices on the Transitional Court, Justices Cifuentes, Hernández, Martínez, and Morón were selected to continue on for a full eight-year term.

Early on, progressively minded justices – particularly those with academic backgrounds – at the Constitutional Court gained attention for creating opportunities for legal mobilization by changing understandings about and uses of particular preexisting judicial institutions, including the tutela (Nunes 2010a; Landau 2014; Taylor 2020a). In an

[3] Of course, this is what is "supposed" to occur when a new constitution or a new legal provision is enacted. Empirically, though, we see that this does not always happen. See, for example, the discussion of "sterilization by judicial interpretation" of the 1936 reforms in Chapter 3.

[4] For more detail on these early justices, see Nunes (2010a).

interview with David Landau (2014: 133), Eduardo Cifuentes explained the approach of these progressive justices: "We knew we had one year, because we did not know whether we would be reappointed. We wanted to change as much as we could in one year ... We were not a majority on the Court, but we had influence because we acted together." Ultimately, this came to pass. The progressive orientation of the early Constitutional Court became so ingrained that even conservative judges appear to have put up relatively little resistance upon assuming their positions as Constitutional Court justices. As Néstor Osuna, a former justice in the Superior Council of the Judiciary[5] and alternate Constitutional Court justice explained, "there is a tradition in the [Constitutional] Court of progressivism from day one. Judges of the conservative tradition who came to the Court became moderates at least."[6] This progressivism was manifest in rights-protective stances, particularly in stances that allowed for the justiciability of social rights through the tutela procedure and generated a larger role for the Constitutional Court in the broader judicial system than previously envisioned.[7]

Yet, according to the 1991 Constitution, tutelas could not be used to make claims about social rights violations. Instead, the tutela was meant to serve as a mechanism through which citizens could make claims about civil and political (or "fundamental") rights violations. Article 86 of the Constitution reads:

> Every individual may claim legal protection before the judge, at any time or place, through a preferential and summary proceeding, for himself/herself or by whoever acts in his/her name, the immediate protection of his/her *fundamental constitutional rights* when the individual fears the latter may be jeopardized or threatened by the action or omission of any public authority.

Chapter 1 of the section of the Constitution on "Rights, Guarantees and Duties" outlines these "Fundamental Rights" (including, for

[5] The Supreme Judicial Council oversees the administration of the judiciary.

[6] Elite interview 5 (August 8, 2016). "Hay una tradición de la Corte de ser progresista desde el primer día. Jueces de tradición conservadora al llegar a la Corte se vuelven moderados al menos." A former auxiliary justice in the Sala de Seguimiento de Salud of the Constitutional Court confirmed this view (interview 9, August 18, 2016).

[7] Interestingly, the Colombian Constitutional Court was not formally the head of the judiciary at the time this new constitution was written. The Colombian system featured four high courts, but the *tutela contra sentencias* meant that the Constitutional Court could review the decisions of the other high courts.

instance, the right to life, due process, and freedom of religion), while chapter 2 of that section lists "Social, Economic, and Cultural Rights" (which include the right to health and the right to live in dignity/the right to shelter, among others).

Those involved in the drafting of the Constitution expected that the tutela would be used by Colombians to make rights claims, though not with nearly as much scope or frequency. As Néstor Osuna suggested, "no person at that time had the ability to predict the dimensions that it would have. What we wanted was to have a cheap and simple tool for citizens for simple problems. We did not think that new rights were going to be created. We were [just] looking for a simple tool available to citizens."[8] Juan Carlos Esguerra, the member of the constituent assembly who actually proposed to call this mechanism the "tutela," agreed: "It was not meant to grow that much."[9] Despite this limited set of expectations on the part of the Constitutional Assembly members, those serving on the Constitutional Court in its early years saw an opportunity in the tutela. Justice Eduardo Cifuentes explained that "the idea [was] that it is not enough to consecrate a bill of rights, but that these rights must be surrounded by guarantees through instruments that would make them effective [or claimable]."[10]

The use of the tutela expanded quickly throughout the 1990s and into the 2000s.[11] Decisions on several tutelas that were filed in 1992 set the stage for the development of the justiciability of social rights in Colombia. Early that year, Pastora Emilia Upegui Noreña filed a tutela (T-002/92), claiming a violation of the right to education.[12] Both the lower courts and the Constitutional Court rejected this tutela claim. However, in rejecting

[8] Elite interview 5 (August 8, 2016). "Ninguna persona en ese momento tenía la capacidad de ofrecer las dimensiones que iba a tener. Lo que se quería era tener una herramienta barata y sencilla de los ciudadanos para problemas también sencillos, no pensaba que se iban crear nuevos derechos, se buscaba una herramienta sencilla al alcance de los ciudadanos."

[9] Elite interview 35 (September 23, 2016). Many other interviewees confirmed these points.

[10] Elite interview 1 (July 26, 2016). "La idea de que no es suficiente consagrar una carta de derechos, sino que estas deben estar rodeada de garantías de instrumentos para hacerlos efectivos."

[11] The next five paragraphs, analyzing early tutela decisions, draw directly from Taylor (forthcoming).

[12] Briefly, after the claimant had failed mathematics three times, the Universidad Tecnológica de Pereira refused to allow her to re-enroll in the industrial engineering program.

the claim, the Court asserted that the categorization of rights in the Constitution should be a supplementary rather than determining factor in the decision about whether or not to hear tutela cases.[13] It also suggested that education could, in other concrete cases, be considered a fundamental right. A few months later, in deciding a tutela regarding health, the Court noted, "today, with the new constitution, rights are what judges say they are through tutela decisions."[14] Together, these decisions helped to stake out a larger role for judges in determining the status of constitutional rights. Esguerra suggests that these decisions should be interpreted as an attempt by the Constitutional Court justices make social rights "real" or meaningful in everyday life.[15] Cifuentes similarly notes:

> [This use of the tutela] is not an innovation of the 1991 Colombian Constituent Assembly. Rather, it is a strong and intense seizure of the Constitution by the Colombian Constitutional Court. Everything is [up to] the discretion of the judge … It would be the Constitution [that] obviously introduces the figure and gives possibilities for the constitutional judge to expand it, but the expansion of the tutela, the guidelines of the tutela were not drawn by the Constitution but in my opinion developed [by judges].[16]

13 "El hecho de limitar los derechos fundamentales a aquellos que se encuentran en la Constitución Política bajo el título de los derechos fundamentales y excluir cualquier otro que ocupe un lugar distinto, no debe ser considerado como criterio determinante sino auxiliar, pues él desvirtúa el sentido garantizador que a los mecanismos de protección y aplicación de los derechos humanos otorgó el constituyente de 1991." See the full decision here: www.corteconstitucional.gov.co/relatoria/1992/T-002-92.htm. Further, the decision noted that judges ought to examine constitutional rights with respect to one another rather than in isolation.

14 The complete paragraph is worth quoting here: "Existe una nueva estrategia para el logro de la efectividad de los derechos fundamentales. La coherencia y la sabiduría de la interpretación y, sobre todo, la eficacia de los derechos fundamentales en la Constitución de 1991, están asegurados por la Corte Constitucional. Esta nueva relación entre derechos fundamentales y jueces significa un cambio fundamental en relación con la Constitución anterior; dicho cambio puede ser definido como una nueva estrategia encaminada al logro de la eficacia de los derechos, que consiste en otorgarle de manera prioritaria al juez, y no ya a la administración o al legislador, la responsabilidad de la eficacia de los derechos fundamentales. En el sistema anterior la eficacia de los derechos fundamentales terminaba reduciéndose a su fuerza simbólica. Hoy, con la nueva Constitución, los derechos son aquello que los jueces dicen a través de las sentencias de tutela." See the full decision here: www.corteconstitucional.gov.co/relatoria/1992/T-406-92.htm.

15 Elite interview 35 (September 23, 2016).

16 Elite interview 1 (July 26, 2016). "No se trata de una innovación de constituyente Colombia de 1991. Sino más bien una, una fuerte, un fuerte e intenso apoderamiento

Here, as Cifuentes sees it, judges determined not only that the tutela procedure would expand, but also how it would expand. Strikingly, the justices who wrote these decisions were two of the three academics appointed to the Court, Justices Martínez (T-002/92) and Angarita (T-406/92).

This expansion of the tutela procedure continued, as the Constitutional Court justices began to establish principles for analyzing concrete cases. First, the Court declared that the fundamental status of rights would be evaluated on a case-by-case basis in response to the unique facts presented by an individual tutela, per decision T-406/92.[17] In this case, a resident of the Campestre neighborhood of Cartagena filed a claim asserting that an ongoing public works project violated his rights to sanitation, health, and a healthy environment. The court of first instance rejected the claim on the grounds that these rights were not fundamental rights recognized by the Constitution. The Constitutional Court revoked this decision, granted the tutela, and noted that all future cases with similar fact patterns should be decided in the same manner. The Court sustained this approach in its decision on a case filed by SAS Televisión Ltda, a cable television provider (T-451/92).[18] The company claimed that the denial of a final operating license (it had been granted a provisional license) violated the right to work, to private property, and to culture. The Third Superior Court of Ibagué rejected the claim, and the Constitutional Court upheld that decision.

Within this case-by-case analysis, judges developed two doctrines: the *conexidad* (connection) doctrine and the *mínimo vital* (vital minimum) doctrine. Both allowed for the expansion of progressive rights

a la constitución por parte de la Corte Constitucional colombiano. Todo es la discreción del juez … Sería la constitución obviamente a introducir la figura y da posibilidades para que el juez constitucional pueda ampliarla. Pero la expansión de la tutela, las líneas maestras de la tutela no fueron trazadas por la constituyente sino en mi opinión desarrollada."

[17] "Es importante tener en cuenta que la eficacia de las normas constitucionales no se puede determinar en abstracto; ella varía según las circunstancias propias de los hechos." See the full decision here: www.corteconstitucional.gov.co/relatoria/1992/T-406-92.htm.

[18] Referring back to T-406, the decision holds, "el carácter fundamental de un derecho no se puede determinar sino en cada caso concreto, atendiendo tanto la voluntad expresa del constituyente como la conexidad o relación que en dicho caso tenga el derecho eventualmente vulnerado con otros derechos indubitablemente fundamentales y/o con los principios y valores que informan toda la Constitución." See the full decision here: www.corteconstitucional.gov.co/relatoria/1992/T-451-92.htm.

protections. The connection doctrine refers to the possibility of understanding a nonfundamental right as fundamental, and therefore justiciable, insofar as its violation also results in the violation of a fundamental right. The doctrine derives from decisions made in 1992, starting with T-406/92, which indicated that the right to health could be understood, in certain circumstances, as being essentially connected to the right to life. Later that year, Víctor Narváez Paredes filed a tutela (T-506/92) and claimed the confiscation of his car by the national police not only went beyond the appropriate function of the police, but that it also violated his right to property. The Court denied the tutela, citing doubts about who was the true owner of the car and noting that the authorities appeared to have acted appropriately. Even in denying this property rights claim, the Court nevertheless affirmed the case-by-case approach and the possibility of connecting fundamental rights with nonfundamental ones. The Court – or more accurately, the three academic justices, Ciro Angarita, Eduardo Cifuentes, and Alejandro Martínez, who wrote these decisions – recognized the ability to make tutela claims related to social or cultural rights in some instances.[19] Over time, the connection doctrine was even used to allow tutela claims to unenumerated individual rights, like the right to water (Sutorius and Rodríguez 2015; Páez and Vallejo Piedrahíta 2021).[20]

The second doctrine of justiciability, called *mínimo vital*, emerged in decision T-426/92 (written by Cifuentes), which notes that although the Constitution does not include a right to subsistence, such a right is implied or can be deduced from the existence of other, included rights.[21]

[19] "La posibilidad de considerar el derecho a la propiedad como derecho fundamental depende de las circunstancias específicas de su ejercicio. De aquí se concluye que tal carácter no puede ser definido en abstracto, sino en cada caso concreto. Sólo en el evento en que ocurra una violación del derecho a la propiedad que conlleve para su titular un desconocimiento evidente de los principios y valores constitucionales que consagran el derecho a la vida a la dignidad y a la igualdad, la propiedad adquiere naturaleza de derecho fundamental y, en consecuencia, procede la acción de tutela." See the full decision here: www.corteconstitucional.gov.co/relatoria/1992/T-506-92.htm.

[20] The only explicit reference to water in the constitution comes in Article 366, which reads: "The general welfare and improvement of the population quality of life are social purposes of the state. A basic objective of the state's activity will be to address unsatisfied public health, educational, environmental, and potable water needs."

[21] "Aunque la Constitución no consagra un derecho a la subsistencia éste puede deducirse de los derechos a la vida, a la salud, al trabajo y a la asistencia o a la seguridad social." See the full decision here: www.corteconstitucional.gov.co/relatoria/1992/T-426-92.htm.

Subsequent decisions, such as T-005/95 (again written by Cifuentes), which focused on the rights to health and social security, more fully articulated what was to become the vital minimum doctrine, noting that although health was not a fundamental right, access to medical services were necessary to a life with dignity in the particular case.[22] The standard implied by this doctrine requires that "the petitioner show both that the failure to receive treatment was severe enough to threaten his rights to life, dignity, or personal integrity, and that the petitioner lacked the resources to pay for this treatment or to attain it under some other plan" (Landau 2012: 421). In this conception, otherwise progressively realizable rights (those that are regarded as not immediately applicable) become justiciable, as they are necessary for a minimal standard of living. Ultimately, judges decided to recognize the vital minimum as a right in itself.

Throughout this period, certain Constitutional Court justices actively expanded rights protections, often through the purview of the tutela procedure,[23] viewing the constitutional parameters as artificial limitations on the legal tool that resulted not from societal preferences but political maneuvers and compromises. Cifuentes recalls:

> The challenge was to change the judicial culture ... to demonstrate that the Constitution was a performative constitution ... The Constitution had to be binding on all public powers and private powers, so that constitutional guarantees could effectively address general conditions of citizenship and equality ... That the constitution had to produce a change and a transformation and that this was not simply semantic. That was the idea that I think was shared by colleagues in the Court. The Constitutional Court wanted to ensure that the Constitution permeated the entire judicial arena. In other words, all the judges of the country, the civil judges, the labor and criminal judges, the Supreme Court, all apply the Constitution ... The second challenge of the Court was for rights to mean more power for the weakest ... and for that reason the extension

[22] "El derecho a la salud no es en principio un derecho fundamental de aplicación inmediata. Sin embargo, la Corte ha estimado que este puede ser protegido por medio de la acción de tutela en casos especiales en los cuales se presente conexidad palmaria con un derecho fundamental ... En estas circunstancias, la efectividad de su derecho al servicio médico se encuentra en conexidad evidente con su derecho al mínimo vital indispensable para la subsistencia en condiciones dignas." See the full decision here: www.corteconstitucional.gov.co/relatoria/1995/T-005-95.htm.

[23] Interestingly, many of these extensions were suggested in tutela decisions that actually rejected the original applicant's claims.

> of borders of economic, social and cultural and fundamental rights was guided by the Court directly.[24]

Judges were able to suggest and implement alternate understandings of the proper scope of the tutela procedure and the nature of rights, in part due to their independence and in part due to the continued (and expanding) filing of tutelas by aggrieved citizens. Decisions made by judges in the years immediately following the creation of the new constitution allowed citizens to file tutelas that made claims to a wide variety of social rights. In other words, these expansions did not apply singularly to any one right.[25]

Because all revision decisions are posted on the Constitutional Court's website, I was able to scrape a random sample of these revision decisions, and code and analyze them.[26] The Constitutional Court accepted 62 percent of all tutela claims in my sample (1992–2016) and 68 percent of social rights claims. The Transitional Court

[24] Elite interview 1 (July 26, 2016). "El reto era cambiar la cultura judicial ... El reto era demonstrar ... que la constitución tenía, la constitución era una constitución performativa ... Y la constitución tenía que ser vinculante para todos los poderes públicos y para los poderes privados, que las garantías constitucionales efectivamente buscaban general condiciones real de ciudadanía y de igualdad. Que la constitución había producido un cambio y una transformación y que este era no simplemente semántico. Esa fue digamos con la idea que yo creo que compartía los colegas de la Corte, la Corte Constitucional ... La Corte Constitucional quiere que busca que la Constitución permeé en toda la habita judicial. O sea que todos los jueces del país, los jueces civiles, los jueces laborales, penales, la Corte Suprema, todos aplican la Constitución ... El segundo desafío de la Corte de decía es el de que los derechos significaban más poder para los más débiles ... y por eso la atenuación, la extensión de fronteras de derechos económicos, sociales y culturales y fundamentales fue apro-metía de la Corte directamente."

[25] These early developments should not be taken to mean that all tutelas filed result in positive outcomes, however. Some claims are – rightly or wrongly – denied, and some problems are challenging to name or articulate. Further, a successful decision will not necessarily result in compliance or the delivery of a remedy. An in-depth study of tutela decisions across issue areas found a noncompliance rate of 28 percent, a rate that 71.5 percent of surveyed Colombians deemed unacceptably low (Carlin et al. 2022). Beyond questions of compliance, some claimants may be dissatisfied with the remedy offered by the judge. Among legal professionals there does not appear to be a consensus about whether or not Constitutional Court orders are, in fact, complied with (Juan Carlos Henao, a former Constitutional Court justice, elite interview 62, November 8, 2016; Hernán Olano, a former *oficial mayor* of the Constitutional Court, elite interview 30, September 20, 2016; Pablo Rueda, former auxiliary justice, elite interview 61, November 4, 2016).

[26] This analysis was only possible because of the help of Josh Meyer-Gutbrod.

accepted just over half of the social rights claims made, and each subsequent set of justices accepted a higher percentage of these claims. At the same time, the percentage of lower-court decisions that were overturned increased with each court (at a slightly greater rate than the overturned decisions on nonsocial rights claims), as the Constitutional Court worked to solidify lines of jurisprudence. In this way, a vision of the 1991 Constitution that centered the tutela and newly codified rights came to be legally embedded at the highest court in the country.

5.3 EXPLAINING DIFFERENCES IN JUDICIAL RECEPTIVITY

Legal mobilization provided the opportunity and groundwork for legal embedding, but mobilization alone does not explain the precise contours of the embedding process. We must also look to the development of judicial receptivity to particular kinds of claims to understand why we see variation in claim-making pathways. Notably, although the early Constitutional Court decisions could have applied to all social rights, different rights evolved along different trajectories. Specifically, health tutelas increased more dramatically through the 1990s and early 2000s than tutelas invoking all other social rights combined, though the overall trend lines for all social rights claim-making increase over time (see Figure 5.1).

Differences in social rights claim-making are most apparent when comparing health rights claims to housing rights claims. The official data on tutela claims nationwide compiled by the Defensoría del Pueblo did not initially include disaggregated information on claims to the right to housing, instead including housing in the "other socioeconomic rights" category. That the Defensoría del Pueblo did not separately tabulate housing rights claims until 2016 is evidence of their relative infrequency. In 2016, there were 4,891 housing claims; 3,080 in 2017; 3,536 in 2018; and 3,618 in 2019. Further, my random sample of tutela revision decisions scraped from the Constitutional Court's website indicates that between 1992 and 2016, only 3.4 percent of all reviewed tutelas claimed the right to housing, of which the Court accepted 60.5 percent. Most of these tutelas were accepted on the basis of a right other than housing (each tutela claim can involve multiple rights). In contrast, 25.1 percent claimed to the right to health, and the Court accepted 72.8 percent.

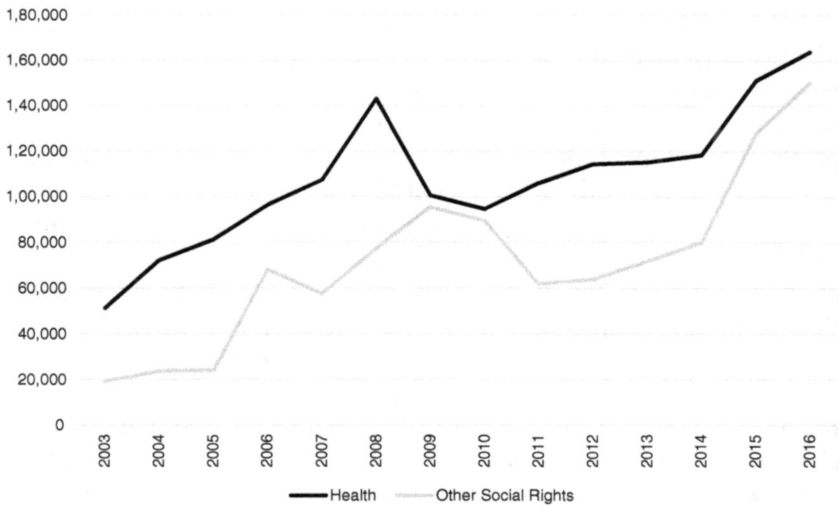

Figure 5.1 Social rights tutela claims.
Source: Author's elaboration using data from the Defensoría del Pueblo.

This disparity in claim-making can be explained, though only in part, by a rise in grievances related to the new healthcare system. Still, it is not immediately clear why other kinds of social rights claims – for instance, housing claims – did not follow a path similar to that of health claims. According to UN-Habitat (2013: 148–9), in 1990, 31.2 percent of urban-dwelling Colombians lived in "slum areas," a percentage that dropped to 14.3 percent by 2009. Thus, there existed a population that *could have made claims* on the basis of housing inadequacy and could have connected those claims about housing to dignity. Whether or not judges would accept these arguments is another story, but it is striking that these kinds of claims have been largely absent in the Colombian context.[27] So, despite the existence of potential grievances in both health and housing, we see substantially more mobilization with respect to the right to health.

Instead, I hold that judicial receptivity, as conditioned by exposure to problems within and outside of the legal system simultaneously, accounts for this difference. The persistence and/or increase of particular kinds of claims can inform judges about an issue, encouraging them

[27] There is evidence, however, that citizens *occasionally* filed tutela claims to this effect (Holland 2017).

to become (more) comfortable with the scope of the problem and to identify with claimants. Over time, this continued exposure to claims triggers a consideration or reconsideration of the correct legal response to the underlying issue, particularly when judges view the issue as comporting with contemporary sociolegal values: in the case analyzed here, when they interpret the issue as central to a dignified life.

Judicial decision-making on health rights followed the path described earlier, with judges first rejecting claims outright, before accepting claims on the basis of the *conexidad* doctrine or the *mínimo vital* doctrine. Eventually, the Constitutional Court declared the right to health to be fundamental in itself (and therefore directly claimable with the tutela). In this case (T-760/08), the Court decided twenty-two separate tutelas together and in the process mandated significant changes to the overarching healthcare policy structure.[28] In 2015, the legislature passed Law 1751, which solidified this understanding of health as a fundamental constitutional right.[29]

An analysis of housing rights claims demonstrates that the expansion of rights claims present in the realm of health was not inevitable. The first of these housing rights tutelas, T-423/92, dealt with "*invasores*," or squatters, who remained on rented property even after their lease had ended. Despite acknowledging the country's housing deficit, the three-judge panel rejected the claim, arguing that the right to housing had to be sought though legal means, that the right to housing was not a fundamental right (therefore falling outside the competence of the tutela), and that "the termination of a lease cannot be considered as a violation of the right to housing."[30] The Court also rejected the only other housing rights tutela it reviewed in 1992 (T-598/92), again pointing to the nonfundamental status of the right to housing.[31]

The most well-known set of legal claims related to the right to housing involved the system of home financing (Unidad de Poder Adquisitivo Constante, or UPAC). Interviewees, including those currently working at the Constitutional Court, consistently referred to the

[28] See full decision here: www.corteconstitucional.gov.co/relatoria/2008/t-760-08.htm.
[29] www.secretariasenado.gov.co/senado/basedoc/ley_1751_2015.html.
[30] See full decision here: www.corteconstitucional.gov.co/relatoria/1992/t-423-92.htm. There was a similarly decided constitutionality case (one not involving a tutela claim): C-157/97. See that decision here: www.corteconstitucional.gov.co/relatoria/1997/c-157-97.htm.
[31] See full decision here: www.corteconstitucional.gov.co/relatoria/1992/t-598-92.htm.

UPAC cases when asked about the right to housing and often failed to identify any other housing rights cases. Initially, citizens organized, marched, and brought tutela claims in the wake the UPAC crisis (Uprimny 2007). Nevertheless, as Pablo Rueda (2010: 46) notes, these tutelas were not decided in favor of the claimants, with the Constitutional Court finding "that an eventual breach of the right to housing was not enough to award protection through [the] *mínimo vital*" standard. In 1999, the Court decided an abstract review case related to UPAC (C-747/99). The Court declared the UPAC system unconstitutional and held that the central bank, not the market, should determine interest rates. Interestingly, two justices expressed hesitancy about issuing such a decision, arguing that:

> The reluctance or incompetence of the relevant organs of state – which should not be tolerated by the people, who can appeal at all times to the instruments of democratic participation – cannot be offered as an excuse for the Court to intervene in the determination or elimination of a public policy, outside of its original function of the review of constitutionality.[32]

While the other justices did not necessarily share this disinclination, their decisions in tutela claims suggest that they, too, saw the tutela as an inappropriate tool to raise claims related to UPAC specifically and housing more generally. Some commentators have suggested that the UPAC cases had a demobilizing impact on claim-making related to housing rights.[33] Further, not only did judges indicate that they would not respond favorably to tutela claims related to UPAC, but financial organizations did not promote the filing of these claims (in contrast to pharmaceutical and insurance companies in the realm of health).

The exposure mechanism helps to explain the differential expansion of rights protections. One clerk put it this way: "It's a bit like the

[32] Justices Cifuentes and Naranjo make this argument in their dissent (para. 14). "El desgano o impericia de los órganos competentes del Estado – que no pueden ser tolerados por el pueblo, que en todo momento podrá apelar a los instrumentos de participación y control que le entrega la democracia – no pueden ofrecerse como excusa suficiente para que la Corte intervenga de fondo en la determinación o eliminación de una política pública, por fuera de su función originaria de control de constitucionalidad." See full decision here: www.corteconstitucional.gov.co/relatoria/1999/c-747-99.htm.

[33] Interview with a former Constitutional Court clerk who practices and teaches law. Elite interview 61 (November 4, 2016).

citizens were knocking on the door to see what the judges were saying. We were very receptive and we opened the door completely … They knocked on the door with many cases of many issues and we as judges opened it [to health claims]." When pressed as to why the Court would have "opened the door" to health claims more readily than other social rights claims, she referred to the state of crisis of the healthcare system, to the "painfulness" of the situation, and the fact that "we suffer physical pain equally, we suffer the pain of seeing a sick relative equally, and we are also equally victims of the health system."[34] Another clerk summarized this situation, saying that the "tutela for social rights [emerged] out of pure necessity of the people, and [they] found that the Constitutional Court was receptive to the needs of the people."[35] As judges continued to be exposed to health claims, they became more comfortable with them and even identified with claimants, and they became more aware of the extent of the problems with the healthcare system and more convinced that these types of claims could or should be resolved by the Court.

Here again, we see the key role of legal mobilization in spurring embedding – and specifically in determining unevenness in embedding. Judges became convinced that some kinds of claims should be resolved by the Court not simply because of the continued filing of health claims (though my sample of tutelas shows that between 1992 and 2016 roughly 25 percent were health claims), but also because the issue of access to healthcare comported with judges' understanding of contemporary Colombian sociolegal values. In other words, judges viewed access to healthcare as central to a dignified life (as evidenced by their willingness to accept health rights tutela claims with the *mínimo vital* and *conexidad* standards). While my interviewees referred to objective factors, such as having sick relatives, the process of recognizing problems and identifying with claimants is contingent and subjective; these judges could just as easily have referenced not health-related issues but housing-related issues as what tied Colombians together,

[34] Elite interview 17 (August 26, 2016). "En la salud el problema es que la … el tema de la salud nos iguala a todos. Ricos y pobres sufrimos por igual los estragos de salud, sufrimos por igual el dolor físico, sufrimos por igual el dolor de ver a un familiar enfermo, y también somos víctimas igualitarias del sistema de salud porque hay momentos en que los costos son tan elevados que no importa si tú tienes dinero o no."

[35] Elite interview 2 (August 4, 2016). "La tutela en todos los derechos sociales es por pura necesidad de la gente y encontró a la corte constitucional que fue receptiva a las necesidades de las personas."

holding instead that "at a minimum, we all need a roof over our heads." They did not, however, share this interpretation of housing and relatively few housing rights claims came before the Court.[36] The shift from experimental to established claim-making featured the growth and acceptance of health rights claims, as potential claimants came to understand health through the lens of the law and judges came to understand health as an issue that should be handled by the courts. That process did not occur for housing rights claims during the same period, leading to one area of unevenness in the constitutional embedding process.

5.4 LEGAL EMBEDDING BEYOND THE CONSTITUTIONAL COURT

Legal embedding at the Constitutional Court level is significant – if we were to see legal embedding anywhere, we would expect to see it there – but everyday Colombians likely never meet Constitutional Court justices. Instead, they file their claims before the lower-court judges who are tasked with the initial tutela decision-making or – less frequently – seek help from lawyers and bureaucrats in government legal offices, like the Personería and Defensoría del Pueblo. I turn now to my interviews with lower-court judges in Medellín and Cali for an additional perspective on the extent to which legal embedding has occurred among lower-court judges outside the Colombian Constitutional Court. I track how judicial receptivity to social rights tutela claims has permeated through the judicial establishment, examining judges' views on the 1991 Constitution, their role, and the tutela, as well as their views on how constrained they are by the Constitutional Court and its jurisprudence. Importantly, these views do not necessarily reflect the modal understanding of lower-court judges, as my interviewees were not randomly selected. However, they offer insights into how some judges who are not part of the immediate Constitutional Court network think about and understand legal culture following the enactment of the country's new social constitution.

These judges uniformly noted that the 1991 Constitution, the rights it enshrined, and the tutela procedure change the nature of their work. Gabriel Roldán, a judge working in the criminal courts in Medellín, explained that "constitutions by themselves do not

[36] Again, only 3.4 percent of reviewed tutelas involved housing rights claims.

transform a society, but they are a starting point." He went on to note that, in this case:[37]

> The 1991 Constitution gave a very important role to the judge in the construction of a social and democratic state of law, precisely through the action of tutela as a constitutional protection mechanism. Judges, I believe that we began to have a greater relevance in society to directly affect the rights of citizens – that seems to me a change of paradigm and perspective compared to the figure of the judge [before].[38]

The judges who I interviewed seemed to appreciate this changed role. For example, when I asked Andrés López, who works in a jurisdiction outside of Cali, about the best part of his job, he pointed to the requirement that he also hear tutela cases, because with the tutela "we are on the other side. In the criminal area, we are [often] putting a poor indigenous person, a poor peasant with few resources [and] without education in jail, and on the other side is the tutela, where people's rights that are violated by health entities are vindicated."[39] Another judge, when I asked about the tutela, explained: "Thanks to our father, creator of the universe, the wise legislator was to bring us in 1991 the tutela, that has been very helpful for many people … In general terms, it has helped defenseless communities a lot."[40] Further, these judges made clear that they did not look down on or dismiss their new constitutional duties (even if they also lamented their workload and other job-related pressures). Cristian Cabezas, a judge working in the criminal courts in Cali,

[37] Elite interview 74 (March 22, 2017). "[L]as constituciones son una carta que por si solas no transforman una sociedad, pero son un punto de partida."

[38] Elite interview 74 (March 22, 2017). "La constitución de 1991 le dio un rol muy importante al juez bajo la construcción de un estado social y democrático de derecho precisamente a través de la acción de tutela como mecanismo de amparo constitucional. Los jueces creo que empezamos a tener una mayor relevancia en la sociedad para incidir de manera directa en los derechos de los ciudadanos, eso me parece un cambio de paradigma y de perspectiva frente a la figura del juez."

[39] Elite interview 83 (April 21, 2017). "[E]stamos en el otro lado. En la parte penal estamos metiendo a un pobre indígena, a un pobre campesino de escasos recursos sin educación a la cárcel, y en el otro está la tutela donde se reivindican los derechos de las personas que son vulnerados por las entidades de salud."

[40] Elite interview 85 (April 25, 2017). "Gracias a nuestro padre creador del universo el legislador sabio fue al traernos en el año 1991 la acción de tutela que ha sido de mucha ayuda para bastantes personas … en términos generales ha ayudado mucho a la comunidad indefensa."

compared his work on criminal matters to his work reviewing tutela claims, telling me that:

> Once the [criminal] hearings are over, around 5 o'clock … I have to go up to the office to look at tutela claims … There are ten-day limits in which to resolve tutelas. Many of them involve matters related to fundamental rights … and these matters cannot wait, in addition to all the criminal matters that cannot wait because they involve people deprived of liberty … We have to protect the rights of people deprived of liberty but also protect the rights of people who claim violations of their fundamental rights, for example, to life, health, human dignity.[41]

Here, Cabezas sets out his traditional judicial work – deciding criminal cases – as equally, not more, important than issuing tutela decisions. He notes that neither criminal matters nor fundamental rights matters can wait; both need to be handled quickly. These quotes provide evidence that the new constitution, with its emphasis on fundamental rights, has become embedded in the minds of lower-court judges.

Another judge went a step further, explaining that sometimes they do work beyond their official duties as judges in order to make real the vision of the 1991 Constitution. For example, they would contact those who have not complied with tutela decisions and say:

> "Hey, why don't you deliver that?" Especially in matters of healthcare. In healthcare I try, sometimes I even go to the healthcare provider here … [There] they say, "oops the judge has arrived," because they are really surprised, right? I ask how they have things and do not deliver them. Here in Colombia, we have a saying, "the face of the saint makes the miracle." The face of the saint makes the miracle. And then they say, "oh, the judge came," [and] sometimes they give [the claimant] the things or the medicines, or the supplies.[42]

[41] Elite interview 80 (April 18, 2017). "Una vez termino las audiencias, más o menos a las 5 … tengo que subir al despacho a mirar todo el aspecto de las tutelas … Las tutelas tenemos unos términos de diez días para resolverlas muchas de ellas tienen asuntos realmente dedicados que comprometen derechos fundamentales. Derechos fundamentales y esos asuntos no dan espera, además de todos los asuntos penales que tampoco dan espera porque tienen personas privadas de la libertad. Tenemos que proteger los derechos de las personas privadas de la libertad, pero también proteger los derechos de personas que reclaman violación de sus derechos fundamentales, por ejemplo: la vida, la salud, dignidad humana."

[42] Elite interview 90 (May 8, 2017). "¿Por qué ustedes no entregan eso? Sobre todo, en materia de tutela de la salud, en las tutelas de salud yo trato, a veces voy incluso yo misma a las EPS aquí. Yo aquí deseé ir allá porque a veces digo: 'Bueno … ' Ellos

They continued, noting that the legal code and expectations regarding judicial work do not require this kind of action. The underlying claim is that the role of judges has expanded beyond their traditional duties of deciding legal claims, as they "all have a social function to fulfill as well. So, we dispense justice, yes, but there are also things that one must do as a member of a society, right?"[43] Traditionally speaking, the judicial role did not involve a close connection with society; yet, a closer connection between citizen and judge was part of the aim of the 1991 constitutional changes.

These interviews also revealed that many lower-court judges kept abreast of Constitutional Court jurisprudence regarding the tutela. Carlos Rodríguez, who hears criminal cases in a town outside of Cali, explained the consequences of lower-court judges following the Constitutional Court's lead: "I believe the mindset about the tutela has changed in that the judges are not so legalistic."[44] He further noted that "little by little, the Constitutional Court has addressed many issues and has given many guidelines on that [the tutela]."[45] Another judge, who also works in a jurisdiction in a small town outside of Cali, explained to me that she needed to pay close attention to the Constitutional Court's tutela jurisprudence, because, for example, "the Constitutional Court has a precedent stating that, in exceptional cases, tutela claims for labor rights can be granted. These very exceptional cases are studied and the precedent is applied, but really there are few opportunities to grant them, even though however there are many tutelas requesting that [labor rights protections]."[46] Johnny Braulio Romero, a judge

cuando llaman y dicen: 'Uy llegó la juez' pues ellos ya se quedan como sorprendidos. Pero yo por lo menos yo digo: 'Pero oiga, ¿Cómo es posible que ustedes tengan las cosas y no las entreguen?' Entonces muchas veces como dicen, acá tenemos un dicho en Colombia que dice: 'La cara del milagro hace al santo.' La cara del santo hace el milagro es que es, al revés. La cara del santo hace el milagro. Y entonces ellos cuando dicen: 'Uy, vino la juez' a veces le entregan las cosas o los medicamentos, o los insumos."

43 Elite interview 90 (May 8, 2017). "Tenemos una función social que cumplir también. Entonces impartimos justicia sí, pero también hay cosas que uno debe hacer como miembro de una sociedad ¿No?"

44 Elite interview 87 (April 25, 2017). "Creo que ha cambiado la mentalidad de la tutela en cuanto a que los jueces no sean tan legalistas."

45 Elite interview 87 (April 25, 2017). "Poco a poco la Corte Constitucional ha abordado muchos temas y ha dado muchas pautas sobre eso."

46 Elite interview 85 (April 25, 2017). "La corte constitucional tiene un precedente señalando que excepcionalmente se conceden esas acciones de tutela para derechos laborales. [Esos] casos muy excepcionales que se estudian y se aplica el precedente, y

working in Medellín, offered an overarching perspective on the dramatic changes in judicial thinking around the tutela from the early 1990s to the present. Specifically, he noted:

> Since 1991, the tutela has been developing, and the changes it has undergone to date have been impressive. That is, things that in 1991, 1992 and 1993 would never have been granted to you at this time a judge grants them without thinking. For example, this tutela that I have here in my hand involves a man who works for a company and has not been paid. That a person requests through the tutela that the company pay him his wages … it would be unthinkable in 1993, 1994. And even in 1996, 1998, it was unthinkable, right? Today there is already a lot of jurisprudence of the Constitutional Court saying that, for example, despite the fact that it is an economic right, yes it can be protected by way of the tutela.[47]

Cristian Cabezas similarly described this expansion of the tutela procedure, saying, "we have, through a tool called *conexidad*, the possibility of treating the violation of a social right as a fundamental rights violation … That has been expanded [over time] and today we speak of 'fundamental social rights.'"[48] Clearly, these judges take Constitutional Court decision-making regarding the tutela seriously.

Overall, then, we see that the lower-court judges I interviewed have largely accepted the tutela, the use of the tutela to make social and economic rights claims, and the Constitutional Court's position at the apex of the judiciary. These judges did point out limitations and

pues realmente se presentan pocas oportunidades en que se conceden, no obstante, son muchas las tutelas pidiendo ese."

47 Elite interview 71 (March 10, 2017). "Desde 1991, la tutela se está desarrollando y los cambios que ha tenido desde que entró a la fecha han sido impresionantes. O sea, cosas que para 1991, 1992 y 1993 jamás te las habrían concedido en este momento ya uno las concede sin pensar. Por ejemplo, esta tutela que tengo aquí en la mano es un señor que trabaja para una empresa como obrero y no le han pagado. Que una persona solicite a través de la tutela que la empresa le pague los salarios que le ha dejado de pagar … sería impensable en 1993, 1994. E inclusive en 1996, 1998, era impensable ¿verdad? Hoy en día ya hay muchísima jurisprudencia de la Corte Constitucional diciendo que, por ejemplo, esto a pesar que es un derecho económico si se pueda amparar por vía de tutela."

48 Elite interview 80 (April 18, 2017). "Nosotros tenemos a través de una herramienta que se denomina la conexidad, la posibilidad de tratar un derecho fundamental a través de acción de tutela siempre que la violación de un derecho social acarre también la de un derecho fundamental, aunque se ha abierto más ese aspecto y hoy hablamos de derecho sociales fundamentales."

inefficiencies in the new system. Some leveled critiques at the tutela, though, notably, no one advocated for the elimination of the tutela or the reversion back to the previous constitutional order. Importantly, even if these judges are simply paying lip-service to the new Constitution and new constitutional order, that lip-service would still be evidence of legal embedding, demonstrating how even judges who otherwise do not share the ideological or normative vision of the Constitution still feel constrained by it. The evidence presented in this section suggests that legal embedding has occurred throughout the Colombian judiciary, not simply within the Constitutional Court.[49]

What about the wider legal sphere, beyond judges? The institutional design of the tutela allows citizens to file constitutional rights claims without needing to formally engage lawyers, but some claimants still turn to private lawyers or state agencies when drafting their tutelas. In 2019, 504,742 tutelas were filed by individuals (81.3 percent), 23,129 by legal representatives (3.7 percent), and a further 53,010 by unofficial agents (8.5 percent); 34,579 were filed by private lawyers (5.6 percent), and 4,782 by state agencies like the Defensoría del Pueblo and Personería (0.8 percent).

The extent to which these state agencies provide citizens with information and/or more formal help filing claims varies substantially. The Personería in Medellín, for example, created the first website through which Colombians could present tutela claims.[50] In 2017, the website allowed only health rights claims, though it has expanded since then to include all fundamental rights. The access tool is not available throughout the country: funding depends on mayoral priorities and resources. Antioquia, the department in which Medellín is located, had the highest number of tutelas filed through the Defensoría and the Personería: about twelve times as many as in Bogotá, though the total number of tutelas filed in both locales in 2019 was around 117,000. Thus, we see evidence of legal embedding in the Personería of Medellín especially. From this wider angle, legal embedding appears to vary significantly across time and space.

[49] Importantly, though, this does not mean that every judge in the country decides every case in a way that is consistent with this social vision of constitutional law. There may be isolated exceptions, but it does appear that legal embedding has permeated the judicial system.

[50] Elite interview 78 (March 29, 2017).

5.5 CONCLUSION

Legal embedding refers to the process by which the legal establishment comes to adopt a particular vision of constitutional law and act as if they are bound by it. In order to determine the contours of legal embedding, we must assess how the institutions, mechanisms, and actors created and empowered by the constitution impact the daily work of law. Further, judicial decision-making that is consistent with this constitutional vision provides additional evidence of legal embedding. Finally, an examination of the broader legal profession – including those actors who were not empowered by the new constitution – can reveal the depth of legal embedding.

Unlike the fate of earlier efforts to infuse Colombian law with a social focus, the 1991 Constitution became legally embedded in Colombia, impacting judicial behavior across different levels of the judiciary. Instead of undermining the new social constitutionalist features through subsequent judicial decision-making (what Manuel José Cepeda has called "sterilization by judicial interpretation"[51]), judges bolstered them. Starting with the justices of the Constitutional Court, judges accepted tutela claims in such a way that they expanded the tutela's purview and incentivized continued claim-making. Importantly, lower-court judges followed the Constitutional Court's lead. In this way, the 1991 Constitution became embedded legally – it became part of what is considered normal, ordinary, or everyday in the practice of judicial decision-making.

This process of embedding did not unfold evenly across issue areas, however. There is variation within legal embedding in terms of the kinds of rights claims to which judges are receptive. In this case, judges were most receptive to health rights claims (a new right recognized in the 1991 Constitution) compared to all other social rights claims. The way that judges were (or were not) exposed to problems within and outside of the legal system simultaneously helps to account for this variation. Judges were exposed to health-related problems consistently and their understanding of those problems conflicted with sociolegal values (i.e., their sense of what it means to have a dignified life). Judicial receptivity followed. This receptivity catalyzed additional claim-making through the tutela, creating a positive feedback loop and furthering both legal and social embedding. Because this process

[51] Elite interview 68 (February 23, 2017).

occurred with respect to the right to health, but not the right to housing, there is some unevenness in constitutional embedding.

Neither legal nor social embedding is inevitable or necessarily permanent. The next three chapters examine challenges to constitutional embedding in Colombia, as well as the extent to which the constitutional order endured. Chapter 6 turns to the limits of legal legibility, or what and whose problems are (and are not) addressed by constitutional rights provisions. Chapter 7 looks to efforts by political actors to limit social constitutionalism and unravel rights protections. Chapter 8 explores the labor of law, or the changes and additions to judges' daily work created by the new constitutional order.

CHAPTER SIX

CHALLENGES TO EMBEDDING

Legal Legibility

One might well ask: Why are we here, in a village of no particular significance, examining the struggle of a handful of history's losers? For there is little doubt on this last score ... There is little reason to believe that they can materially improve their prospects in the village and every reason to believe they will, in the short run at least, lose out, as have millions [...] before them.

The justification for such an enterprise must lie precisely in its banality.[1]

James Scott (1985: 27)

Not everyone benefits equally from the emergence and embedding of social constitutionalism. This chapter examines the promise of Colombian social constitutionalism and those it leaves behind. State efforts to expand access to citizenship goods, whether by the creation of new rights or the extension of existing policy, are often partial and uneven: what happens to those who do not qualify for these goods but believe they should? In other words, what happens to those who are disadvantaged both politically and economically, but are not understood as deserving in legal terms? These challenges – what I call challenges to legal legibility – can undermine the process of constitutional

[1] Scott justifies his focus on the banal experiences of history's losers because, in his view, "these circumstances are the *normal* context in which class conflict has historically occurred." Often this group of people is overlooked unless or until some surprising political outcome occurs (e.g., collective defiance or rebellion). I do not deny that possibility – indeed, this kind of marginalization has been discussed as a factor that led some Colombians to join armed guerrilla movements – but I want to claim that in the case of constitutional rights, these perceptions and experiences of marginality, exclusion, and/or disaffection matter, even if no "surprising" political outcome follows.

embedding. As shown in previous chapters, citizens have been able to attempt to attain access to healthcare services and compel official responses to information requests by filing tutela claims. They have also been able to file tutela claims to seek benefits offered to those who can document that they were victims of the armed conflict.[2] Yet, many marginalized citizens are unable to document victim status and instead are viewed as simply "poor," rather than direct victims, but they nonetheless feel abandoned by the state.

It is precisely "history's losers" (to use Scott's term) who the universalizing promise of the constitutional recognition of social citizenship seeks to serve. In the social constitutionalist model, all citizens, regardless of employment status or connections to elites, should be able to gain access to the goods and services necessary to fully participate in political and social life as a matter of constitutional rights. Yet, often the expansion of legal protections, especially as they relate to social service or welfare provision, has both formally and informally involved the construction of notions of the deserving versus the undeserving poor.[3] The idea is that only those who are particularly deserving – whether because of something they are understood to have done (or not done) or because of something they are understood to be (or not be) – should have access to those protections. Rights, then, become contingent not only on the ability of citizens to make claims to them but also on whether or not claim-makers are understood to be deserving.

When folks understand themselves to be deserving, but formal institutions do not,[4] that tension can present a challenge for constitutional embedding. In the context of social constitutionalism, there is a promise of significant change, but what is actually delivered might instead be the reification of difference. Further complicating matters is the fact

[2] The Victims and Land Restitution Law 1448 (2011) set out to "establish a group of judicial, administrative, social and economic measures, individual and collective, to benefit the victims of the violations referred to in Article 3 of this Law, within a framework of transitional justice, that will allow the enjoyment of their rights to truth, justice and reparation with guarantee of non-repetition, for them to be recognized as victims and to be dignified through the realization of their constitutional rights."

[3] Merry (2003) similarly identifies the distinct between "good" and "bad" victims of domestic violence. She details how the construction of different kinds of "victims" shapes if and how battered women turn to the law.

[4] This disjuncture maps onto what Merry (1990) calls a "process of cultural domination." As McCann (1994: 284) notes, in describing Merry's work, "legal discourses tend to privilege some meanings but to silence, undermine, or transmute others."

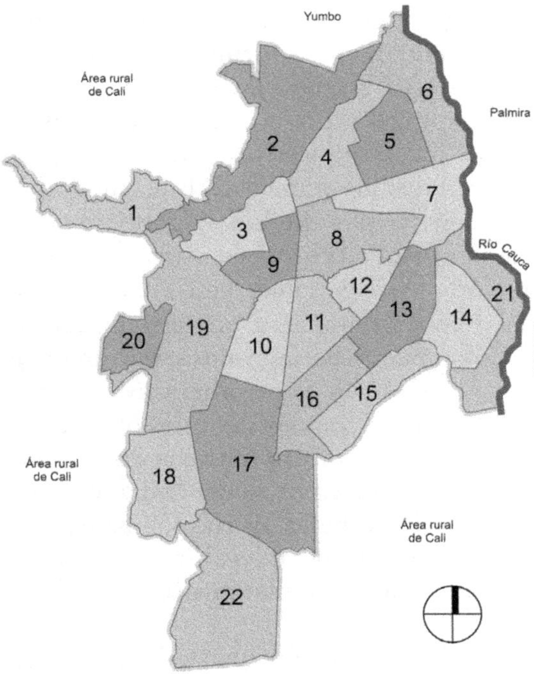

Figure 6.1 *Comunas* in Cali, Colombia.
Source: Wikimedia commons, SajoR.

that this kind of reification can occur on some issues, while substantive change is made on other issues – a process than can trigger the growth of an expectations gap and a sense of comparative grievance (Kruks-Wisner 2021) or informed disenchantment (Gallagher 2006, 2017). The underlying frustration remains the same across mechanisms: the process is not working for me. With respect to comparative grievance, this frustration is directed at a perceived inequality: the process is not working for me, but it is working for other people. With informed disenchantment, on the other hand, the frustration is directed at the disconnect between how the process is promised to work and how it actually does (or does not) work.

This chapter turns to the meaning of the 1991 Constitution and the tutela procedure in a marginalized neighborhood on the outskirts of Cali, Colombia called Comuna 14. Comuna 14 is located in the district of Agua Blanca, which is comprised of Comunas 13, 14, 15, and 21 (see Figure 6.1). Agua Blanca is home to about 700,000 people. The district is infamous for its poverty and high levels of violence. In April and May of 2017, I conducted twenty-four unstructured individual and group interviews with a total of forty-three people in Agua Blanca.

My interviews provide an empirical window into the relationship between law, rights, and social incorporation, and the lived experience of unrealized promises and disillusionment. While this empirical window is particular in many ways – the highly politicized and polarizing 2016 peace agreement had recently been signed, rejected in a contentious popular vote,[5] renegotiated, and enacted;[6] the decades-long internal armed conflict was still ongoing in certain parts of the country; the Colombian legal apparatus was uniquely accessible given the tutela procedure – in many other ways it is not. Marginality and dislocation are all too common features of everyday life for people around the world, specifically for citizens who are not treated as such (and for those are who are not recognized as citizens, even on paper). This chapter seeks to build on the robust body of scholarship that examines the limits of liberal legalism in confronting the structural realities of unequal class relations (e.g., McCann and Lovell 2020).[7]

With respect to the 1991 Constitution and the tutela, there are overlapping sets of concerns. Who does the Constitution actually benefit? What kinds of problems are tractable with the tutela, and what kinds of problems are ill-suited to it? Building from that, are certain kinds of people more likely to have problems that are tractable with the tutela and therefore the new Constitution?

I engage my interviews and observations in Agua Blanca to investigate the politics and lived experience of the relative "have-nots" (Galanter 1974), the marginalized, those whose problems fall outside legal recognition, and the remedies offered by the 1991 Constitution. Paradoxically, the addition of new legal recognitions and protections for citizens may generate a sense of disaffection and leave some with the perception that they are even more vulnerable, as expectations gaps and relative losses grow – which in turn can cut against constitutional

[5] The results showed 50.2 percent against the agreement and 49.8 percent in favor.

[6] After the renegotiation, both houses of Congress approved the agreement, and it was not put to another popular vote. The Constitutional Court approved this "fast-track" plan consisting of an expedited vote in Congress and no additional plebiscite.

[7] McCann and Lovell (2020) present a clear discussion of these limits as they play out in the case of labor activism in the twentieth-century United States. See also Nonet and Selznick (2001), among others.

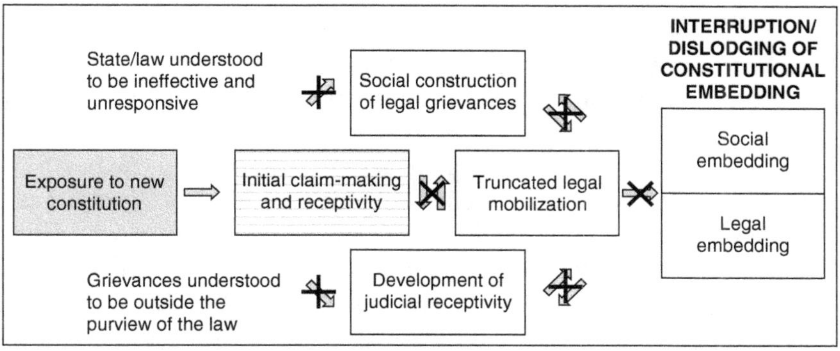

Figure 6.2 The interruption of constitutional embedding by legal illegibility.

embedding. Here, the process of constitutional embedding can be truncated, in terms of both its legal and social components, at least for certain communities (as shown in Figure 6.2). After exposure to the new constitution, if people understand the state and the legal system to be ineffective or unresponsive to their specific needs, and if those needs remain outside the realm of the law according to the legal establishment, the feedback loops that push constitutional embedding will not emerge.

In the case of residents of Agua Blanca, however, it is not clear that such an expectations gap ever emerged. If someone never believed in the promises of the state or the new constitution (or never seriously considered those promises as things that could impact their life), then partial rights protections or even the complete absence of rights protections will not trigger pushback. While folks in Agua Blanca were deeply knowledgeable about the tutela and how one can use it to gain access to some healthcare, that knowledge did not readily translate into the language of rights or increased expectations regarding rights fulfillment. In Agua Blanca, the consequences of social constitutionalism seem to be limited to the bureaucratization of rights; to the turning of grand promises into paperwork.[8] The constitution may not be embedded in this particular community, but the risk to overall embedding in Colombia is limited. Put simply, the very marginality that defines the lives of residents of Agua Blanca also works to confine the limits of constitutional embedding to the margins.

[8] Here, the result is piles of parchment, not just parchment promises.

6.1 INTERVIEWS IN AGUA BLANCA

Before moving to my investigation of legal legibility and constitutional embedding, a few words on the interview process and the interviewees are in order. A local interlocutor, who I will call Daniela,[9] connected me with each interviewee and was an active participant in the majority of these interviews. In fact, much of the time we simply walked around the neighborhood and stopped in, chatting with whomever was home, and moving to an official interview if folks were interested and felt comfortable. The interviewees, thus, were part of Daniela's social network and are not necessarily representative of the district as a whole. Further, the concerns of those in Agua Blanca are not necessarily representative or even indicative of everyone who feels left out of the new constitutional order. These interviews, however, present a unique opportunity to learn something about how one particular group of marginalized folks think about the 1991 Constitution and the problems in their lives. To return to Scott's justification at the outset of this chapter, my hope is that the unfortunate banality of the situation that folks in Agua Blanca find themselves in will provide "portable insights" into the promises and limitations of constitutional embedding.[10]

All twenty-four interviews took place in or right outside respondents' homes and more often than not took the form of informal conversations about justice in Agua Blanca or in Colombia more broadly. Frequently, family members, friends, or neighbors of the primary person we were speaking with wandered into the room in which we were conducting the interview. At times, some of them would decide to join in. Most of the people we spoke with noted that they have inconsistent ties to the formal labor market, tending to work informally or on short-term contracts. They also told us stories about interactions with potential employers that faltered as these employers became reluctant or unwilling to hire them after finding out that they live in Agua Blanca.[11] Violence

[9] I first met Daniela during one of the Caravan for Peace, Life and Justice events in Cali.

[10] Simmons (2016: 31) explains the value of seeking "portable insights" in her discussion of contextualized comparisons: "We choose cases where we see similar dynamics or processes at work, allowing ourselves the flexibility to identify complex causal processes as they unfold. From this in-depth knowledge, we can develop portable insights. These insights are not contingent on problematic assumptions about what the theoretically relevant variation that needs to be controlled is or whether the same empirical phenomena work in the same ways across contexts."

[11] Agua Blanca interview 21.

was ubiquitous. One resident lamented that "here, one buys a gun just like they're buying a pen. And the police know."[12] Further, most of their interactions with the state involved interactions with the police, interactions which often left them and/or their children bruised or even worse off. Another described the police as treating young people in Agua Blanca inhumanely, saying: "They take them and beat them and hit them without any justification, without any reason. They mistreat them, they kick them, they hit them in the face."[13] Some interviewees rolled up their sleeves, pulled up their shirts, or scrolled through photos on their phones to reveal bumps, bruises, and scars that they attributed to violent treatment at the hands of the police. In short, these folks understand themselves to be largely excluded from the benefits of both political and economic life, despite the universalizing promises of rights protections under the new constitution.

The interviews primarily focused on folks' experiences with the formal legal system and particularly the tutela procedure. Though I had not originally intended to discuss the 2016 peace process or the internal armed conflict it was meant to resolve, frustration with the underlying assumptions of this process repeatedly came up. This frustration centered on the ideas that the *guerrilleros* were being treated differently (i.e., better) than people in the neighborhood and that only certain people were given access to state resources (those who could document "victim" status and those who had been active participants in the conflict), though everyone was affected by the conflict. In what follows, I share findings from these interviews, first in relation to rights, the tutela, and the 1991 Constitution, and then in relation to poverty and the armed conflict.

6.2 CONSTITUTIONAL LAW IN AGUA BLANCA

As documented in previous chapters, with the introduction of the 1991 Constitution, its expansive set of rights recognitions, and the tutela procedure, Colombians were able to make claims about potential rights violations relatively easily. However, this ability on paper doesn't mean

[12] Agua Blanca interview 6. "Aquí compra un arma como compra un lapicero. Y la policía saben."

[13] Agua Blanca interview 1. "El trato que les dan a los jóvenes de aquí en el distrito de Agua Blanca, es inhumano porque los cogen y los golpean y los pegan sin ninguna justificación sin ningún motivo. Los están maltratando, les pegan patadas, les pegan en la cara."

that folks viewed the problems in their lives as legal in nature or thought that they could advance their own claims through the courts. Problems are not innately "legal," and problems that could be resolved through the legal system are not always viewed as such.[14] William Felstiner, Richard Abel, and Austin Sarat (1980) and Richard Miller and Austin Sarat (1980) lay out this situation in the form of the "dispute pyramid," with "unperceived injurious experiences" at the base and formal legal disputes at the peak. As documented in Chapters 4 and 5, the process of legal recognition – or of moving from an unperceived injurious experience to a legal claim that might be accepted – is interactive and iterative, involving the social construction of legal grievances, or how problems come to be understood as legal grievances, and the development of judicial receptivity, or how judges come to understand problems as properly resolved in the formal legal sphere. While repeated legal claim-making has broadly led to the right to health becoming legally legible to everyday citizens and judges alike in Colombia, that legibility falters when we look to Agua Blanca and Comuna 14, where poverty, discrimination, and bureaucratic rules complicate access to healthcare services.

The accessibility and perceived necessity of the use of the tutela are core features that facilitated the social embedding of the 1991 Constitution, particularly as the tutela related to health. The connection between the tutela and access to healthcare are just as strong in Agua Blanca as elsewhere in the country. Almost everyone spoke of the tutela only in reference to health claims. As is the case throughout Colombia, perceptions of the tutela are often imbued with a sense of ambivalence: filing a claim may or may not work; it has helped some people, but not everyone; you can't count on it. As Verónica, a nurse, explained:

> My opinion on the tutela? It has benefited many people for treatments and surgeries, yes. In other words, the tutela has helped a lot for high-cost treatments or high-cost medications. Many people have benefited, right? But there are other people who haven't. People who haven't have to go to the media, to the radio, to television to get their problem resolved.[15]

[14] See also Tait (2022) on this point.

[15] Agua Blanca interview 18. "Mi opinión sobre la tutela, ha favorecido mucha gente, ¿sí? Para los tratamientos y las cirugías. Sí. Ósea la acción de tutela ha servido mucho para que es tratamientos de alto costo o medicamentos de alto costo. ¿Muchas personas han favorecido, cierto? Pero, hay otras personas que no. Personas que no, que tienen que ir a los medios de comunicación, al radio, a la televisión para poder que lo atienden."

On the topic of healthcare specifically, she noted:

> In Colombia, healthcare is very poor and is getting worse … Medications are bad, treatments are bad. You have to file tutela claims, you have to be suing, you have to be harassing them to give you a good medicine. [Without the tutela] all they give you is acetaminophen, ibuprofen, naproxen, blood pressure pills, and nothing more. That is what matters to them [the tutela claim]. The rest [of patients], they die.[16]

Teresa, who I referenced at the start of this book and who lived down the road, shared a story with me that echoed Verónica's. She told me about a time when she had trouble breathing. She did not have formal employment and could not afford private medical treatment. Facing this barrier in access to healthcare, she filed a tutela claim. And she won. However, the decision required the subsidized health insurance regime to provide her with creams and diapers. The remedy was wholly detached from the problem: what good would diapers and creams do for a breathing problem?[17] Not everyone fared even this well. Mari shared that she had been encouraged to file a tutela claim by the clinic where her mother was seeking treatment. She explained:

> I filed a tutela claim, because my mother had spent a lot of time in a clinic. The clinic was bankrupt and didn't take care of my mother. She died fifteen days later … My mom died because of negligence … I filed the tutela, but the clinic never did anything.[18]

These experiences, however, did not dissuade Mari or Teresa from asserting that they would use the tutela again.[19]

The folks I spoke with viewed this a compound issue, inextricably linked with poverty. Not only has the tutela become the effective entry

[16] Agua Blanca interview 18. "En Colombia la salud muy mala en salud ahora es lo que más mal está. El estado no hace nada por que las clínicas salgan de los déficits fiscales que tienen. Los medicamentos son malos, los tratamientos son malos, hay que poner tutelas, hay que estar demandando, hay que estar acosando para que le den un medicamento bueno, todo lo que hacen es acetaminofén, ibuprofeno, naproxeno las pastillas de la presión y no más. Eso es lo más que les importa a ellos, de resto, que se muera todo el mundo."

[17] Agua Blanca interview 6.

[18] Agua Blanca interview 13. "Yo tutelé lo de mi mamá que estaba mucho tiempo en la clínica, y la tutelé porque la clínica estaba en quiebra y no le corrieron mucho a mi mamá y mi mamá falleció en 15 días; y yo la tutelé y todo; y pues la verdad ellos mandaban las demandas, pero nunca hubo así que corrieras no. Y mi mamá murió por negligencia de la clínica."

[19] For more on this ambivalence, see Taylor (2018).

point for healthcare services, and not only do healthcare service providers encourage the filing of tutela claims before potentially offering services (things that in themselves draw out the process of gaining access to health). What's more, those with less must use the subsidized healthcare system (because they do not have the ability to pay for private medical services), and the subsidized healthcare system is staffed by less qualified and less invested people. This last statement is not one that I verified, but its accuracy is less important than the fact that folks shared it with me; that folks believed it.

Laura similarly pointed to the connection between poverty and health when sharing the difficulties her daughter faced in even getting an appointment scheduled:

> The public healthcare providers here don't attend to people. They don't give them medicine. It's a problem for them to give one an appointment. Just look at the case of my daughter. It took a year and a half to get her a rheumatology appointment and she needs it. She suffers from rheumatoid arthritis. Look, a year and a half to make an appointment?[20]

Her neighbor, Leonor, saw things the same way. When I asked how she felt broadly about the healthcare system, she explained that "it has improved a little bit, but it is still a 50 out of 100 – and that is for the upper class. Poor folks die sitting in a chair waiting for the doctor to see them."[21] Part of this perspective comes from an experience she had just days before we spoke: "I was at the clinic on Thursday. It was an emergency. My husband had pain for over a month, and we went to the doctor. [They just said,] 'Take this Amoxicillin.'" He wasn't getting better, so they returned to the clinic, where they were told he would be an "urgent priority." However, he wasn't. In Leonor's words:

> We went back on Friday and they operated on him yesterday [Saturday] at dawn. When we were in the surgery room, the surgeon told me, "I went down more than four times to look for your husband. I've been here since five in the morning and they said he wasn't here." But he

[20] Agua Blanca interview 5. "[T]odas esas EPS de aquí no atienden a la gente, no les dan los medicamentos, eso es un problema para que le den una cita a uno. Mire no más, mi hija, año y medio para que le dieran una cita de reumatología y ella la necesita, porque ella sufre, ósea, de, es artritis reumatoide. ¿Y mire que año y medio para que le hagan una cita?"

[21] Agua Blanca interview 9. "Entonces la atención ha mejorado un poquito ¿no? Pero le falta, del cien, están en el cincuenta. Y eso, que, en estratos altos, en los bajos usted se muere esperando ahí en una silla a que un médico lo quiera revisar."

> had been sitting in a chair for two nights. Why? Because nurses don't focus on the priority [patients], but rather on other things. Doctors and everyone have become indolent.[22]

This kind of experience was not unique to Laura's daughter or Leonor and her husband.

Another neighbor, Claudia, had also recently been faced with the limitations on the healthcare services available to residents of Agua Blanca. She told me:

> Look yesterday night, [I went to one of the public hospitals]. My niece fell from a second-floor window, through the glass. She landed on some rocks, so they took her to the medical clinic and do you know what they said? That they couldn't take care of her because they didn't take care of minors, [not even] a girl who was wounded and her head broken open. They did nothing for her. They sent her to another hospital, another clinic and they did not treat her [there either], because she did not have money to pay the clinic. Her health insurance card did not work there.
>
> So, they had to take her to Carlos Holmes [a medical center].[23] In Carlos Holmes, they had her there and they didn't want to attend to her. A police officer she knew from childhood had to call for the girl to be attended to, because the girl's body was all wounded and they hadn't treated her yet. She was dripping blood, and she was unconscious for more than half an hour, and they didn't treat her. That's when they came to treat her and then there was no ambulance to take her, they didn't know if they could take her to the hospital. [The health insurance company] had not given authorization.
>
> When a girl falls from a second floor, it is something serious![24]

[22] Agua Blanca interview 9. "Estuve jueves en la clínica era por urgencia. Mi esposo tuvo un dolor más de un mes y fuimos al médico. En la semana sacamos cita, no eso es una pequeña infección. Tómate esta Amoxicilina … Fuimos el viernes y lo operaron ayer a la madrugada y era prioritaria y cuando ya estuvimos en sala de cirugía me dice el cirujano yo baje más de cuatro ocasiones a buscar a tu esposo, yo estoy desde las cinco de la mañana acá y dijeron que no estaba. y él en una silla sentado dos noches atrás. ¿Por qué? Porque las enfermeras no se concentran como en lo prioritario, sino que están en otras cosas. Se han vuelto indolentes los doctores y todas las personas."

[23] Another interviewee told me that there was a saying about Carlos Holmes in the neighborhood: "It is 'Carlos Holmes Trujillo Hospital,' and they call it the 'Dead Carlos Hospital.' If someone goes there for any little thing [they die]." Agua Blanca interview 21. "Hay un hospital que le dicen es el 'Carlos muerto,' se llama 'Hospital Carlos Holmes Trujillo' y le dicen el 'Hospital Carlos muerto,' que él llega allá por cualquier cosita sale."

[24] Agua Blanca interview 2. "Mira ayer anoche, [ayer fui a uno de los hospitales departamentales] la sobrina mía se vino de un segundo piso con el vidrio y abajo la recibió

Forgetting that the situation had not been resolved, I asked, "and what happened in the end, is she okay?" Claudia responded, "already this morning, they sent her to the public hospital, to do an exam. We are waiting to see the result of the exam."[25] She quickly transitioned back to her frustrations with the healthcare system:

> Of course, they must treat you whether you have money or not, or whatever insurance card you have. It's an emergency! What if she's a baby? What then? Not here. They leave you to die … [and] it's worse in these neighborhoods [the Comunas of Agua Blanca]. One must run from side to side [of the district]. For example, the insurance card we have is good for Carlos Holmes, but we are closer to López [a different medical center]. If we have an emergency and go to López, which is closer, because if I wait for Carlos Holmes, the patient might die, but [at López] they tell you, "No, no, I can't attend to him because we don't take the insurance card." What is that? This world is turned upside down.[26]

This difficulty in gaining access is not something that the tutela procedure can readily remedy. Claudia's niece could not file a legal claim and

unas piedras, entonces ella la trajo, la llevaron para la clínica médica y ¿Sabes lo que le dijeron? Que no la podían atender porque no atendían menor de edad, una niña que va herida y la cabeza rota, con heridas. No le hicieron nada, de ahí la remitieron para otro hospital para otra clínica y no la atendieron porque no tenía para pagarle el valor de la clínica, el carnet no le servía para ella entonces la tuvieron que llevar para el Carlos Holmes, en el Carlos Holmes la, la, la revisaron, no en el Carlos Holmes la tenían ahí y no la querían atender, tuvo que ir un policía que tuvo que llamar para que atendieran a la niña, porque la niña con el cuerpo todo herido y no la atendían todavía y chorreando sangre y viendo que la niña duró más de media hora inconsciente y no la atendían, ahí fue que la vinieron a atender y después que no había ambulancia para dirigirla, que no sabían para que hospital la pudieran llevar, en Emssanar no habían dado autorización. // Cuando una caída de un segundo piso de una niña es algo grave."

25 Agua Blanca interview 2. "Ya, esta mañana la remitieron para el departamental, para hacerle un examen. Empezamos estamos esperando a ver el resultado de un examen, entonces para mí eso, si un niño va herido, me parece a mí que, que en esta vida lo primordial son los niños, entonces así uno tenga cualquier carnet, en el hospital que tu vaya, deben de atender."

26 Agua Blanca interview 2. "Claro, deben de atenderlo así usted tenga plata o no tenga plata o tenga el carnet que tenga. Pero es una urgencia ¿y si es un bebé?, ¿Qué? No, aquí lo dejan a morir … y peor que es en estos barrios, uno corre de lado a lado por ejemplo el carnet a nosotros nos sirve para, para el Carlos Holmes, y a nosotros nos queda más cerca el de López, tenemos una emergencia el López que está más cerca, porque si me espero al Carlos Holmes se me muere el paciente, entonces no corres para acá pero que le digan a uno, no, no, yo lo puedo atender porque el carnet no le sirve a quien sea bueno muchachos ¿eso qué es? Esto, este mundo está patas para arriba."

wait ten days for a decision. She needed immediate medical attention. Further, filing a claim does not mean that one will receive a positive or useful response. As Daniela told me: "Yes, we file tutela claims, but they don't care. They put our demands aside, because we are poor people with little means … They dismiss the demands."[27] The value of the tutela – however limited it might be – appears to be limited to the realm of health for folks in Agua Blanca, and the economic conditions of their lives overshadow that value.

After hearing these specific stories of loss and deprivation and the inadequacy of the tutela to address the harms in their lives, I asked if the 1991 Constitution had changed anything in their lives. The answer was a resounding no; that constitutional law felt far away, outside of everyday life. Paula, a woman who survived cancer and whose husband had to threaten to use the tutela to ensure that the insurance company cover the requisite care, told me: "No, I don't pay attention to such things."[28] Laura, who, in addition to trying to help her daughter navigate the healthcare system and attain care for her rheumatoid arthritis, also ran a community organization and had faced multiple threats to her life, explained: "To me it seems like there is a great distance between the Constitution and life. It's one thing that the Constitution says and another thing that what they do … And rights always go. Rights are violated every day, violated every day."[29] For the family of Kike, a young man who had recently been beaten to death, the question did not seem to make sense at all. Daniela stepped in and reiterated my question: "What has the Constitution changed?" Again, the question was met with silence. Eventually, Kike's mother asked: "What's that?" I tried to explain: "The new constitution was a huge change in law, but … It is one of the most progressive in the world, but [what about] in everyday life?"[30] After another pause Daniela answered, "[yet,] we're dying more every day."[31] The others in the room murmured in agreement.

[27] Agua Blanca interview 1. "Sí, pero a ellos no les importa ellos hacen esa demanda a un lado, pero como nosotros somos personas debajo recurso y pobres nos ponen cuidado … se desechan la demanda."

[28] Agua Blanca interview 14. "Yo nunca me he interesado por esas cosas."

[29] Agua Blanca interview 5. "Para mí me parece como hay una gran distancia dentro de la Constitución y la vida. Una cosa es lo que dice la Constitución y otra cosa es lo que hacen … y siempre uno se va que los derechos, los derechos, los derechos y los derechos todos los días los violan, todos los días los violan."

[30] Agua Blanca interview 1. "¿Es una constitución nueva fue un gran cambio en la ley, pero … ¿Es como la más progresista en el mundo, pero en la vida … ?"

[31] Agua Blanca interview 1. "Nos estamos muriendo cada día más."

Thus, the everyday problems faced by folks in Agua Blanca do not appear to be ones that can be addressed by the 1991 Constitution, at least not in the view of residents of the district. The issue here is not simply the absence of rights consciousness or a lack of information. Residents of Agua Blanca have a great deal of knowledge on how one uses the tutela, and they have strongly held and often well-informed views on Colombian politics, especially related to the conflict, as Section 6.3 describes. Here, we see the emergence of "informed disenchantment" that results not from experiencing the legal claim-making process and losing faith in it, but instead from having a good deal of knowledge about that process but feeling excluded.

6.3 POVERTY AND THE CONFLICT

But what can these everyday problems be attributed to, and how might they be resolved? Should they be legally legible? According to folks living in Agua Blanca, the disconnect between poverty and formally recognized experiences of suffering due to the armed conflict account for these problems – problems that have become both intractable and part and parcel of the government's approach to people like them. They see the new constitutional infrastructure as not offering them much of anything.

Before moving further, a note on the armed conflict and the legal recognition of victimhood in Colombia is needed. Article 3 of the Victims and Land Restitution Law (or Law 1448) of 2011 defines victims as "those persons who individually or collectively have suffered damage from events occurring from January 1, 1985, as a result of violations of international humanitarian law or serious and flagrant violations of international standards of human rights that occurred because of the armed conflict." Folks who wish to be identified as "victims" must initiate the process of recognition by contacting a Victims' Unit office in person, by mail, or over the phone.[32] They must present personal identification, two witness statements, and a description of the victimization and when it occurred. A representative of the Victims' Unit then attempts to verify the information in the application with the Red Nacional de Información (National Information Network).[33] Each

[32] Formally, victims enter what is called the Registro Único de Víctimas.

[33] "Red Nacional de Información – RNI: Unidad Para Las Víctimas," www.unidadvictimas.gov.co/es/direccion-de-registro-y-gestion-de-la-informacion/red-nacional-de-informacion-rni/37825.

application should receive a response indicating whether or not they qualify within 120 days.[34]

From the perspective of everyday Colombians, there are tensions within the program as to who qualifies as a victim and what qualified as victimization. So-called "ordinary crimes" do not apply, though it can be challenging to differentiate ordinary crimes from conflict-related crimes given the diffuse nature of the conflict. Further, not all victims – even those recognized under the law – are treated the same. As Paula Martínez Cortés (2013: 13–14) explains:

- The victims of forced displacement and human rights abuses committed before 1985 may only benefit from symbolic reparations, and not from land restitution or economic compensation.
- The victims of human rights abuses committed between 1985 and 1991 have the right to receive economic compensation but not land restitution.
- Victims whose lands were unlawfully taken or occupied through human rights abuses after 1991, but before the expiration of the law, have the right to land restitution …
- Illegal armed actors who have suffered human rights violations or infringements of international humanitarian law cannot be acknowledged as victims …
- In cases of illegal killings committed by the state security forces, which usually claim that the victims belonged to an illegal armed group, relatives are only recognized as victims if a criminal investigation confirms that the deceased person was not part of one of those organizations. Given the difficulties in clarifying such membership, it may be impossible for relatives to obtain compensation.

Elsa Voytas and Benjamin Chrisman (forthcoming) show that in areas where violence was carried out more frequently by state-affiliated actors victim registration is lower than in areas associated with violence by nonstate actors. This may be because those negatively impacted by the state are less likely to turn to the state for redress or it could signal intentional or unintentional exclusion by the Victims' Unit. Frequently, folks – whether they are recognized as victims or not – report disillusionment and negative evaluations of the registration process (Pham et al. 2016; Cronin-Furman and Krystalli 2021).

[34] For more on these documents and the documentation process, see Cronin-Furman and Krystalli (2021).

Victim status is not legible or tractable outside of this particular social-political-historical moment. While there are precise laws defining who does and does not count as a victim in Colombia, the category of victim is not like the category of refugee. One can be a refugee for a variety of general reasons in different times and different places. Not so for officially designated "victims." Further, the remedy offered is broad, moving beyond truth and accountability to also address the conditions of daily life and the ability to live well or make choices about how to live: the goal is the realization of constitutional rights.[35] There are many reasons that one might find oneself in this position of constraint, poverty, and desperation, yet victim status is treated differently. While Law 1448 sets out a clear dividing line between who is and is not a victim, social understandings of victimhood do not necessarily align with the formal legal definition, especially considering the diffuse nature of the conflict and people's perceptions about what actually happened, who was at fault, and who suffered harm. Further, do those who find themselves in suboptimal life circumstances for other (structural) reasons *not* deserve protection? And what about those who cannot, for whatever reason, document the devastation that the conflict imparted on their lives? Or those who were negatively impacted by the conflict before 1985?

These questions are ones that many of the residents of Agua Blanca implied in their conversations with me. To be clear, the complaint is not that the government should not support victims of the armed conflict, but that those who fought against the state seem to be getting state support, while not all those who suffered from the conflict do. Further, poverty is understood to be connected to the displacement caused by the armed conflict; yet, poverty is seemingly not legible to the law – certainly not in the perspective of many people from Agua Blanca.[36]

Leonor shared that although her family had experienced violence and displacement, and although her mother had participated in the

[35] See Article 1 of Law 1448.

[36] The Constitutional Court has actually decided tutela cases on the basis of *mínimo vital* doctrine, which suggests that "non-fundamental" rights should be considered "fundamental" (and thus applicable to the tutela procedure) when the violation of the "nonfundamental" right would threaten the vital minimum or the minimum conditions necessary for a dignified existence. See Landau (2012) for a full discussion of *mínimo vital*.

peace process (including an attempt to claim victim status), her family had not received any benefits, or even an official response, from the state. She described that experience as follows:

> Well, you see, I lived through violence for a long time, from a very young age. We were displaced from our farm. We arrived here in Cali, and a brother of mine was taken by the guerrillas when he was thirteen years old. The guerrillas killed him because he was going to run. My mother went, she spoke with them, and we are participating in the peace process now, but it has not worked. They have not yet given us an answer.[37]

She concluded by telling me that justice did not exist for the poor in Colombia. Many others suggested something similar: "Justice is for those who have money; that is, there is the law of money."[38] Now, it's possible that Leonor's family does not meet the criteria outlined in Law 1448, and it's also possible that they do but the process simply has not been completed yet. Leonor's understanding, however, was that her family was being unjustly excluded, despite their deservingness.

For some, this sense that justice was not for the people of Agua Blanca stemmed from unequal punishments for violations of the law. As Verónica explained, "nowadays if you steal a cell phone, they put you in jail, they punish you. If you kill a person, they sentence you to two, three years. And in a year, you get out ... This is not justice."[39] Paula held that this inequity in punishment went even further:

> If a boy is caught stealing or something, they send him to jail, to die in the yard, but those white-collar criminals, who don't just steal cheese or milk or cell phones, who [instead] steal to buy 200 cell phones, millions of pesos, they steal from the state, they give [the white-collar criminals] a house as a jail or they assign them a room in with a television,

[37] Agua Blanca interview 9. "Pues vea, yo viví la violencia mucho tiempo, desde muy pequeña, desde la finca que nos desplazaron. Llegamos aquí a Cali aquí en Cali un hermano mío se lo llevó la guerrilla cuando tenía trece años y a él la guerrilla lo mató porque se iba a volar. Mi mamá fue, habló con ellos, pero nunca, estamos en el proceso sobre lo de la paz que está viviendo ahora, pero no ha funcionado todavía no han dado respuesta."

[38] Agua Blanca interview 1. "La justicia es pa' que tiene dinero, ósea existe la ley de dinero."

[39] Agua Blanca interview 5. "Le digo yo es que hoy en día si te robes un celular, dejan a la cárcel, castigan. Si te matan a una persona, castigan, dos, tres años, tareas en la cárcel y en un año te salen ... Esto no es justicia. La justicia te castigo real."

> a refrigerator, that is, an apartment in a jail and there they take care of them and send them the newspaper.[40]

Laura also shared that she believed that "prisons should be educational centers, centers of reform, but here that doesn't exist. The young men come out worse."[41] What then happens is that young people turn to committing more and more serious crimes.

The perception is that poverty – and thus delinquency – stems from government inattention and neglect, as well as the conflict. Laura explained: "No, I do not trust these people [the government] because they have defrauded us. And the problem here is that, due to poverty, no, it is true, that there are many people who sell themselves for a plate of food."[42] Part of the challenge is the connection between poverty and the conflict, or poverty and displacement. Gloria lamented:

> People arrive [in Cali] without an opportunity. It's overcrowded … We are going to have more crime, because as long as there is no opportunity, as long as there is no respect. They are moving from their land, where people have their food, have their lives made and they come here to face a life that is the most horrible thing that can happen to them. I say the most horrible, because I count myself as displaced.[43]

She then told her story of displacement: "We left our land that had everything, where we lived well, to suffer here in the city. To the people here, we are an annoyance." While the river near where she used to live provided fish after fish, in the city "you have to buy some little fish heads and they have to share them with up to thirty people." As long

[40] Agua Blanca interview 14. "Si a un chico lo cogen robando o algo, lo mandan para la cárcel allá dentro a que se mate con todo el patio, pero a esos ladrones de cuello blanco, que no roban el queso ni la leche ni el celular, esos se roban para comprar 200 celulares, millones, roban el estado y a ellos le dan casa por cárcel o le asignan una habitación o una cárcel con televisor, con equipo, nevera, ósea un apartamento en una cárcel y allá los cuidan y les mandan el periódico."

[41] Agua Blanca interview 5. "Las cárceles deben ser centros educativos, de reformación, pero aquí no hay eso. Los muchachos salen peores."

[42] Agua Blanca interview 5. "No, yo no tengo confianza en esa gente porque nos han defraudado y el problema aquí es que, debido a la pobreza, no, es cierto, que hay mucha gente se vende por un plato de comida."

[43] Agua Blanca interview 21. "[E]sas personas que llegan sin oportunidad, llegan a un hacinamiento … vamos a tener más delincuencia, porque mientras no haya oportunidad, mientras no haya respetos, mientras, no, se esté desplazando de su terruño, donde la gente tiene su comida, tiene su vida hecha y llegan aquí a enfrentarse a una vida que es lo más horrible que le puede pasar, yo digo lo más horrible porque yo me cuento como desplazado."

as that is that case, "then crime will continue … look, as long as Cali is hungry, there cannot be peace."[44]

For others, the issue was more that the government appeared to be focused on helping the guerillas instead of investing in noncombatants, in those negatively impacted by the conflict, those understood by residents of Agua Blanca to be rightfully deserving. Diana held that "if you are from the guerrillas, the president … gives you a house. Yes, for the guerrillas. But for us, the poor, no."[45] Francia explained:

> Those people were murderers, the FARC, and they are not going to pay, they are not going to pay anything! The guerrillas are going to earn more than a worker, an employee who is earning a minimum wage. The minimum wage is 700 and something pesos. And do you know how much each member of the FARC is going to earn? 1,800 for sitting around doing nothing! And where does this come from? Our money, from the people![46]

Verónica agreed:

> The current [Santos] government has focused on what? On peace, peace, peace, and everything is in the doldrums in Colombia. Colombia is a

[44] Agua Blanca interview 21. "Salimos de nuestra tierra con todo, vivíamos bien, a sufrir aquí a la ciudad, porque para la gente que vive aquí en la ciudad, nosotros somos un estorbo, para nosotros que vinimos de un campo libre, es horrible llegar a un ciudad dónde uno no conoce, dónde uno está acostumbrado a que si va a comer, uno va a desayunar, y uno quiere desayunar con pescado, se va al rio el rio está así, y saca un pescado así grande y sí se lo quiere comer todo, se lo come, se lo come, y aquí hay que comprar unas cabecitas de pescado y tienen que compartirlas hasta con 30 personas, entonces va a seguir la delincuencia, … vea mientras Cali esté sin hambre puede haber paz, mientras Cali esté con hambre, con el estómago vacío, nadie tiene paz y tranquilidad, y nadie piensa bien, porque usted con hambre no va a pensar bien, ni trabaja bien, ni piensa bien, ni duerme bien, ni vive bien, eso es verdad."

[45] Agua Blanca interview 1. "Si usted es de la guerrilla, el presidente … le da casa. Sí, para la guerrilla. Pero para nosotros, los pobres, no."

[46] Agua Blanca interview 10. "Esa gente eran unos asesinos, las FARC, y ellos no van a pagar, ¡no van a pagar nada! … Los guerrilleros van a ganar más que un asalariado. Un asalariado se está ganando un mínimo. Un mínimo que son 700 y pico, ¿Y sabe cuánto se va a ganar cada miembro de las FARC? Mil ochocientos, por estar sentado haciendo nada, ¿y esto sale de dónde? del dinero de nosotros, del pueblo." Francia went further, explaining that folks like her voted against the peace agreement and that the government did not listen to them. "Y la verdad, así como yo, hay mucha gente que no está de acuerdo con esto, mucha gente no está de acuerdo con esto. Entonces, por eso se votó, se votó por el no haber si la verdad hubiera, ahí había un cambio aquí, pero no, no sirvió para nada. Porque no lo tomaron en cuenta." Interestingly, she did not blame the Constitutional Court and did not connect the efforts to push the peace agreement through despite the results of the plebiscite.

> horrible country now, because there is no government. The government we have is all bad, and the mayors are the same. They always favor the upper or middle classes. The poor are not favored at all.[47]

Claudia brought up something similar in a separate interview: "What the government did was, what they did was screw us. [President Juan Manuel] Santos screwed us. This story of peace. Peace screwed us. It's peace for him, not for us. All he wants is to win the Nobel Prize."[48] Daniela chimed in: "He won the Nobel Prize for knowing how to rob the poor."[49] I then asked Claudia what peace would mean for her. She replied, "peace for me is equality of all, that is peace. Santos does not want equality for us. What he does have is a preference for the guerrillas, because what he is giving them is being taken away from us poor people."[50] Here, she was referring to the increase in the value added tax from 16 percent to 19 percent that the Colombian Congress had approved a few months before we spoke, in December 2016.

6.4 WHAT DOES THIS MEAN FOR CONSTITUTIONAL EMBEDDING?

This chapter has detailed the perception that rights serve some and not others, that there is unfair discrimination built into institutions meant to guarantee universal protections. Ultimately, these perceptions serve as a challenge to constitutional embedding, though perhaps more at a theoretical level. Julieta Lemaitre – who went on to serve as a justice in the Special Jurisdiction for Peace – offers a vision of a state defined

[47] Agua Blanca interview 18. "El gobierno de ahora se ha centrado ¿en qué? En que la paz, la paz, la paz y todo está de capa caída en Colombia. Colombia es un país horrible ahora porque no hay gobierno. El gobierno que tenemos es re malo todo y los alcaldes igual, siempre favorecen las clases altas o medias y los de las clases populares no las favorecen para nada."

[48] Agua Blanca interview 2. "Eso lo que hicieron fue el gobierno, lo que hizo fue jodernos, ese Santos nos jodió. Tipo de cuento de la paz, nos jodió la paz, la paz para él, para él porque para nosotros eso no es paz. Aquí lo único que quiere es ganarse el premio Nobel." Note that the interview took place in April 2017, some four months after President Santos was awarded the 2016 Nobel Peace Prize.

[49] Agua Blanca interview 2. "Él se ganó el Premio Nobel por saber robar a los pobres."

[50] Agua Blanca interview 2. "La paz para mi es una igualdad de todos, eso es una paz. Santos no tiene igualdad con nosotros. Él lo que tiene, es una preferencia por los guerrilleros, porque lo que le está dando a ellos no los está quitando a nosotros los pobres."

by the inversion of the phrase often attributed to Getulio Vargas, "for my friends, anything; for my enemies, the law." By contrast, Lemaitre envisions a state constrained by the law, a state that offers everyone the benefits and protections of the law. This kind of state would be:

> [A] state capable of being a "friend" of the people whom it has historically abandoned. It is not with roads and buildings, nor with the army, that the state successfully expands. It is when ordinary officials echo the values of reconstruction from below, and offer the care and security provided by the best community leaders, not by shadowy powers, that the state successfully expands, that it manages to delegitimize its rivals, and regulate social relations within the law, rather than outside it. Doing this, and doing it openly, within the law, learning from mistakes and successes, is the correct way to expand the Colombian state and make a good life possible for all, the "life loved by all." Only with such a state can we one day offer the law to our friends as well. (2019: 199–200)[51]

This beautiful vision seemingly remains quite far in the distance for those in Agua Blanca. Near the end of my stay in Cali, Daniela told me, "si la justicia fuera justicia, este país sería muy diferente." This is to say that law, rights, justice, and citizenship in practice – perhaps especially for residents of Comuna 14 – do not live up to their promises, a reality that has been documented across contexts (e.g., Scheingold 1974; Thompson 1975; McCann 1994). To imagine a Colombia in which law on paper matches law in practice means imagining a very different Colombia.

The 1991 Constitution is less embedded in Agua Blanca than elsewhere in Colombia, and this limited embedding and limited legibility signals a weakness in social constitutionalism, that it is not living up to its grandest of promises. To be fair, if perfection is the standard,

[51] "[U]n Estado capaz de ser 'amigo' de las personas a las cuales históricamente ha abandonado. No es con carreteras y edificios que se extiende con éxito el Estado; tampoco con el Ejército. Cuando el Estado se extiende con éxito, cuando logra deslegitimar a sus rivales, y regular las relaciones sociales con la ley y no por fuera de ella, es cuando estos funcionarios de a pie hacen eco de los valores de la reconstrucción desde abajo, y ofrecen el cuidado y la seguridad que brindan los mejores líderes comunitarios y no pocas veces los poderes a la sombra. Hacer esto, y hacerlo de manera abierta, dentro de la ley, aprendiendo de los errores y de los aciertos, es la manera correcta de expandir el Estado colombiano y hacer posible, para todos, una vida Buena, la 'vida querida por todos.' Solo con un Estado así podremos algún día ofrecer la ley también a nuestros amigos."

any intervention will surely fail, and other forms of political engagement have not sufficiently served this population either. As Francia put it, "we poor people have neither a voice nor a vote in this country. Here we only have a voice and a vote when politicians come to neighborhoods to ask for votes, for us to vote for them ... [But then] they forgot about the people, so nothing really happens here."[52] Some of the time, folks can mobilize and create poor people's movements and solidarity-based community organizations, even in the absence of formal or at least regular employment that might form the foundation for union-informed modes of collective action (e.g., Piven and Cloward 1977). Claudia, Daniela, Gloria, and Laura, in fact, were active participants in these kinds of organizations. My goal here is not to try to weigh the relative benefits of different forms of political participation against one another, but to note that folks in Agua Blanca appear to have relatively few options when it comes to gaining access to state (or alternative) goods and services.

Even if the 1991 Constitution and the tutela procedure only result in access to some medications and long-delayed medical appointments, that's better than nothing – especially compared to previous levels of access and possibilities to contest the nondelivery of medical services. That said, the new constitutional infrastructure is not understood to address the primary burdens faced by residents of Agua Blanca, especially those harms that we might call "diffusely economic" in nature, including poverty (as compared to stolen wages, for example).[53] If the goal is to fully realize rights, this disconnect is significant. If the focus is on overall constitutional embedding in Colombia, however, it is not. The limitations of constitutional embedding in Agua Blanca have not prompted a new expectations gap[54] and have not destabilized

[52] Agua Blanca interview 10. "Nosotros los pobres, no tenemos ni voz ni voto en este país, acá solamente tenemos voz y voto cuándo los políticos vienen a los barrios así a venir a pedir que votos, para que voten por ellos ... se olvidaron de la gente. Entonces aquí no pasa nada la verdad."

[53] This line of thought merits broader consideration (i.e., consideration beyond the Colombian case that provides the basis for this project). What are the contours of the "legal legibility of harm" (and issue adoption/nonadoption), who or what determines them, and how have they changed over time? Further, who is the burden on to prove that particular harms do or do not count or are not relevant?

[54] Instead, the expectations seem to better fit Viktor Chernomyrdin's aphorism: "We hoped for better, but it turned out like always." I am grateful to Lauren McCarthy for pointing this out.

the aggregate, country-level processes (namely, legal mobilization through the social construction of legal grievances and development of judicial receptivity to particular kinds of claims) that serve to embed social constitutionalism in Colombia. Considering, however, that the National Center for History Memory (2013) estimates that 17 percent of Colombians directly experienced violence of some kind during the armed conflict, legal legibility or illegibility will likely remain a challenge for constitutional embedding moving forward.

CHAPTER SEVEN

CHALLENGES TO EMBEDDING

Power Struggles

As a new constitution comes to be embedded socially and legally, the landscape of power and relevance shifts. Some actors will prefer the previous status quo over the incoming system defined by new rights protections, new citizen expectations, and new judicial roles. As a result, these actors will have incentives to push back against constitutional embedding. This chapter explores power struggles in the midst of constitutional embedding in Colombia, examining how actors within the executive, legislative, and judicial branches of government attempted to contest the growing power of the social constitutionalism in the country, particularly in its most visible features: the Constitutional Court and the tutela procedure. To date, these actors have failed to curb the impact of the 1991 Constitution, in large part because of the extent to which social and legal embedding have taken root and continued to reinforce one another.

In the early 1990s, the newly created Constitutional Court was one of four apex courts, and while tutela decisions ended at the Constitutional Court, other kinds of legal claims were understood to be settled upon decisions rendered by the Supreme Court, the Council of State, or the Superior Council of the Judiciary. As the years progressed, these various high courts jockeyed for position at the height of the judicial system. Each of these clashes became known as a "*choque de trenes*" (literally, a train wreck). In addition to increasing its power by facilitating tutela claims related to social rights (Taylor 2020a), the Constitutional Court also expanded its role by allowing tutela claims against judicial decisions (*tutela contra sentencias*) and by developing the idea of an

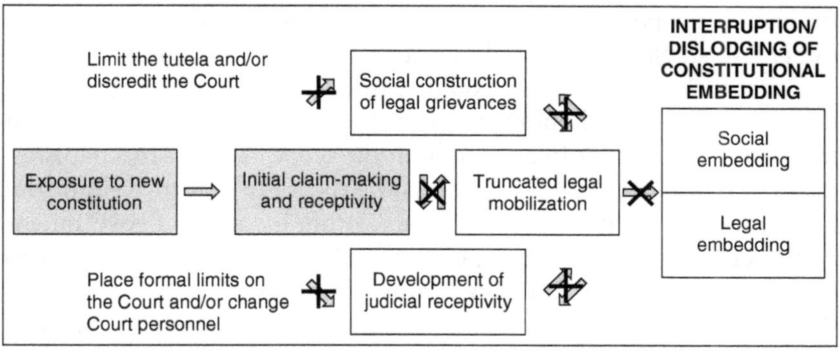

Figure 7.1 Powerful actors' efforts to thwart constitutional embedding.

unconstitutional state of affairs (*estado de cosas inconstitucional*), which could then be remedied through structural decisions (Rodríguez Garavito 2009, 2011). These maneuverings (which we might understand as successful efforts at legal embedding), alongside popular support (which is the result of successful social embedding), allowed the Court and the new constitutional order to weather criticisms and conflict within the judicial system. While some of these criticisms may be valid, my goal in this chapter is not to evaluate the relative merits of the criticisms of the Constitutional Court or the 1991 Constitution. Instead, I intend to track how the Court and the Constitution managed to maintain prominent positions in social and legal life in Colombia.

At various times, executive and legislative branch actors likewise attempted to limit the impact of the 1991 Constitution, particularly the tutela procedure and the Constitutional Court. These efforts took the form of outspoken criticisms, proposals to reduce the scope or even eliminate the tutela, and what some observers describe as attempts to game the appointment system for the Constitutional Court. Once again, however, the constitutional order has – at least so far – weathered these challenges, due to the institutional culture developed within the Court (a byproduct of legal embedding) and popular support, or what David Landau (2014) describes as the creation of a "middle-class constituency" for the Court and the tutela procedure (again, evidence of social embedding). Figure 7.1 shows how these various power struggles could interrupt or dislodge constitutional embedding, inhibiting the further social construction of legal grievances, the development of judicial receptivity, and/or the interplay between the two, effectively truncating the positive feedback process described in Chapter 2 that is integral to stable or longstanding constitutional embedding.

Constitutional embedding could be interrupted along the upper path (because of successful efforts to discredit the Constitutional Court in the eyes of everyday citizens or to limit the scope of access mechanisms, in this case, the tutela), the lower path (successful efforts to limit the Constitutional Court's power relative to other branches of government and/or change out personnel), or both. The rest of this chapter turns to these efforts by the judiciary beyond the Constitutional Court and the other branches of government to limit the power of the constitutional order. It closes with a discussion of how social constitutionalism in Colombia endured despite these challenges.

7.1 *CHOQUE DE TRENES* AND THE RISE OF THE CONSTITUTIONAL COURT

As noted earlier, when the 1991 Constitution went into effect, there were four apex courts in Colombia: the newly created Constitutional Court, the Supreme Court, the Council of State, and the Superior Council of the Judiciary. Under this configuration, there is arguably a hardline separation between matters of ordinary and administrative jurisdiction and constitutional matters. The Supreme Court is the highest authority in matters of ordinary (i.e., civil, criminal, and labor) law, the Council of State in matters of administrative law, and the Constitutional Court for constitutional matters. However, the tutela procedure, as set out in Article 86 of the 1991 Constitution, could be used to assert potential fundamental rights violations (though act or omission) by any public institution in the country.

As early as 1992, some Colombians tried to use the tutela procedure in response to judicial decisions they disagreed with: they "tutela-ed" the other apex courts, asking the Constitutional Court to reconsider some element of the decision another court reached or the process by which it reached that decision. In fact, the first tutela decision reviewed by the Constitutional Court, T-006/92, included a challenge to a Supreme Court decision. As the majority of the three-justice panel, Eduardo Cifuentes and Alejandro Martínez (José Gregorio Hernández, dissented) revoked the Supreme Court's decision, noting that "excluding the tutela action regarding the sentences of one of the Chambers of the Supreme Court of Justice means that, in this field of public action, so closely related to the protection of fundamental rights, there is no means of control of its constitutional behavior."[1] Six other T-cases (tutelas) and one C-case (abstract review cases) dealing with the notion of tutelas against prior judicial decisions came before the Court in that year (T-223, T-413, T-474, T-492, T-523, T531, and C-543).[2] These decisions set out what became known as the *vía de hecho* doctrine.[3] Cifuentes was involved in six of these T-cases, Alejandro Martínez in four, and Ciro Angarita in three.[4]

José Gregorio Hernández, writing for the majority in C-543/92, outlined the possibility for constitutional review of prior judicial decisions under certain circumstances, namely when a judge has allowed or created an unjustified delay in coming to a decision, when fundamental rights are ignored or threatened, and when "irremediable damage" may occur.[5] He cautioned, though, that "it is not within the powers of the

1 "Excluir la acción de tutela respecto de sentencias de una de las Salas de la Suprema Corte significa que, en este campo de la actuación pública, de tan estrecha relación con la protección de los derechos fundamentales, no existe ningún medio de control de su comportamiento constitucional." See the full decision at: www.corteconstitucional.gov.co/relatoria/1992/t-006-92.htm.

2 Tabulated by Bermudez Maya and Gomez Mejia (2016).

3 Jan Boesten (2016: 133) explains: "The figure of the *via de hecho* originates in the question of what constitutes a *cosa juzgada* (judged case) in the new Constitution, and is central for legal certainty, because it stipulates that legal questions already settled in a completed legal process cannot be reopened. Under the rule of law and the centrality of habeas corpus only legal processes establish 'legal truths'. From the same premise follows the principle, 'non bis in idem', which provides legal security to the individual by imposing that an individual cannot be prosecuted and judged twice for the same crime. In the Anglo-Saxon realm this is referred to as the prohibition of double jeopardy. The dissent in the decision disputed the interpretation of the *cosa juzgada* and its application to the procedure of the tutela. Magistrates Cifuentes, Angarita, and Martinez contended that the imposition of a time limit in judicial processes, implicit in the principle of *cosa juzgada*, is in no way disputed in the application of the tutela against judicial decisions. Rather, the *tutela contra sentencias* simply means that in the case of fundamental rights violations the Constitutional Court suspends this time limit until after the conclusion of the tutela review. Since there cannot be tutelas against tutelas, it does not constitute a prolongation of the legal process *ad infinitum*. Crucially, in the case of the tutela, the litigated issue is not the concern of the deliberation in the Court, but rather whether a fundamental right of the plaintiff was violated by a court's decision. Therefore, the constitutional judge who revises the accused judge's legal decision does not undermine the autonomy of the latter in taking her decision."

4 José Gregorio Hernández, was involved in six as well, though he dissented in five.

5 "Así, por ejemplo, nada obsta para que por la vía de la tutela se ordene al juez que ha incurrido en dilación injustificada en la adopción de decisiones a su cargo que proceda a resolver o que observe con diligencia los términos judiciales, ni riñe con los preceptos

tutela judge to interfere in a judicial process already in progress, adopting decisions parallel to those previously issued, since such a possibility undermines the concepts of functional autonomy and independence."[6] In this particular case, Hernández believed that these conditions were not met. Eduardo Cifuentes, Ciro Angarita, and Alejandro Martínez – the three justices on the Transitional Court who came from academic backgrounds (as discussed in Chapter 5) – offered a dissenting view, arguing that this tutela should proceed, precisely because this claim suggested a potential violation of fundamental rights through the previous decision. In other words, their view was that this particular claim did not reopen a settled legal matter, but instead posed a new question relating to fundamental constitutional rights.

This kind of claim came to be known as the *tutela contra sentencias*,[7] which reflects that the dissenting view eventually won out. In fact, during the following year, Cifuentes, Hernández, and Martínez, in T-079/93, allowed a tutela claim against a prior judicial decision to move forward, though they ultimately affirmed the Supreme Court's decision. At least five other decisions in 1993 by the Constitutional Court further bolstered the possibility of *tutelas contra sentencias*. In T-158/93, Justices Vladimiro Naranjo, Jorge Arango Mejía, and Antonio Barrera reiterated the *vía de hecho* doctrine, which holds that "the tutela action is appropriate when it is exercised to prevent public authorities, through de facto means, from violating or threatening fundamental rights."[8] By 1994, all members of the First Court

constitucionales la utilización de esta figura ante actuaciones de hecho imputables al funcionario por medio de las cuales se desconozcan o amenacen los derechos fundamentales, ni tampoco cuando la decisión pueda causar un perjuicio irremediable, para lo cual sí está constitucionalmente autorizada la tutela pero como mecanismo transitorio cuyo efecto, por expreso mandato de la Carta es puramente temporal y queda supeditado a lo que se resuelva de fondo por el juez ordinario competente (artículos 86 de la Constitución Política y 8° del Decreto 2591 de 1991)." See the full decision: www.corteconstitucional.gov.co/RELATORIA/1992/C-543-92.htm.

6 "Pero, en cambio, no está dentro de las atribuciones del juez de tutela la de inmiscuirse en el trámite de un proceso judicial en curso, adoptando decisiones paralelas a las que cumple, en ejercicio de su función, quien lo conduce, ya que tal posibilidad está excluida de plano en los conceptos de autonomía e independencia funcionales." See the full decision: www.corteconstitucional.gov.co/RELATORIA/1992/C-543-92.htm.

7 For more information on the *vía de hecho* doctrine, see Bermudez Maya and Gomez Mejia (2016).

8 "Es procedente la acción de tutela cuando se ejerce para impedir que las autoridades públicas, mediante vías de hecho vulneren o amenacen derechos fundamentales. El

(1993–2000), regardless of left–right ideology, affirmed the possibility of the *tutela contra sentencias*.[9] Just over ten years later, in C-590/05, the Constitutional Court issued a decision that expanded the list of appropriate instances of the use of the *tutela contra sentencias* to eight situations.[10]

The broader legal establishment was slower to adopt the *tutela contra* sentences. In a careful analysis of tutela claims involving the Supreme Court and the Council of State during the 2000s, Manuel Quinche Ramírez (2007: 292) concludes that these "judges, when faced with the dilemma of choosing between substantive law and the interpretation of form, prefer[red] the latter, even if fundamental rights are violated with the choice."[11] In fact, he notes that two chambers of the of the Supreme Court, the Labor Cassation Chamber and the Criminal Cassation Chamber, were especially reticent. Citing Óscar Dueñas Ruiz (1997: 42–59), Quinche Ramírez explains that the "ideological tendency" of judges who sat in these chambers had "historically been in favor of restricting the rights of Colombians" (Quinche Ramírez 2007: 291).[12] The Supreme Court and the Council of State made five main arguments as to why the *tutela contra sentencias* should be limited (Quinche Ramírez 2007: 307–9). I paraphrase those arguments here:

1. There is no defined hierarchy among the "high courts." Therefore, each high court should have the final say on whatever matters fall within their jurisdictions. The *tutela contra sentencias* thus undermines the structure of the judiciary.
2. The principle of *res judicata* ought to stand: if a matter has been decided, it should not (or cannot) be reopened by the same parties. The *tutela contra sentencias* does exactly that.

caso que nos ocupa enmarca cabalmente dentro de los parámetros de esta excepción, por cuanto existe en él evidencia de una flagrante violación de la ley, constitutiva de una vía de hecho, en detrimento del derecho fundamental al debido proceso." See the full decision: www.corteconstitucional.gov.co/relatoria/1993/t-158-93.htm

[9] A survey of experts placed the justices along a 1 (left) to 10 (right) scale. Gaviria 2.186, Martínez 3.262, Cifuentes 4.762, Morón 5.69, Barrera 5.923, Mejía 6.625, Hernández, 6.628, Herrera 6.737, and Naranjo 7.784 (Rodríguez-Raga 2011: 161).

[10] See Loaiza Henao (2014) for a discussion and examples of these eight instances.

[11] "[Estos] jueces, al enfrentar el dilema de escoger entre el derecho sustantivo y la exégesis de las formas, prefieren éstas, aún si con la escogencia resultan vulnerados derechos fundamentales."

[12] "[L]a tendencia ideológica de aquellas dos salas ... se han mostrado históricamente partidarios de restringir los derechos de los colombianos."

3. Judges should have functional autonomy. The *tutela contra sentencias* allows for (unconstitutional) interference by constitutional judges into matters than have already been examined and interpreted.
4. Judges have independent legal specialties and functions. Those specialties (e.g., administrative law) have their own universe of norms and arguments. With the *tutela contra sentencias*, constitutional judges could revise or reverse a process that had been constitutionally compliant (that fell outside of their specialty).
5. The Constitution and constitutional principles must be defended. The *tutela contra sentencias* can violate constitutional principles and specifically allows for impunity.

Quinche Ramírez highlights a provocative statement issued by the full chamber of the Supreme Court on March 24, 2006 to illustrate the fifth argument:

> Faced with the new gap opened by the Constitutional Court to impunity, the Supreme Court of Justice calls on the judges across the country, without being discouraged, to continue to apply the Constitution and the law with full independence and autonomy, and absolute respect to the human story of the accused, whatever it may be, but guided by the impartiality imposed on them by their condition as representatives of the Estado Social de Derecho [social state under the rule of law] that governs us.[13]

Here, the Supreme Court not only grumbled about the *tutela contra sentencias*, but explicitly called on judges sitting on lower courts to adopt an alternative view of constitutionalism and rights protections than the one promoted by the Constitution Court.

In a similar vein, the Council of State, following a tutela against one of their sentences in November 2015, claimed that actions of the Constitutional Court "constitute[d] a de facto route and lack[ed] validity." The Council of State further argued that their original decision "is unchangeable, unchallengeable and definitive." They even called for copies of their statements to be sent to "the Commission of Accusations

[13] "Frente a la nueva brecha abierta por la corte constitucional a la impunidad, la Corte Suprema hace un llamado a los jueces de todo país para que, sin desanimarse, continúen aplicado la constitución política y la ley con plena independencia y autonomía, y absoluto respeto por el drama humano de los procesados cualesquiera que sean, pero guiados por la imparcialidad que les impone la condición de representantes del Estado social de derecho que nos rige."

of the House of Representatives, so that they could initiate a criminal process against the magistrates of the Constitutional Court" (Quinche Ramírez 2020: 97). Rather than addressing the broader judicial community, here the Council of State appealed (unsuccessfully) to members of Congress to check the Constitutional Court's power.

In the face of these criticisms, the Constitutional Court continued to affirm the *vía de hecho* doctrine and the legitimacy of the *tutela contra sentencias*. From the perspective of justices on the Constitutional Court, the Constitution explicitly tasked the Court with defending fundamental rights, and the new constitutional order gave primacy to constitutional legal matters over all others. Examining a violation of due process during a proceeding does not reopen settled questions of law from the proceeding; instead, it allows for the narrow consideration of whether or not fundamental rights were protected. For example, Manuel José Cepeda, writing in SU-1219/01,[14] held:

> The [Constitutional] Court notes that the judges are independent and autonomous. It also underlines that this independence is to apply the rules, not to stop applying the Constitution. A judge cannot invoke his independence to avoid the rule of law, much less, to stop applying the supreme law that is the Constitution. The alternative, unacceptable in a constitutional democracy, is that the meaning of the Constitution changes according to the opinion of each judge.[15]

Read uncharitably, this view would seem to contradict a 1992 tutela decision referenced in Chapter 5 (emphasis added):

> There is a new strategy to achieve the effectiveness of fundamental rights. The coherence and wisdom of the interpretation and, above all, the effectiveness of the fundamental rights in the 1991 Constitution, are ensured by the Constitutional Court. This new relationship between fundamental rights and judges means a fundamental change in relation

[14] SU stands for *sentencias unificadas*, which are issued when there are divergent judicial decisions on the same issue that must be settled to ensure legal certainty for future judicial decisions.

[15] "La Corte, advierte que los jueces son independientes y autónomos. Subraya, también, que su independencia es para aplicar las normas, no para dejar de aplicar la Constitución. Un juez no puede invocar su independencia para eludir el imperio de la ley, y mucho menos, para dejar de aplicar la ley de leyes, la norma suprema que es la Constitución. La alternativa, inaceptable en una democracia constitucional, es que el significado de la Constitución cambie según el parecer de cada juez." See the full decision here: www.corteconstitucional.gov.co/relatoria/2001/SU1219-01.htm.

> to the previous Constitution. This change can be defined as a new strategy aimed at achieving the effectiveness of rights, which consists of giving priority for the responsibility for the effectiveness of fundamental rights to the judge, and not to the administration or the legislator. In the previous system, the effectiveness of fundamental rights ended up being reduced to their symbolic force. *Today, with the new Constitution, the rights are what the judges say through the tutela.*[16]

More charitably, we might understand these two positions as in congruence, suggesting that only constitutional judges should be involved in the interpretation of constitutional rights and constitutional law. Beyond these constitutional defenses, the Court also pointed to the principle of universal jurisdiction and the practices of international courts as well as courts in other Latin American countries as undercutting the arguments against the *tutela contra sentencias* that involved reopening settled matters.[17]

Many of the judges and lawyers who I interviewed expressed some sympathy for the positions of the Supreme Court and Council of State, if not outright agreement, even when they were otherwise limited in their criticisms of the Constitutional Court and the new constitutional order. For example, Hernando Herrera, who had served as an assistant during the Constitutional Assembly and later as a *conjuez*, or alternate justice, in the Council of State, explained that the Constitutional Court has become a "super court," because the *tutela contra sentencias*

[16] "Existe una nueva estrategia para el logro de la efectividad de los derechos fundamentales. La coherencia y la sabiduría de la interpretación y, sobre todo, la eficacia de los derechos fundamentales en la Constitución de 1991, están asegurados por la Corte Constitucional. Esta nueva relación entre derechos fundamentales y jueces significa un cambio fundamental en relación con la Constitución anterior; dicho cambio puede ser definido como una nueva estrategia encaminada al logro de la eficacia de los derechos, que consiste en otorgarle de manera prioritaria al juez, y no ya a la administración o al legislador, la responsabilidad de la eficacia de los derechos fundamentales. En el sistema anterior la eficacia de los derechos fundamentales terminaba reduciéndose a su fuerza simbólica. Hoy, con la nueva Constitución, los derechos son aquello que los jueces dicen a través de las sentencias de tutela." See the full decision here: www.corteconstitucional.gov.co/relatoria/1992/T-406-92.htm.

[17] Quinche Ramírez (2007: 311) points to Argentine and Uruguayan cases in which the courts later annulled decisions that had been issued during the 1980s or retried cases that had been resolved by amnesty laws (e.g., the Argentine police officer Miguel Oswaldo Etchacolatz, accused of illegal detention, torture, and murder, was originally sentenced in 1986, then granted amnesty under the *obediencia debida* and *punto final* amnesty laws, and retried in 2006 and sentenced to life imprisonment).

allows it to revise the decisions of other courts. He outlined the perspectives of both sides in the following way:

> It is all very well for citizens to disagree, but not for magistrates and judges to fight, and this is a war of scope [or competence]. I understand the concern of the Supreme Court and the Council of State ... "If I am the most important body in my jurisdiction, how can another judicial body come and tell me that what I did was wrong? With respect to what I am doing, nobody is supposed to handle it better, to the extent that there are specialized jurisdictions here." And on the other hand, the Constitutional Court says, "yes, but I have the job of guaranteeing the rights of all citizens and the constitution gives me the possibility of reviewing tutela claims, and then I can choose the tutelas related to sentences of the high courts."[18]

José Bonivento – who had served as a justice on and president of the Council of State, the Civil Cassation Chamber of the Supreme Court, and the Superior Council of the Judiciary, in addition to being nominated but not selected for the Constitutional Court in 1993 – reflected on the *tutela contra sentencias* and the *choque de trenes*, saying:

> That was indeed one of the great disputes, confrontations ... [The Supreme Court and the Council of State] consider that their decisions cannot be touched and that there is no room for tutela, but the [Constitutional] Court has done it. It is being done haphazardly and piercing everything. And the truth is that today the Constitutional Court reviews.[19]

[18] Elite interview 39 (September 27, 2016). "Porque uno advierte que está muy bien que los ciudadanos peleen, pero no que los magistrados y los jueces peleen, y esta es una guerra específicamente de competencia. Yo entiendo la preocupación de la Corte Suprema y del Consejo de Estado, sobre todo, más que del consejo superior de la judicatura, ellas dicen si yo soy organismo de cierre, si yo soy un organismo más importante en mi jurisdicción por qué puede llegar otra corporación distinta y decirme que lo que yo hice estuvo mal hecho. Cuando además lo que yo estoy haciendo, se supone nadie lo maneja mejor, en la medida que aquí hay jurisdicciones especializadas. Y por otro lado, la corte constitucional dice sí, pero es que yo tengo la función de garantizar los derechos de todos los ciudadanos y a mí la constitución me da la posibilidad de escoger las tutelas, y entonces yo puedo escoger las tutelas relacionadas con sentencias de las altas cortes."

[19] Elite interview 18 (September 1, 2016). "Esa sí fue una de las grandes disputas, enfrentamientos, porque ... ellos consideran que no pueden ser tocadas sus decisiones y que no cabe par la tutela pero la Corte lo ha hecho y ahí está en curso y se hace a la buena y taladrando todo. Y lo cierto es que hoy en día la Corte Constitucional revisa."

He draws a clear connection between the tutela and the power to review the decisions of other courts. In his view, the Constitutional Court has embraced this function and has claimed the status of the superior court. Juan Carlos Esguerra highlighted a further critique of the Court, stating that, essentially, "lawsuits do not end in Colombia … [because there are] seven opportunities to decide the same thing."[20] Constitutional Court justices might push back against Esguerra's characterization, but undoubtedly, the *tutela contra sentencias* does provide another opportunity to challenge the process underlying legal cases.

That said, as Manuel Quinche Ramírez explained to me in an interview in 2016, while the "*tutela contra sentencias* had once been considered sacrilegious, now it is something common and accepted."[21] Lina Mogollón, who has experience working at each of the three high courts that figure prominently in this chapter – the Constitutional Court, Supreme Court, and Council of State – concurred, saying:

> Right now, it's a little easier. It was very difficult at the beginning. I think that is because of the nature of the judges. We had very established judges, who had studied law from a positivist perspective, only the law … At the beginning it started many clashes. They [the different high courts] delegitimized each other … [But] it has been twenty-six years, and the perspective is already changing – a little because the judges [on the bench now] are new judges. They are judges who have been studying constitutional law since the 1991 Constitution.[22]

This view comports with that of Juan Carlos Henao, who served as a justice on the Constitutional Court between February 2009 and April 2012. He recollected feeling "discomfort, obviously, because the other magistrates [on the other high courts] do not like it, no way … but that

[20] Elite interview 35 (September 23, 2016).

[21] Elite interview 2 (August 4, 2016). "La tutela contra sentencias judiciales, eso era un sacrilegio, ahora es algo común y corriente."

[22] Elite interview 41 (September 28, 2016). "Si, fue muy difícil, ahorita es un poco más sencillo. Fue muy difícil al principio también yo pensaría por la naturaleza de los jueces teníamos jueces muy adultos, también que habían estudiado el derecho desde la perspectiva positivista, solamente la ley … Al principio comenzó mucho, muchos choques, se deslegitimaban unos con otros … ya llevamos 26 años y ya va cambiando la perspectiva. También un poco porque los jueces son nuevos jueces, son jueces que ya estudian derecho constitucional desde la Constitución del 91 y ya comienzan a ampliar esa noción, entonces ya permiten la tutela. No siempre, pero si ya van avanzando de a poquitos. Entonces ha sido un discurso que ha ido avanzando y se ha ido posicionando."

is the way the system has worked in Colombia. That is developed by very clear jurisprudence and the legislator has never wanted to change that. It has always allowed the Constitutional Court to have that possibility [of reviewing *tutelas contra sentencias*]."[23] The process by which Henao arrived at the Constitutional Court is notable: he was nominated by the Council of State, after having been both a clerk and an alternate justice in that body.

Mario Cajas, a law professor and historian of the Colombian Supreme Court at the Universidad ICESI, suggested that the tension was real, but perhaps not reflective of actual confrontations between the high courts. He told me:

> When one reviews the jurisprudence, the cases are not that many. Some work that a colleague of ours did in 2008 showed that there were forty sentences in a year of a thousand and something that were produced. There were not that many and the cases where the [Constitutional] Court reversed Supreme Court decisions were much less than 10 percent. What happens is that these cases are cases of prominence.[24]

These high-profile cases shape discourse, if not everyday practice. Cajas further noted that in practice the Supreme Court has seemed to shift in its approach to these kinds of cases:

> If you do a review of those twenty-odd years you can also see where, for example, the Criminal Chamber has tended to get closer to the constitutional guidelines. The Labor Chamber is the one that is furthest away, and the Civil Chamber is in the middle. But we went from a moment where the three were far apart [from constitutional guidelines] and now they are getting closer.[25]

[23] Elite interview 62 (November 8, 2016). "Pues se produce un malestar, obviamente, porque los otros magistrados no les gusta como así que va … pero esa es la forma en que ha funcionado el sistema en Colombia, eso está desarrollado por la jurisprudencia muy clara y el legislador nunca ha querido cambiar eso siempre ha permitido que sea la Corte Constitucional la que tenga esa posibilidad."

[24] Elite interview 27 (September 16, 2016). "Cuando uno revisa la jurisprudencia los casos no son tantos, es decir, algún trabajo que hizo un colega nuestro en el 2008, mostraba que eran 40 sentencias en un año de mil y pico que se producían, no eran tantas y que los casos donde la Corte revertía o revocaba las decisiones de la Suprema Corte eran mucho menos del 10%. Lo que pasa es que los casos a los que se enfrentan son casos de renombre."

[25] Elite interview 27 (September 16, 2016). "Si tú haces una revisión de esos veinte y pico de años también puedes como fijar algunos momentos en donde por ejemplo,

Francisca Pou Gimenez (2018) has also documented the shift of the other high courts to fall more in line with the Constitutional Court's stance relative to rights protections, specifically with respect to the rights of nature (or of rivers and forests being rights-bearers).

Nothing about the initial discourse between the other high courts and the Constitutional Court suggested that either was likely to back down from their oppositional positions. However, the Supreme Court and Council of State could not eliminate the *tutela contra sentencias* on their own. That would require legislative action.

7.2 POLITICAL ATTACKS ON THE CONSTITUTIONAL COURT AND TUTELA

In addition to facing skepticism and even hostility from the other high courts, the Constitutional Court and the new constitutional order were also subject to challenges from the executive and legislative branches of government, particularly during the presidencies of Ernesto Samper (1994–1998) and Álvaro Uribe (2002–2010). Samper's proposals focused on eliminating the *tutela contra sentencias* and the ability of the Constitutional Court to review declarations of states of "internal commotion" (which would allow the executive a broader range of powers to deal with the emergency situation). As David Landau (2014) documents, however, the Samper administration only had narrow majorities in both houses of the legislature and could not count on disciplined party voting.[26] Samper faced an impeachment vote in 1996 and his popularity plummeted as evidence connecting his campaign to the Cali cartel mounted.[27] His proposed reforms did not make it out of the committee stage without fundamental revision. The Council of State and Supreme Court sponsored their own reform proposals, which made it past the committee stage, but could not garner the required majority of House votes. The then-president of the Council of State, Juan de Dios Montes, vented publicly about feeling disrespected by

la Sala Penal ha tendido más a acercarse más a los lineamientos constitucionales; la Sala Laboral es la que más está alejada y la Sala Civil, digamos que está en la mitad. Pero pasamos de un momento en donde las tres estaban alejadas y ahora se van acercando."

26 This paragraph draws heavily on research conducted by Landau and summarized in his 2014 dissertation.

27 For information on the scandal and investigations, see Dugas (2001a).

members of the House and his frustration that the president of the Constitutional Court, Antonio Barrera, had framed the proposal as "a conspiracy against the tutela," "inciting the population" in the process (Gutierrez 1997).

The story of the Uribe-era reforms is much the same. Rodrigo Uprimny (2005: 8) summarizes five strategies undertaken by the Uribe administration to reduce the power of the Constitutional Court:

1. Exclude the high courts from processing tutelas, due to the congestion that afflicts these courts;
2. Limit the tutela in the case of social rights, due to the economic imbalances caused by judicial interventions in this field;
3. For reasons of legal certainty, prohibit the *tutela contra sentencias*;
4. Limit the use of the tutela in labor matters; and
5. Prohibit tutela decisions from involving modifications to budgets or national or local development plans.[28]

The most notable of these ultimately unsuccessful efforts were mounted in 2002, 2004, and 2006. Looking to Legislative Act 10 of 2002 in the Senate as an illustrative example, the act sought to reconfigure the judicial realm, its practices, and its appointment procedures. Quinche Ramírez (2007: 321) explains that the part of this reform oriented toward the 1991 Constitution seemed to have "a single objective: to make the tutela a merely nominal action of minimal effectiveness."[29] The reform would limit due process claims through the tutela and the *tutela contra sentencias*, in addition to eliminating tutela claims for social and economic rights, specifically undercutting the *conexidad* doctrine.[30]

[28] Uprimny (2005: 7) writes: "Frente a la tutela, los borradores gubernamentales han propuesto sistemáticamente tres estrategias: (i) excluir a las altas cortes de su conocimiento, debido a la congestión que aqueja a esos tribunales; (ii) limitar la procedencia de la tutela en caso de derechos sociales, debido a los desequilibrios económicos provocados por las intervenciones judiciales en ese campo; y (iii), por razones de seguridad jurídica, prohibir la tutela contra providencias judiciales. En algunos de sus borradores, el gobierno ha planteado otras dos reformas: (iv) excluir la tutela para asuntos laborales y (v) que las órdenes judiciales de tutela no puedan modificar los presupuestos ni los planes de desarrollo nacionales o locales."

[29] "[U]n único objetivo: el de hacer de la tutela una acción simplemente nominal de mínima eficacia."

[30] For more on the *conexidad* doctrine, see Chapter 5.

In an interview with Everaldo Lamprea, Manuel José Cepeda, who served on the Constitutional Court between 2001 and 2009, reported that all of the justices on the Court came together regardless of their ideological positions to oppose these reforms. They took a proactive approach, attending academic events and issuing statements to the media about the value of the tutela procedure.[31] For example, the president of the Court at the time, Eduardo Montealegre, gave an interview with *El Tiempo* (Amat 2003), in which he critiqued these proposals, holding that Minister of the Interior Fernando Londoño's real goal was to "end the Constitutional Court":

> But the road goes further: Minister Londoño intends to break the Constitution, with a clear strategy of dismantling the fundamental principles of the Constitution of '91. I say dismantle because he is doing it in parts, in pieces. If one begins to join those pieces, one discovers that he is going after a totally different model of state.

The efforts of the Constitutional Court justices were successful: none of these proposed reforms ever became law.[32] Though Uribe retained much more popular support than Samper, and though his political coalition was often successful in pushing policy through Congress, his attempts to reform the constitutional order also failed. The Uribe administration withdrew the 2002 and 2004 proposals before either was put to a vote (Landau 2014).

That the Uribe administration opposed the Constitutional Court's power and actively undertook efforts to limit it should not be read as implying a harmonious relationship with the other high courts. Javier Revelo-Rebolledo (2008) has documented the extent to which the Uribe administration attempted to influence the working of the Supreme Court in particular, from changing the law as it pertains to sedition (to counteract a Supreme Court decision finding that the crime of sedition did not apply to paramilitary actors) to Uribe himself calling the president of the Supreme Court, César Julio Valencia, to "check on" the status of investigations into the conduct of his cousin. What's more, the Department of Administrative Security (DAS), the state security and intelligence agency, surveilled and

[31] Cited in Lamprea (2015: 87).

[32] The Constitutional Court further declared the government's anti-terror legislation to be unconstitutional and stood in the way of the government's effort to expand its state of emergency powers in 2004.

illegally wiretapped Supreme Court justices while those justices were opening up investigations on members of Congress for their connections to paramilitary groups.[33] Rodrigo Uprimny (Freedom House Freedom House 2011) reports that:

> By July 2011, more than 110 members of Congress were being investigated by the judiciary, especially by the Supreme Court, which is charged with conducting criminal investigations of legislators: 36 have been convicted, 41 were on trial, and 36 more were under formal investigation. Most, though not all, of the investigated or convicted politicians formed part of President Uribe's coalition. Uribe and other officials responded with frequent, vociferous rhetorical attacks on the court – and with or without the president's knowledge – retaliation by the DAS.

Thus, while the Uribe administration and the Supreme Court and Council of State may have shared some goals (e.g., the elimination of the *tutela contra sentencias* and the reduction in the Constitutional Court's powers), they did not form a stable coalition to push for these changes.

In more recent years, as many of the lawyers and legal academics that I interviewed noted, members of Congress who supported these reform efforts seem to have developed a new strategy to try to reduce the power or effect of the Constitutional Court, through "mediocrity-packing." In other words, rather than trying to limit the Court through changes in the institutional structure or through the nomination of formalistic or conservative judges, some members of Congress have tried to cut off the sense of connection between the Constitutional Court and the people by nominating judges who are not viewed as "superstars."[34] It remains to be seen whether or not this strategy will pay off. For now, though, the Constitutional Court and its proponents have won social and political battles throughout the

[33] Activists and opposition leaders were also subject to this surveillance.

[34] Elite interview 20 (September 6, 2016). Some commentators have documented a clear conservative shift in the preferences of nominated judges (Graaff 2012); however, it remains to be seen the extent to which that shift translates into Constitutional Court decisions. Again, the Court's internal culture is understood to be progressive on rights issues, and it appears that conservative justices in the past moderated their views upon appointment to the Court (elite interview 5, August 8, 2016). The absence of "superstar" justices does not, in itself, suggest that so-called normal justices would seek to alter the Court's practices, tendencies, and jurisprudence.

1990s and 2000s that have ensured that social constitutionalism has remained embedded in Colombia.

7.3 *PAIS DE TUTELA* AND THE ENDURANCE OF THE CONSTITUTIONAL ORDER

So, what exactly happened? Why did these criticisms and proposed reforms ultimately fail to meaningful alter the power of the Constitutional Court, the scope of the tutela, or the stability of the constitutional order? In short, constitutional embedding had occurred, in both its social and legal forms. The social element reinforced the legal, as citizens conveyed broad support for the tutela and the Constitutional Court, and the legal element reinforced the social, as judges (especially the justices of the Constitutional Court) legitimated citizen use of the tutela and spoke out in favor of the constitutional order. Attitudes and interests overlapped and compounded one another, such that relatively powerful actors in the legal and political spheres could not chip away at or disembed social constitutionalism in Colombia.

In his 2014 dissertation, David Landau identifies and catalogues the ways in which the Constitutional Court was able to garner public support and weather politically motivated attacks on its power. He explains that "the Court cultivated a number of different bases of support, and these bases of support – elements of the academic community, civil society, and the general public – have protected the Court at key moments" (Landau 2014: 129). Efforts to cultivate these bases of support included direct and indirect efforts at communication with the public, through symbolic decisions, public audiences, and monitoring commissions of civil society groups. The use of these mechanisms allowed the Court to "construct a mobilization of civil society that [would] then pressure the other branches of government" (Landau 2014: 210). In other words, these efforts – rather than "independence by design" or the existence of political fragmentation – enabled the Court to exercise judicial independence and protect itself from both court-curbing and court-packing efforts.

The Constitutional Court also sought to broaden its powers to issue structural decisions in response to tutela claims, through something called the "*estado de cosas inconstitucional*," or state of unconstitutional affairs (Rodríguez Garavito 2009, 2011). The underlying idea is that the individual tutela claims that make it to the Constitutional Court reflect deeper, structural conditions of rights violations – so a structural decision is necessary to remedy those violations. Eduardo Cifuentes wrote the decisions that outline such a state. First, in SU-559/97, a case regarding pensions for educators, he noted that the situation under investigation amounted to a "state of affairs that is openly unconstitutional."[35] In T-153/98, Cifuentes settled on the language of the *estado de cosas inconstitucional*:

> [The Court] has used the unconstitutional state of affairs in order to seek a remedy for situations of violation of fundamental rights that are of a general nature – insofar as they affect a multitude of people – and whose causes are of a structural nature – that is to say that ... their solution requires the joint action of different entities. Under these conditions, the Court has considered that given that thousands of people are in the same situation and that if they all resorted to the tutela, they could unnecessarily congest the administration of justice, the most appropriate thing to do is to issue orders to the competent official institutions with the so that they put into action their powers to eliminate this unconstitutional state of affairs.[36]

Eleven other decisions in 1998 invoked the unconstitutional state of affairs (C-229, SU-250, T-068, T-289, T-296,T-439, T-535, T-559, T-590, T-606, T-607). T-024 of 2004, a case having to do with the rights of internally displaced persons, solidified the figure of the unconstitutional state of affairs. Further, as described in Chapter 5, the Court also issued a structural decision on the healthcare system with T-760/08 (without declaring an unconstitutional state of affairs). Each of these structural decisions undoubtedly impacted public policy and

[35] "[U]n estado de cosas que resulta abiertamente inconstitucional." See the full decision: www.corteconstitucional.gov.co/relatoria/1997/SU559-97.htm.

[36] "Esta Corporación ha hecho uso de la figura del estado de cosas inconstitucional con el fin de buscar remedio a situaciones de vulneración de los derechos fundamentales que tengan un carácter general – en tanto que afectan a multitud de personas – y cuyas causas sean de naturaleza estructural – es decir que, por lo regular, no se originan de manera exclusiva en la autoridad demandada y, por lo tanto, su solución exige la acción mancomunada de distintas entidades. En estas condiciones, la Corte ha considerado que dado que miles de personas se encuentran en igual situación y que si todas acudieran a la tutela podrían congestionar de manera innecesaria la administración de justicia, lo más indicado es dictar órdenes a las instituciones oficiales competentes con el fin de que pongan en acción sus facultades para eliminar ese estado de cosas inconstitucional." See the full decision: www.corteconstitucional.gov.co/relatoria/1998/t-153-98.htm.

government spending,[37] at once propelling the Constitutional Court into debates typically resolved in the legislature rather than the courts and demonstrating to the Colombian citizenry that the Court could be responsive even when other branches of government faltered.

The Court could not have made such aggressive moves in countering the Supreme Court, Council of State, and various presidential administrations had citizens not embraced the Court, which they did primarily through the tutela mechanism. In the early 1990s, citizens did not necessarily understand the purpose, promise, or limits of the tutela, but nonetheless experimented with it. As Julieta Lemaitre describes, "it was more an expression of despair and hope than anything."[38] Yet, as documented in Chapter 4, citizens moved beyond the experimentation stage quickly and adopted use of the tutela into their everyday practices. In an interview in 2016, Diana Fajardo – who worked as a clerk at the Constitutional Court between 2009 and 2013, and who would be appointed to the Court as a justice in 2017 – explained to me that:

> The citizens took ownership of the Constitution, which had never happened before. That is, before only law students read the Constitution. No more. Now you have the common citizen, everyone. It is impressive, they feel their constitution as a birthright, and the tutela is even more untouchable for the Colombian citizen.[39]

In other words, the citizenry embraced the tutela, which rendered the tutela politically untouchable (which in turn ensured a large role for the courts in Colombian life). In an op-ed in *El Espectador* in 2010, Alejandro Gaviria – then the minister of health – lamented

[37] Rodrigo Uprimny (2007) reports that: "According to a report from the Budget Directorate of the Ministry of Finance, presented in October 2004 at a seminar on the topic, the ruling on displaced persons could cost approximately one trillion pesos, that is, nearly 400 million dollars at a revalued rate of 2500 pesos per dollar. And the decision on prisons cost around 300 billion pesos in operating expenses and some 260 billion in investments, that is, a total 560 billion pesos, which is equivalent to approximately 230 million dollars."

[38] Elite interview 20 (September 6, 2016).

[39] Elite interview 40 (September 28, 2016). "[L]os ciudadanos se apropiaran de la Constitución que eso no había ocurrido nunca, es decir, quiénes leían la Constitución, los estudiantes de derecho, no más. Pero ahora tú tienes el ciudadano del común, todo el mundo. Es impresionante, sienten su constitución como un patrimonio y la acción de tutela aún más es una garantía como intocable para el ciudadano colombiano."

that Colombia had become "*el país de la tutela*," or the country of the tutela.[40] Whether one supports the tutela or finds it troubling, its centrality in the Colombian social and legal imaginaries cannot be disputed. The combination of the newly empowered Court and newly empowered citizens – or, stated differently, the combination of legal and social embedding – safeguarded the expansive model of social constitutionalism in Colombia.

[40] His broader critique involves the concern that responding to issues in healthcare after the fact, through the tutela, inhibits effective public health policymaking (Interview 56, November 2, 2016).

CHAPTER EIGHT

CHALLENGES TO EMBEDDING

Workload

The social and legal embedding of the 1991 Colombian Constitution empowered the Constitutional Court with respect to the country's other high courts and the executive and legislative branches of government, as documented in Chapter 7. These other actors at times challenged the constitutional order and sought to reshape the relative power of the Constitutional Court and the tutela procedure. Thus far, though, these challenges have not been sufficient to dislodge social constitutionalism in Colombia.

This chapter turns to an additional set of challenges created by the advance of social constitution and the broadened role it entails for ordinary judges. Ordinary judges are tasked with the daily labor of hearing tutela claims in the first and second instances on top of their other duties. Not only does the tutela bring more work, but tutela decisions also must be given priority over other kinds of cases. Judges have ten days to decide tutelas in the first instance and twenty days in the second, while other legal claims do not come with express time limits. Ordinary judges are the first step in the process of constitutional claim-making through the tutela procedure that eventually leads to the Constitutional Court. If, as shown in Figure 8.1, they are unable or unwilling to keep up with the workload of social constitutionalism – and again, in the Colombian case, that workload is particularly onerous – judicial receptivity to the social constitutionalism at the Constitutional Court and the social construction of legal grievances will not be sufficient to propel a feedback loop and continued claim-making. Citizens may initially make claims and judges may initially be receptive to these claims, but these dynamics may not endure. Whether intentional

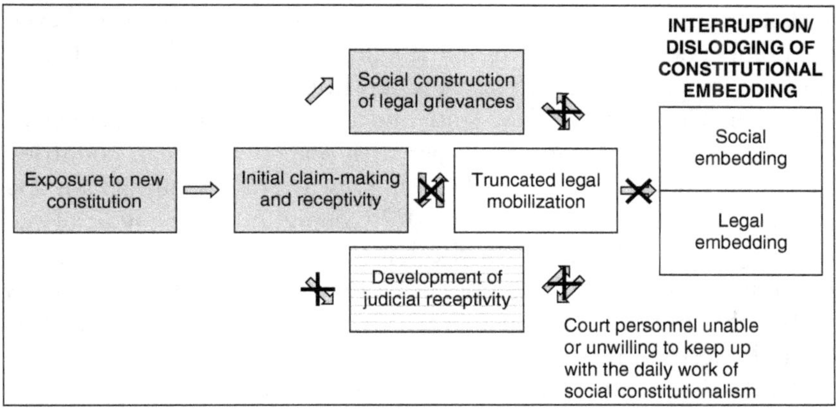

Figure 8.1 Judicial workload and constitutional embedding.
Source: Author's elaboration using data from the Consejo Superior de la Judicatura.

or not, if judges do not provide the procedural experience (i.e., fair, efficient, etc.) or outcomes that claimants seek, the conditions for continued claim-making could break down.

The rest of this chapter documents the daily work of social constitutionalism, tracking geographic and temporal variation where possible. It also chronicles how judges at different levels of the judiciary understand this work and the difficulties that come with it, before moving to a discussion of the consequences of overwork and underdelivery. The chapter closes by noting how social constitutionalism in Colombia endured despite these work-related challenges.

8.1 DAILY WORK: WHAT'S CHANGED?

The 1991 Constitution introduced the new Constitutional Court and the tutela procedure, in the process reshaping the duties of judges throughout the judicial hierarchy. The addition of a new court meant a rearrangement of the judiciary that involved a great deal of tension between the various Colombian high courts (as documented in Chapter 7). For the majority of judges in the country, however, the introduction of the tutela procedure had a much bigger impact. The obligation to offer quick decisions on tutela claims soon came to dominate the daily work of ordinary judges, not just those working in the newly created Constitutional Court.

Every year, the judiciary submits a report to the Congress, which includes a variety of statistics, including the number of judges per

100,000 people, the number of different kinds of claims filed, and even the number of women working in the judiciary. Between 2001 and 2021, these reports noted that there were ten to eleven judges per 100,000 people in Colombia, and at least one judge in every municipality.[1] For perspective, this ratio is on par with several European countries, including France (11.2), Italy (11.9), Norway (11), Spain (11.2), and Sweden (11.6), according to the 2022 Council of Europe judicial systems report.[2] Looking within the Latin American region, the number of judges per 100,000 people in Colombia appears to fall squarely within the middle of the spread: Chile has 6.5 at the low end, while Costa Rica sits at the high end with just under twenty-two.[3]

While the number of judges remained relatively consistent over time, the number of legal cases that these judges were asked to process did not. In 1996, Colombians filed 2,676 legal claims per 100,000 people. That number increased to 4,773 by 2021.[4] This pattern is even more pronounced when we look to tutela claims in particular. There was a slow but steady increase in tutelas from 1992 to 1998, and then the number of claims per year jumps significantly until about 2015. By 2015, Colombians were filing over 600,000 tutela claims each year, in addition to more traditional kinds of legal claims.

What's more, many who filed tutela claims also filed what are called *incidentes de desacato*, or contempt orders, when they believed that the decision in their tutela claim had not been complied with. In 2017 – the first year that such a statistic was included in the report to Congress – about 43 percent of the time those who filed tutela claims also filed *incidentes de desacato*.[5] The rate of filing *incidentes de desacato* has remained relatively steady since then (in 2021 it was 41 percent[6]). The 2021 report suggests that "[t]he high filing rate of *incidentes de desacato* is related to the practice of complying with tutela orders once the contempt claim is in progress, but prior to sanction."[7] The filing of *incidentes de desacato* is particularly common after receiving a positive response to a health tutela claim.

1 Data for years before 2001 are spottily referenced in reports from 2001 and later.
2 According to data collected in 2020 by the European Commission for the Efficiency of Justice (Council of Europe 2002: 46).
3 According to data collected by the Centro de Estudios de Justicia en las Américas in 2008–2009 and published by the Corporación Excelencia en la Justica in 2018.
4 Consejo Superior de la Judicatura (2001: 51; 2021: 20).
5 Consejo Superior de la Judicatura (2017: 14).
6 Consejo Superior de la Judicatura (2021: 72).
7 Consejo Superior de la Judicatura (2021: 74).

Looking subnationally, we see variation in the number of tutela claims filed. Figure 8.2 shows the monthly average number of tutelas filed per 1,000 people in each department between 2003 and 2019, according to judges in the ordinary jurisdiction (i.e., excluding the specialized jurisdictions).[8] These data were collected from the judicial statistics reports posted on the Rama Judicial website. While the rate of claims filed is fairly consistent in some departments, in others we see significant periods of growth or even single-year spikes. The mean number of tutelas filed per 1,000 people per month is 7.1. The highest reported monthly average was 40.3 over the course of 2017 in Caquetá. We also see spikes in tutela claims filed in Antioquia in 2015, Bogotá in 2015, and Sucre in 2010. In short, the workload created by tutela claims is not evenly distributed across the country, and it changes over time in ways that are likely challenging for judges to keep up with or adjust to. We might reasonably expect judges to adapt to the increased workload brought about by the tutela procedure when claim-making rates remain relatively consistent over time, and even when rates increase steadily. What Figure 8.2 shows, however, is that, at least in some years in some departments, there are periods of steep – and potentially unexpected – increases.

It also is clear that claim-making is not simply the product of those living in major cities. While claim-making is prevalent in the departments of Bogotá (home to the country's largest city, Bogotá) and Antioquia (home to the country's second-largest city, Medellín), it is certainly not limited to these two departments. After accounting for population, we see increasingly high rates of claim-making in departments like Caldas, Caquetá, Norte de Santander, and Risaralda. Further, eleven departments (of thirty-three) experienced at least one year in which the average monthly rate of tutelas filed per 1,000 people exceeded fifteen: Antioquia (ten times); Caquetá (nine times); Caldas and Putumayo (five times each); Meta, Quindío, and Risaralda (four times each); Norte de Santander and San Andres y Providencia (three times each); Bogotá and Tolima (twice each); and Arauca, Magdalena, and Sucre (once each).

Figure 8.3 standardizes the claims per 1,000 people filed by the number of ordinary courts in each department.[9] The mean number of tutelas filed per month per ordinary court is 10.5 according to data

[8] In 2016, 86.7 percent of tutelas were initially presented in the ordinary jurisdiction (Consejo Superior de al Judicatura 2016: 153).

[9] No data reported for Amazonas, Guainia, Guaviare, Vaupes, or Vichada.

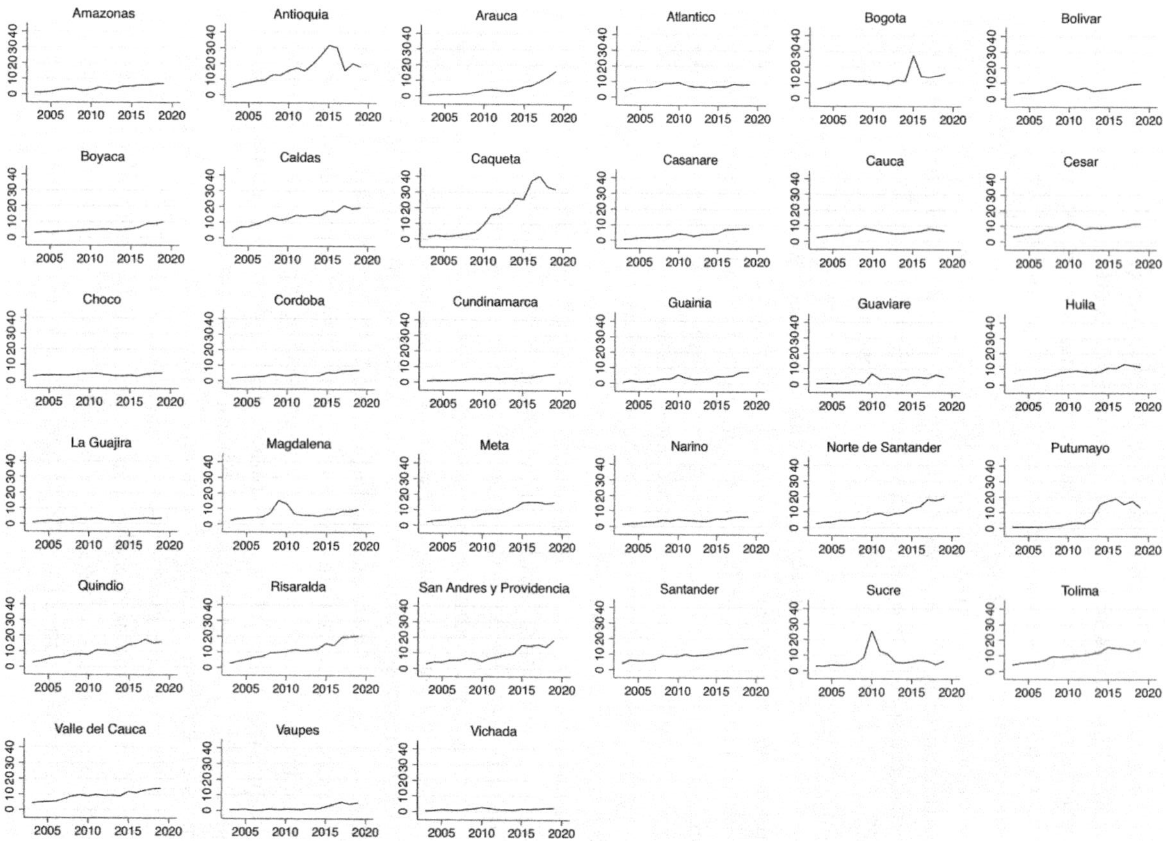

Figure 8.2 Tutela claims per 1,000 people (monthly average).
Source: Author's elaboration using data from the Consejo Superior de la Judicatura.

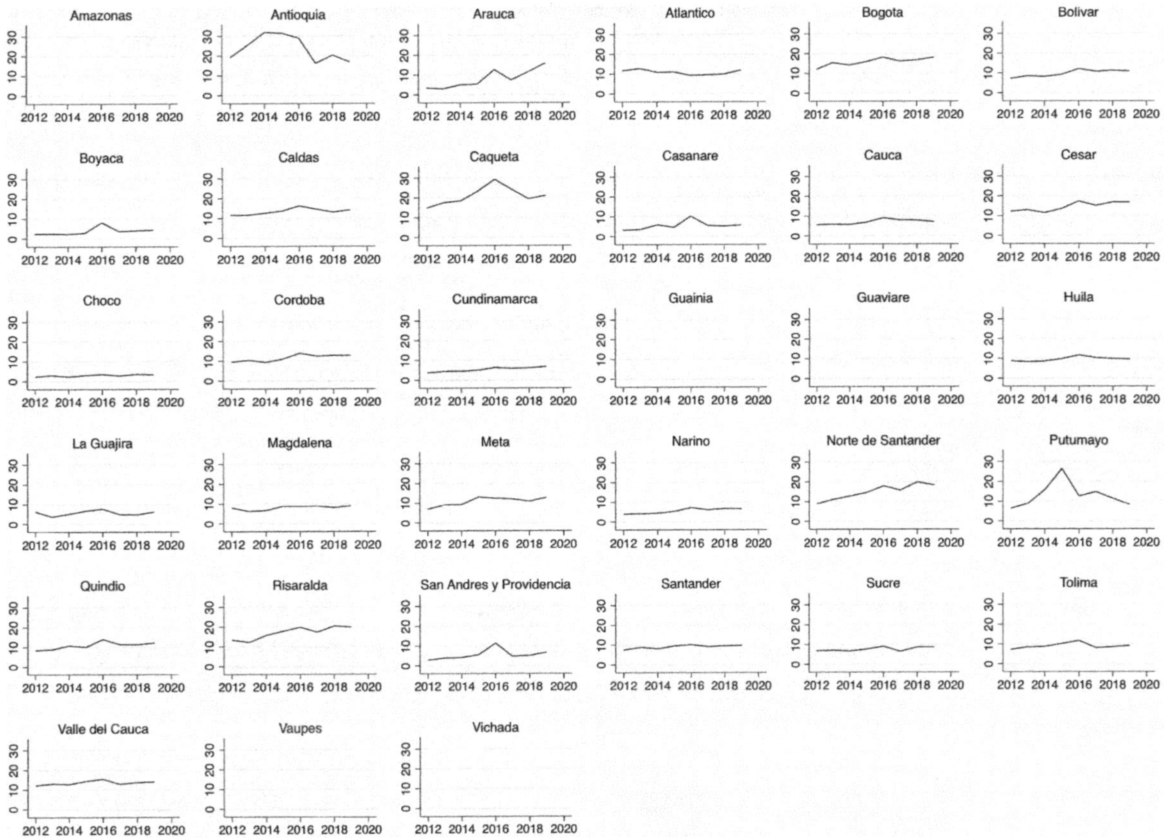

Figure 8.3 Tutela claims per ordinary court (monthly average).
Source: Author’s elaboration using data from the Consejo Superior de la Judicatura.

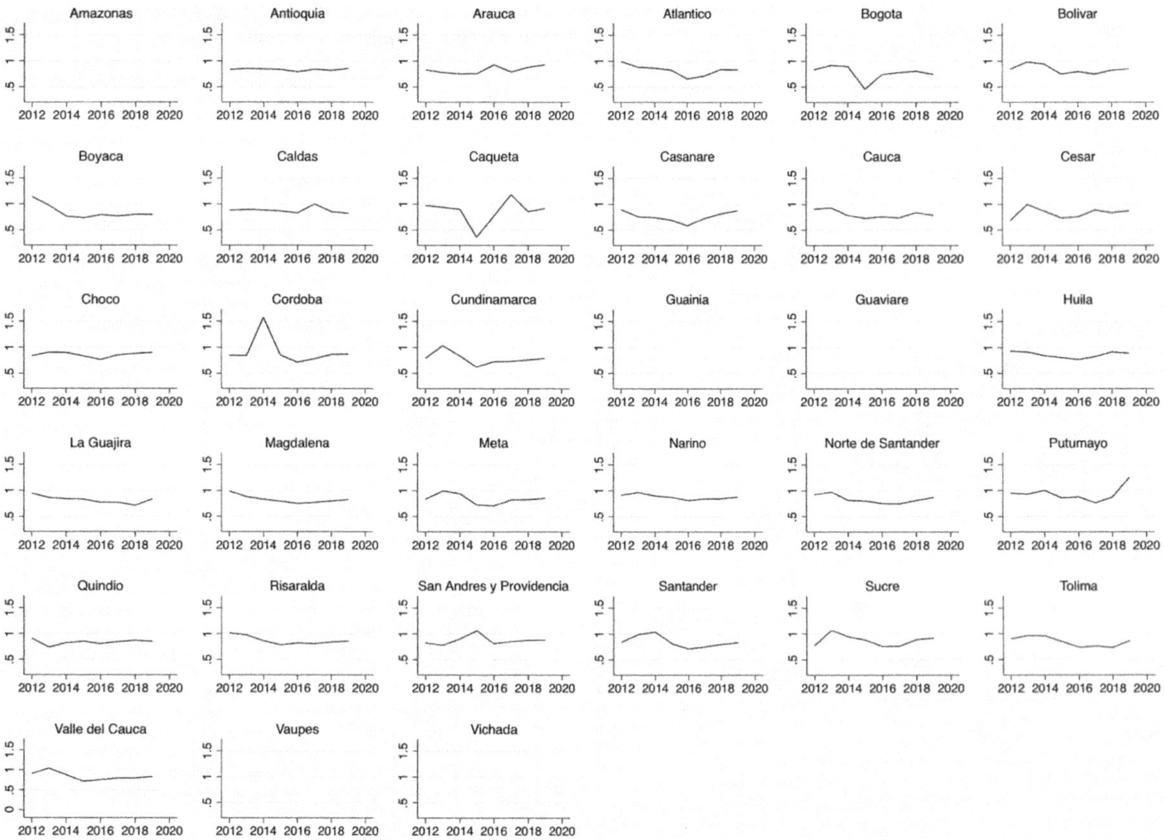

Figure 8.4 Proportion of *procesos* and tutelas cleared (monthly average).
Source: Author's elaboration using data from the Consejo Superior de la Judicatura.

provided by the judges of the ordinary courts, and 8.7 according to data provided by the Defensoría del Pueblo. The maximum number of tutelas filed per month per ordinary court was thirty-two according to the ordinary judges' reports, and thirty-four according to the Defensoría del Pueblo reports. Even partially accounting for the differential opportunity to file claims (theoretically, if there are more courts and more judges, one could more easily file claims), there are differences across departments and over time. For instance, we see more than twenty-five tutelas filed per month per ordinary court in just three departments: Antioquia in each year between 2013 and 2016, Caquetá in 2016, and Putumayo in 2015.

In 2019, the ordinary courts reported an average of 57,854 tutelas coming in each month across the country and 155,154 *procesos* (legal proceedings for claims other than the tutela). Tutelas, thus, made up about 27 percent of the incoming cases for ordinary judges, up from about 24 percent in 2012 (the earliest year for which data reported by ordinary judges are available). Figure 8.4 shows the rate of legal claims *filed* (both tutelas and *procesos*) compared to *decided* each month in each department, as reported by judges working in the ordinary jurisdiction.[10] At least for the period of 2012 to 2019, clearance rates do not seem to be getting worse, and in most departments, the rate seems to be consistent. On average, 85 percent of the legal claims coming in were resolved each month, though there is some variation across courts and departments. While disaggregated data on these trends in earlier years are not available, the Superior Council of the Judiciary reports that in 1997, tutelas made up only 3 percent of total incoming cases, compared to 27 percent in 2019, suggesting a major increase in the proportion of judges' daily work taken up by tutela claims.[11]

8.2 IN THEIR OWN WORDS: ORDINARY JUDGES ON THEIR WORK

Undoubtedly, the introduction of the tutela has created more work for ordinary judges, and that work is not distributed evenly across the country. But to what extent does this extra work pose a problem for judges?

[10] No data reported for Amazonas, Guainia, Guaviare, Vaupes, or Vichada.

[11] Consejo Superior de la Judicatura (2016: 151). See also statistics from spreadsheets posted on the following website: www.ramajudicial.gov.co/web/estadisticas-judiciales/ano-2019.

I turn now to my interviews with lower-court judges in Medellín and Cali for an additional perspective on how judges outside the Colombia Constitutional Court – ones who are tasked with the initial tutela decision-making – understand this work. Importantly, these views do not necessarily reflect the modal understanding of the tutela procedure among lower-court judges, but they do offer insight into some of the challenges posed by the tutela procedure for judges.

First, the quantity of the work is overwhelming at times. Further, many interviewees noted that lower-court judges have not necessarily studied constitutional law or the specific subjects invoked in tutela claims. This concern came up for many of the criminal law judges I interviewed. For example, Albeiro Marín explained how this workload can come to be all-encompassing. He noted that "tutelas, criminal proceedings, sentences, incidents of contempt, all of this is resolved simultaneously. There are too many tasks at the same time, so another issue appears that seems very important to me is the judicial error, the great possibility of judicial error."[12] Cristian Cabezas stressed the gap in knowledge that many judges will have on matters related to tutela claims:

> Not all judges are experts in constitutional law … Through the tutela action we can get involved in all the processes that involve fundamental rights. A criminal law judge like me, who knows and has specialized in criminal law, who works every day in criminal law, may be forced to resolve a matter of labor law, civil law, social security, administrative law.[13]

Similarly, Juan Sebastián Tisnés noted the potential costs of this lack of expertise:

> The cost is sometimes very serious. I am not necessarily an expert in health, right? So, I think that there should be specialized judges in

[12] Elite interview (April 25, 2017). "[T]utelas, procesos penales, sentencias, la tutela tiene a su vez el incidente de desacato y todo eso se resuelve de manera simultánea eso simultáneo es muy importante porque son demasiadas tareas al mismo tiempo de modo que aparece otro tema que me parece muy importante es el error judicial la gran posibilidad del error judicial."

[13] Elite interview 80 (April 18, 2017). "No todos los jueces son expertos en derecho constitucional. Hay un problema y tiene algo que ver con un aspecto que es el siguiente, como a través de la acción de tutela podemos involucrarnos en todos los procesos que involucren derechos fundamentales un juez penal como yo, que sabe y se ha especializado penal, que todos los días trabaja derecho penal puede verse obligado a resolver un asunto de derecho laboral, de derecho civil, de seguridad social, de derecho administrativo."

> tutelage but since there are not, and we cannot deny justice, we have to learn [on the job] ... There are areas in which you are more comfortable, in my case, for example, criminal law. I prefer to go to those hearings all day than to decide tutela claims, because there I feel like a fish in water. When deciding tutelas, not so much, but because I have to do it, because it is part of my job, I do it.[14]

In addition, Cabezas noted that:

> I spend all day processing the criminal cases, and the I must race to process the tutela claims. Many times, I cannot spend the same amount of time on the tutela as I do on the on analysis that I do for the criminal processes. On many occasions, tutelas solutions may not protect rights to the extent that they should, but it precisely has to do with the workload. If we process seven criminal proceedings a day and then all the tutelas sentences, that implies a great load. The tutela has an impact, I would not dare to say negatively, but it has an impact on the workload.[15]

The risk here is that mistakes might occur, or that some judges may choose to cut corners given this crunch. In fact, one person who worked in the Constitutional Court as a law student shared with me her frustration that many incoming tutelas seemed to include passages

[14] Elite interview 72 (March 15, 2017). "Creo que debería haber jueces solo de tutelas, es decir, jueces que se dediquen solo a fallar tutelas particularmente porque es una especialidad como lo digo difícil, los derechos que se discuten o lo que está en entredicho, es algo que le cuesta a la gente y cuando digo que le cuesta es que la decepción a veces es muy grave no hablo necesariamente de salud ¿cierto? Entonces pienso que sí debería haber jueces especializados en tutela pero ya que no los hay nosotros no podemos denegar justicia pues tenemos que aprender pienso que la labor que a uno la encomienden uno la debe cumplir y si tu como juez no eres capaz de ser juez de tutela vete, lo digo porque hay cosas en las que nos movemos más fácil que en otras, mi caso por ejemplo es el derecho penal, prefiero ir a audiencia todo el día que sacar tutelas porque me siento ahí como pez en el agua en las tutelas no tanto pero ya que lo tengo que hacer y que es parte de mi trabajo lo hago pero si considero que debería haber jueces de tutela."

[15] Elite interview 80 (April 18, 2017). "Estoy todo el día tramitando los procesos penales y subo a la carrera a tramitar los procesos de tutela, muchas veces no se tiene el mismo tiempo de análisis del proceso penal para el de tutela; en muchas ocasiones las soluciones de tutela tal vez no protegen los derechos en la medida que debieran hacerlo pero precisamente tiene que ver con esa carga laboral, si tramitamos siete procesos penales al día y tengo que dictar sentencia, siete sentencias penales y además todas las sentencias de tutela, eso implica una gran carga. La acción de tutela impacta, no me atrevería a decir que negativamente, pero impacta la carga laboral."

that had been copied and pasted from previous claims (with the wrong names and facts).[16]

Other judges suggested that the time crunch also worked in the opposite way: responding to so many tutela claims inhibited their ability to devote as much time as they would have liked to the other legal claims they were tasked with adjudicating. One succinctly asserted that the quantity of tutela claims "leads to the neglect of other processes." While these other claims are not tutelas, "claimants have their right to have their problems solved, because if they come here to seek solutions to problems, it also requires a quick solution."[17] Here, the claim is that the extra workload created in tasking judges with deciding both tutela claims and typical legal claims at once puts judges in a difficult position, as they have to decide where to cut corners.

Viviana Bernal, a judge working in the labor courts in Cali, concluded that in order to be a good judge of the tutela, you must be something of an autodidact, "because the tutela actions are so unpredictable, and they require your immediate attention. You do not know what will happen, and you do not know what [kinds of requests] people are going to present to you."[18] Carlos Rodríguez, a criminal law judge, concurred, explaining that "you have to review constitutional jurisprudence daily. The Constitutional Court is always giving an interpretation of fundamental rights and how they apply to each specific case."[19] In order to avoid making errors, deciding cases incorrectly, and doing a disservice to claimants, ordinary judges across specialties must study constitutional matters.

Another judge commented that one of the most difficult parts of his job was "the drama of the tutela and *incidentes de desacato*, which

[16] Fieldnotes (March 30, 2017). I do not have a good sense of how frequently this kind of thing occurred, but others also suggested that this may have happened from time to time.

[17] Elite interview 85 (April 25, 2017). "Porque las tutelas es la mayor carga laboral que tiene un juzgado, siendo la mayor carga laboral que tiene un juzgado da lugar a que se descuide los otros procesos dónde también, aunque no son tutelas los usuarios tienen su derecho a que se les solucionen sus problemas porque si vienen acá a buscar solución de los problemas, también requiere que sea una solución rápida."

[18] Elite interview 79 (April 6, 2017). "Yo diría que es un requisito para tu ser un buen juez de tutela pues primero porque existe la forma autodidacta de aprenderlo y segundo porque las acciones de tutela son tan imprevisibles que requieren de tu compromiso en el momento. No sabes que te va a llegar y no sabes con qué se te va a presentar la gente."

[19] Elite interview 87 (April 25, 2017). "Usted diariamente tenga que revisar jurisprudencia constitucional. La Corte Constitucional siempre esté dando una interpretación de los derechos fundamentales y cómo se aplican a cada caso concreto."

do not stop being dramatic – that a person needs a health service and they are denied it."[20] He was alluding to the fact that oftentimes, one tutela order is not enough to ensure compliance, even though the medicine or procedure sought might be time-sensitive. Instead, the claimant must seek a contempt order in the hope that the second order or a more severe penalty will prompt compliance. Not only does this impact the claimant, but it also increases the workload of the judges involved.

Andrés López, a judge working in Puerto Tejada, explained in detail some of the challenges that come with contempt orders. For one, the teeth behind the contempt order lie in the ability to arrest someone for noncompliance. However, in order to deprive someone of liberty (i.e., arrest them) in this case, the judge must notify that person directly:

> [For example,] I personally must notify a man [whose company is based] in Bogotá and he is never there, so it is useless for me to send the notification to the company's address, not if he has to be present to receive it ... Sometimes the tutela even gets canceled. The Circuit Court cancels tutelas, because they say that I did not notify the implicated person, I did not guarantee the right of defense ... because I had to notify them personally there in the entity that there was a tutela. Then there are [other] notification problems because one calls an entity to fax it and everything, to the manager, let's say in Popayán [a city located about 100 kilometers from where López works], and they say that the fax does not go through, that there is no fax. You have to notify them quickly, and if you send it by official mail and it takes many days, so you would have to resort to sending it by private mail.[21]

[20] Elite interview 72 (March 15, 2017). "El drama de las tutelas y los incidentes de desacato, que no deja de ser dramático que una persona necesite un servicio de salud y se lo nieguen porque sí, me parece dramático eso."

[21] Elite interview 83 (April 21, 2017). "El problema ha sido que en el incidente de desacato para privar de la libertad la corte también ha buscado la garantía de la persona y como es una privación de la libertad usted debe notificarlo personalmente, como notifico personalmente a un señor por Bogotá y que no está nunca allí entonces no me sirve que le mande la notificación a la dirección de la empresa, no que tiene que ser presente, y cómo si eso es absurdo, a veces se pasan de la garantía. Considero que por ejemplo en esas situaciones, pasa también con los correos electrónicos y a veces el circuito me ha anulado tutelas porque dicen que no lo notifiqué, no garanticé el derecho de defensa de la entidad ... porque debía notificarlo personalmente allá en la entidad de que había una tutela entonces hay problemas de notificación porque de pronto uno llama a una entidad para pasarlo por fax y todo, al gerente digamos que en Popayán y dicen que no pasa el fax, que no hay fax, y uno tiene que notificarla rápido, entonces uno lo manda por correo oficial y este se demora muchos días por eso se tendría que recurrir por mandarlo por correo particular."

From there, you would need to get some kind of assurance that the mail was both delivered and received. Email does not seem to work either, frustrating López even further: "It does not make sense if we are in the twenty-first century and technology is designed to speed up things like this. They give me an email for an entity that provides public services … I don't care if the person working there saw it and didn't read it. That's his problem."[22] But, of course, it is López's problem too, given the rules around notification, and there is no blanket policy that will perfectly balance the protection of the rights of the accused and prevent the manipulation of procedural rules by those who wish to avoid legal sanction. Other judges told me about making phone calls to try to ensure that tutela orders were received and understood, and one even described making regular trips down to the various medical offices to follow up on his orders.

All of this extra work must happen on a judge's own time, in addition to carrying out their other duties. Some judges may enjoy and have time for this extra work, but others may not, creating another source of inconsistency and inefficiency in the tutela process. As Albeiro Marín, who works in the town of Palmira, explained:

> One of the delicate things as a judge is that one is a human being, a human being full of needs, [needing] to be with the family on the weekend, to go out and have a little leisure time, like any normal person. Something complicated happens here, you work from Monday to Friday officially from eight in the morning to five in the afternoon, but you have to take work home at night and on Saturday and Sunday, too. So not only is it the workplace but also the personal sphere that is totally permeated and affected by your job.[23]

[22] Elite interview 83 (April 21, 2017). "No tiene sentido si estamos en el siglo 21 y la tecnología está diseñada para agilizar las cosas cómo me dan a mí un correo electrónico de una entidad que presta servicios públicos y tengo que considerar que con el solo envío él tiene su deber de revisar su correo a mí no me interesa si lo vio y no lo leyó ese es problema suyo."

[23] Elite interview (April 25, 2017). "Una de las cosas delicadas para uno como juez es que es uno es un ser humano elemental, un ser humano lleno de necesidades sí, de familia, de estar con la familia el fin de semana, de salir a recrearse un poco como cualquier funcionario normal; aquí pasa una cosa complicada se trabaja de lunes a viernes oficialmente de 8 de la mañana a 5 de la tarde pero tienes que llevar trabajo a tu casa en la noche y el sábado y domingo también de manera que digamos que caemos en otro ámbito ya no en el laboral sino en el ámbito personal que está totalmente permeado y afectado por la situación laboral."

This work overload is exacerbated by the particular conditions judges face in their jurisdiction. Marín continued, explaining that no matter how intelligent or diligent a judge is, the workload can be too much:

> How is a reasonable amount of work for a judge going to be determined in Colombia? Because it is not possible. A judge in Palmira, for example, which experiences so much crime, receives 1,000 cases, and a judge from Buga, which is a quieter town, can easily have [just] 200 cases, no more, yes? So how do they demand so much of me? So, for example, here we were three judges bearing that extremely high load, all with an average until recently of 800 cases, 400 prisoners, plus tutelas, incidents of contempt, and other series of activities that you also have to be studying.[24]

Not everyone I interviewed faced these kinds of pressures, and some spoke about making tutela decisions as relatively routine, rather than burdensome. What is key here is that at least some judges in some parts of Colombia see the tutela as creating additional work that makes it challenging for them to do their jobs effectively – in deciding matters that fall within their specialty (like criminal or civil matters) and in deciding tutela claims.

Overall, though, the introduction of the tutela presented new challenges to judges as they sought to carry out their daily work. The timing of tutela decisions as well as the subject matter pushed judges to do not only more work than they had previously but also to engage in different legal topics that some of the time might be outside their expertise. To sum up his views on the effects of the tutela procedure, one judge referenced the phrase made famous by the poet Guillermo Valencia during Rafael Uribe Uribe's funeral – "blessed be democracy, even though it may kill us" – suggesting "blessed be the tutela, even though

[24] Elite interview (April 25, 2017). "¿Cómo se va a determinar una carga razonable para un juez en Colombia? Porque no es posible que un juez en Palmira por ejemplo que es tan de alta delincuencia le lleguen 1000 carpetas y a un juez de Buga que es un pueblo más tranquilo y el juez puede tener tranquilamente 200 carpetas no más ¿sí? Entonces cómo me exigen a mí tanto, cómo me hacen exigente esa carga laboral cuando no hay parámetros entonces por ejemplo aquí éramos tres jueces soportando esa carga altísima todos con un promedio hasta hace poco de 800 carpetas, 400 presos, más las tutelas, los incidentes y otras series de actividades que también hay que estar estudiando luego en el día uno puede hacer cincuenta mil cosas y todo tan normal pero rápido, claro estoy de acuerdo si el juez está capacitado puede exigírselo pero un momento hay parámetros porque también la fatiga del ser humano está allí patente por más inteligente que sea."

it may kill us."[25] Typically, interviewees – both those working at the Constitutional Court and those working elsewhere in the legal system – evaluated the tutela positively, pointing to the immense advances in access to justice brought about by the mechanism, though many also recommended revisions to the way that tutelas are processed in the hopes of reducing congestion in the legal system. The most common suggestion involved the creation of a specialized set of judges whose only job would be to review and decide tutela cases.

8.3 OVERWORK, UNDERDELIVERY, AND THE ENDURANCE OF SOCIAL CONSTITUTIONALISM

The concern here as it relates to the stability of the constitutional order is twofold. First, if judges are unable or unwilling to keep up with the work of tutela decisions, the tutela and rights claim-making may lose significance in people's everyday lives. Equally important is the issue that judges cannot compel compliance, even with contempt orders. To the extent that tutela decisions are understood to be insufficient (whether because judges offer the "wrong" remedies or because of non-compliance), unmet expectations may come to undermine social constitutionalism. If people turn away from legal mobilization, from using the tutela, the feedback processes that serve to embed social constitutionalism will falter. However, thus far, these challenges related to work and workload have not overcome the countervailing, embedding forces behind the 1991 Constitution.

In terms of the first concern, it appears that much of the time judges are, in fact, keeping up with the extra work of social constitutionalism. Referring back to Figure 8.4, at least for the last ten years or so, judges have been relatively consistent in terms of the percentage of both tutela claims and *procesos* they clear each month (despite some variation across departments). We might think that this relative consistency is due to the combination of normative and coercive incentives. Most of the judges I spoke with shared a desire to do a good job and indicated that they viewed their job as an especially important one. Many also reflected that they were constrained by the rules regarding the tutela. Carlos Rodríguez explained that the tutela primarily impacted his work

25 Elite interview 74 (March 22, 2017). "Me ha gustado que he dicho algo como emulando a un viejo político colombiano que decía él 'bendita sea democracia así nos mates' y yo diría 'bendita seas tutela así nos mates.'"

in that, when a tutela claim is filed, "you have to put aside many things you are doing to dedicate yourself to that issue, and the tutela covers any possible issue … it can be pension issues, purely labor issues, social security issues that are very technical, issues related to the right to water, [or] right to public services that are very technical."[26] If you failed to do so, you might be subject to serious penalties. Jorge Montes, who worked in a judge's chambers in Cali, described a similar concern:

> What we fear the most is violating the terms of the tutela. That is why the tutela has been effective, because we fear that. So, there is no excuse. I'll give you an example, when I was an assistant to a judge, I could have four or five tutelas that needed to be decided in one day. It was no excuse to say, "I have five tutelas." You had to do them. I had to take tutelas home [after my normal workday].[27]

Finalizing the tutela decision late was not an option. Johnny Braulio Romero shared what happens if he submits tutela decisions late (i.e., after more than ten days):

> I can be suspended from my position for a month, two months, a year, depending on how serious the offense was. In the case of the tutela, as it is about defending fundamental rights, it is assumed that they cannot wait. I cannot decide [those claims] whenever I want. If there is one thing that the judges respect in Bogotá, Amazona, the coast, wherever, it is the term to resolve a tutela, because being a day late means that they can sanction you, and the sanctions are very severe, and nobody wants that.[28]

[26] Elite interview 87 (April 25, 2017). "Uno tiene que dejar muchas cosas que está haciendo para dedicarse a realizar ese tema y digamos la tutela abarca cualquier tema posible … puede ser temas de pensiones, temas netamente laborales, de seguridad social que es muy técnico, temas digamos del derecho al agua, derecho al servicio público que son muy técnicos."

[27] Elite interview 84 (April 24, 2017). "Lo que más le tenemos miedo es violar los términos del fallo para la acción de tutela. Por eso es que la tutela ha sido efectiva, porque nosotros le tememos a eso. Entonces no hay excusa. Te pongo un ejemplo, cuando yo era el asistente de un juez con el que trabajaba, yo podía tener para un mismo día cuatro o cinco tutelas. Pues no había excusa de decir: 'Es que yo tengo cinco tutelas.' Tú las tenías que sacar o sacar. Me tocaba llevarme tutelas para la casa."

[28] Elite interview 71 (March 10, 2017). "Me pueden suspender del cargo por un mes, dos meses, un año dependiendo de qué tan grave fue la falta, tratándose de tutela como se trata de defender derechos fundamentales se supone que esto no da espera entonces no lo puedo decidir cuando quiera, si hay una cosa que los jueces respetan en Bogotá, Amazona, Costa, donde sea es el termino para resolver una tutela, porque pasarse un día implica que te pueden sancionar, y las sanciones son muy fuertes y nadie quiere eso."

While not every judge brought up possible suspension, all noted that the tutela decisions must be made within ten days and that the decisions must be in line with the Constitutional Court's jurisprudence. It appears that judges have kept up with the work of the tutela, at least well enough. The rules regarding the tutela and the expectations judges have about their work have ensured that judicial receptivity endures.

Further, the interconnections between the tutela, health, and the new constitution seem to have mitigated the second concern about perceptions of judicial work. Many folks continue to view the formal legal system as too slow, as corrupted, or as otherwise ineffective overall, and that does drive some to seek alternatives. As Juan Sebastián Tisnés told me:

> When I worked in a small town, someone asked me, "Judge, I have a bill of exchange that Don Carlos owes me, how long does that process take here [if I try to resolve it through the courts]?" So, I told them, "It depends, but it will last eight months or a year." They said, "*yo mejor voy abajo*" [literally, I better go downstairs]. To go downstairs is to go to the guerrillas. It is faster there, and I say this without blushing, all the principles established in the civil code, the guerrillas respected, except if you take the case there, they charge you, but otherwise all concentration, speed, everything was carried out … There was coercion because people could lose their lives for not paying the debt … There are things that prevent people from having a good image of us [the judiciary], for example, the time it takes for judicial decisions to be pronounced, the accumulation of cases that then causes the postponement of hearings, the corruption that exists in the judicial branch.[29]

[29] Elite interview 72 (March 15, 2017). "Cuando trabaje en pueblito la gente le preguntaba a uno 'juez tengo una letra de cambio y un título en efectivo que me lo debe Don Carlos ¿Cuánto tiempo demora ese proceso aquí?' entonces les digo 'depende de algunas vicisitudes propias del proceso durará ocho meses o un año' y la gente decía 'yo mejor voy abajo' abajo es la guerrilla porque allá es más rápido y lo digo sin sonrojarme, todos los principios que establece o establecía el código de procedimientos civiles allá en la guerrilla se respetaban excepto gratuidad porque si llevabas el caso allá te cobraban pero de resto todo concentración, celeridad, todo se cumplía porque eran juicios de una y si había coacción porque la gente podía perder la vida por no pagar la deuda entonces todos los principios excepto, insisto gratuidad. Hay cosas que impiden que la gente tenga buena imagen de nosotros por ejemplo el tiempo para toma de decisiones judiciales para proferirse eso también esta mediado por el cumulo de procesos que tenemos por todo lo que aplazan las audiencias, por la corrupción que hay en la rama judicial."

This frustration and disenchantment that citizens express about the formal legal system, however, has not spilled over into the realm of the tutela. Instead, as described in Chapter 4, thinking about the use of the tutela seems to be more ambivalent than anything – folks are not sure it will work, but they might as well try (see also Taylor 2018). The 1991 Constitution has become embedded in people's understanding of their social worlds, yet that embedding has not come with raised expectations. As a result, expectations have not been undercut or unmet and hopes have not been dashed. So far, ambivalent legal mobilization and its influence on how everyday Colombians and judicial officials understand the 1991 Constitution has been able to counteract the challenges presented by the everyday work of social constitutionalism.

CHAPTER NINE

PARTIAL CONSTITUTIONAL EMBEDDING

The Case of South Africa

On the one hand, I think people think that the Constitutional Court and the law are very powerful things and then the other hand, do they really translate into effects for anyone?[1]
Former clerk for Constitutional Court Justice Bess Nkabinde

The preceding chapters of this book theorized the concept of constitutional embedding and documented how both of its components – social and legal embedding – occurred in Colombia, such that the 1991 Constitution could weather strong challenges to its status and influence. The key argument of the book is that constitutional embedding is necessary for constitutional rights to be meaningful in everyday life. It holds that constitutional embedding comprises two dimensions: social and legal. The social dimension of constitutional embedding references the degree to which individuals and groups come to understand and relate to the Constitution in an intimate and everyday way, and legal embedding references the degree to which actors in the formal legal sphere accept and share a particular vision of constitutional law. Where the social and legal dimensions of constitutional embedding reinforce one another, a constitutional order will be likely to endure and difficult to dislodge.

This chapter, drawing on one year of fieldwork in South Africa – including eighty interviews with eighty-eight judges, lawyers, professors, and activists, an original survey, and participant observation – conducted between 2017 and 2018, extends the argument of this book to the case of the 1996 South African Final Constitution. In South Africa, we see clear

[1] Elite interview 121 (August 29, 2017).

evidence of legal embedding, with Constitutional Court justices and their law clerks – who would go on to serve as prominent members of the legal profession – adopting and developing a particular vision of constitutional law that would be at once responsive to citizens' needs and largely deferential to the executive branch's policy preferences. Social embedding, however, has lagged. While NGOs and legal aid organizations supported some litigants in harnessing the power of the law, rights claiming through the courts did not become a fixture of everyday life outside of law schools and courtrooms. Without each type of embedding reinforcing the other, the depth of the impact of constitutional change is limited. The constitutional text still promotes a transformative vision, but imagined – and imaginable – social and legal changes are hampered by this partial embedding.

9.1 WHY LOOK TO SOUTH AFRICA?

Colombia, South Africa, and India have long been held up as models of social constitutionalism (see, e.g., Bonilla 2013). While the Indian constitution recognizes social rights only as directive principles, both Colombia and South Africa adopted new constitutions in the early to mid-1990s that recognized a wide range of rights, including social rights, and offered opportunities to make legal claims to those rights before new constitutional courts. The key difference between Colombia and South Africa in terms of their social constitutionalist impulses lies in the Colombian adoption of the tutela procedure that allows individuals to make rights claims without the need for a lawyer or the ability to pay fees. Judges must process these claims within ten days. While South Africa did adopt various strategies to increase access to justice, they fall well short of the tutela procedure in terms of speed and cost.

Further, Colombia and South Africa appear very similar with respect to the structural indicators measuring economic (upper-middle income and increasing) and human development (high and increasing), inequality (high and relatively stable), and levels of violence (high but decreasing) over the last three decades. Yet, even in the midst of these structural similarities, the two countries have been defined by substantially different state configurations, different party systems, and different historical legacies. The South African National Party implemented apartheid in 1948, developing a state that at the same time was highly legalistic, violent, and discriminatory toward nonwhite South

Africans, while featuring an interventionist, welfare-oriented economy policy for white South Africans (see, e.g., Abel 1995; Meierhenrich 2010; Nattrass and Seekings 2011). Just ten years later, a different form of exclusionary governance was formed in Colombia, with the National Front Agreement, which mandated power sharing between the Liberal and Conservative parties and further marginalized those outside of these traditional networks of power. Around the same time, guerrilla groups took up arms in a revolutionary challenge to the state (e.g., Palacios 2006; Tate 2007). Apartheid and the anti-apartheid struggle indelibly marked South African political development, as did the protracted war between the revolutionary left and the state, albeit in different ways. Following the end of apartheid, the African National Congress (ANC) has dominated South African politics, certainly at the national level and to a large extent at the provincial level, rendering the country a de facto one-party democracy.[2] On the other hand, the historical dominance of the Liberal and Conservative parties in Colombia has faltered, with the Colombian party system veering toward deinstitutionalization (Mainwaring 2006; Morgan 2013; Albarracín et al. 2018).

Citizens in both Colombia and South Africa pushed for fundamental changes to the state, and especially its foundational legal order, in the early 1990s, and in response, policymakers adopted new constitutions in both countries. As in South Africa, Colombia had been historically defined by its longstanding – if differently operationalized – commitment to formalism in law. Yet, the combination of decades of war between leftist guerrillas and the state that showed little sign of abating, a consistently unresponsive legislature, and the emergence of a student movement, comprised largely of law students, resulted in demand for a new legal experiment that would ultimately recognize a new set of rights and empower the judiciary (Dugas 2001b; Lemaitre 2009). Interestingly, as Jens Meierhenrich (2010) demonstrates, in South Africa, features of the apartheid state actually promoted shared stabilizing expectations among the elites, many of whom trained as lawyers, about the role of law in the transition to inclusive democracy. In this context, a basic level of confidence in the idea of law and constitutional rights permeated throughout society, regardless of race. Further, the Constitutional Court – at least initially – was understood and understood itself to be engaging in a joint constitutional project

[2] This dominance has faltered of late, however.

with the other branches of government (Fowkes 2016). Considering these factors, the empowerment of the courts, the recognition of social rights, and citizen trust in the legal process are less surprising that they might initially appear.

The rest of the chapter turns first to the emergence of social constitutionalism in South Africa, before looking to legal embedding and then social embedding. It closes with a discussion of the consequences of partial embedding.

9.2 THE EMERGENCE OF SOCIAL CONSTITUTIONALISM IN SOUTH AFRICA

Much like the 1991 Colombian Constitution, the South African Final Constitution of 1996 (building on the 1993 Interim Constitution) set out a social orientation for law that its designers hoped would help the country to transform.[3] In South Africa, as in Colombia, transnational ideas about rights and constitutionalism – specifically regarding the entrenchment of social rights and the creation of constitutional courts – found fertile ground following domestic pressure for legal and social change (Klug 2000). Various facets of the anti-apartheid movement called for a refounding of the South African state, specifically a fundamental change in the legal architecture of the state. During the constitutional negotiations, the language of internationally or "universally" accepted rights was commonplace. Political elites and appointed experts explicitly sought examples from international law, as well as from the Canadian Charter and the German Basic Law, setting the stage for the adoption of a social constitution. In what follows, I provide an overview of the debates around social constitutionalism during the constitutional negotiations of the early 1990s in South Africa, which will then allow me to assess the extent to which this vision of constitutional law has become embedded socially and legally in the country.

These negotiations took place between 1990 and 1993, and they included the Conventions for a Democratic South Africa and the Multi-Party Negotiating Process.[4] The resulting Interim Constitution of 1993 introduced judicial review, created the Constitutional Court,

[3] For more on "transformative constitutionalism," see Klare (1998).

[4] For more detailed accounts of these negotiations, see Mandela (1995), Sparks (1995), Klug (2000: chapter 4), and Meierhenrich (2010), among numerous other sources

and established a Bill of Rights.[5] This Bill of Rights did not include robust social rights protections, but neither did it preclude them from being added later in the Final Constitution, which is precisely what occurred. Following the establishment of the Interim Constitution, a constitutional assembly consisting of both houses of the newly elected Parliament was convened to draft a Final Constitution, which would be certified by the newly created Constitutional Court.

As part of this final drafting process, the major political parties established several theme committees, which were tasked with providing expert advice on constitutional design questions, including on the inclusion and scope of rights protections. Theme Committee 4 handled these rights questions. The First Report of Theme Committee 4 in January 1995 notes that all of the parties to the Constitutional Assembly agreed in principle that the Universal Declaration of Human Rights (1948) and the International Covenants on Civil and Political Rights and Economic, Social, and Cultural Rights (1966) could "be used as important references for identifying universally accepted fundamental rights," that "[t]he Bill of Rights should be entrenched, justiciable and enforceable," and that the final list of included rights should not be limited to the rights listed in the Interim Constitution (41–42). This last point was important in that the Interim Constitution recognized a rather limited set of social rights (including basic education and an "environment which is not detrimental to … health or well-being").

All of the major parties submitted documents outlining their preferences regarding constitutional rights protections to the Theme Committee 4. The ANC's preliminary submission to the committee, entitled "Our Broad Vision of a Bill of Rights for South Africa,"[6] indicated deep support for a substantive set of social rights, as well as a clear role for the courts in helping to realize those rights (48–49). The Inkatha

[5] For Ginsburg (2003: 55), South Africa's adoption of judicial review was a "textbook example of the insurance theory," wherein minority veto players seek out judicial review to protect their interests from a dominant majority in the future. Yet, insurance theory cannot account for the shift to social constitutionalism in particular – white South Africans may have sought limits on the ANC's power, but they were not expressly concerned with the broad realization of the rights to health, housing, or education, for example.

[6] This document is distinct from the document, "A Bill of Rights for a New South Africa," referenced at the start of this section. Part of the Constitutional Assembly Theme Committee 4 Fundamental Rights Report on Block 1 (Constitutional Court archives, 46–48).

Freedom Party (IFP) and Pan African Congress (PAC) also advocated for the inclusion of justiciable social rights, expressly noting that the Bill of Rights should be geared toward supporting the well-being of citizens. The IFP's proposal suggested that the Constitution should allow for "the updating and evolution of human rights protections, which are historically an ever changing field of law," and called for the Constitution to recognize "all fundamental human rights and all those other rights which are inherent to fundamental human needs and aspirations as they evolve with the changes and growth of society" (59).[7] The PAC called for the creation of "an institution modeled along the lines of the European Human Rights Commission" to help with what they called the "practical enforceability" of rights.[8]

The Democratic Party, on the other hand, raised a number of concerns about the separation of powers and enforceability of rights. Their submission held that "policy formation – from the detailed provision of health services to the allocation of housing – is preserve of parliament, not the constitution" and suggested that relatively few civil and political rights be explicated in the Bill of Rights. They also noted, however, that "because the promises of a Bill of Rights could be empty, cruel words echoing in a wasteland of deprivation and denial, the Bill must provide for a standard of justification which empowers the citizen to obtain from government the entitlements to the means of survival" (51).[9] The National Party also raised strong concerns about social rights, stating that "the inclusion of more socio-economic rights [presumably beyond those included in the Interim Constitution] in the bill of rights itself, is legally untenable and will, moreover, give rise to immense practical problems for government" and advocated for the use of "alternative mechanisms" to address issues related to social rights, such as "directive principles" (66–67).[10]

[7] Part of the Constitutional Assembly Theme Committee 4 Fundamental Rights Report on Block 1 (Constitutional Court archives, 57–62).

[8] Part of the Constitutional Assembly Theme Committee 4 Fundamental Rights Report on Block 1 (Constitutional Court archives, 68–71).

[9] "Submission on Constitutional Principle 2: Fundamental Rights," part of the Constitutional Assembly Theme Committee 4 Fundamental Rights Report on Block 1 (Constitutional Court archives, 49–56).

[10] Part of the Constitutional Assembly Theme Committee 4 Fundamental Rights Report on Block 1 (Constitutional Court archives, 63–67). The Vryheidsfront Party also expressed skepticism about socioeconomic rights: specifically whether or not they were "universally accepted" and whether or not they were enforceable in

While there was significant disagreement as to the scope and application of the Bill of Rights in these initial submissions, it is important to note that all parties framed their proposals in terms of international human rights discourse, not as a result of coercion or even explicit suggestion by external actors, but as a result of a shared understanding among domestic elites of the legitimate sources of constitutional examples. Further, these debates were less heated than those regarding the question of land and property. As one expert involved in the drafting process as a member of the Technical Committee to advise the Constitutional Assembly on Drafting of Bill of Rights noted: "The debate on property rights was much more vigorous and intense … Social and economic rights went through quite easily. The ANC supported social and economic rights, and the Technical Committee was unanimous in its support … We did keep that very separate from the property rights issue."[11,12] In fact, the Technical Committee achieved early consensus. The same expert recalled: "The Committee unanimously supported the inclusion of socioeconomic rights in the Bill of Rights. That is how the decision was taken. And then came the drafting … We relied heavily on the Covenant [on Economic, Social, and Cultural Rights]." He went on to say: "There was no great philosophical debate … We were all lawyers."[13]

Further, another expert advisor on the Technical Committee holds that by the time that the Constitutional Assembly negotiations were in full swing, "the debate at that point focused on the justiciability issue and where the courts should have a specific role" in the adjudication of social rights. That same expert also notes that for some, including many ANC members, "the idea was to see the Bill of Rights as a tool to transform society." Others, including members of the National Party and the Democratic Party, were more skeptical (for varying reasons). However, there "was a convergence because they also saw [that] the more you've got in the Bill of Rights, the more protection there would be for minority groups as well."[14] Generally speaking, then, elite political

practice. The African Christian Democratic Party submission noted that the party would support the rights of any generation, as long as they were "not condemned by the Word of God" (Constitutional Court archives, 45).

11 Elite interview 118 (August 25, 2017).

12 Though land and property may logically fit within the conceptual category of social and economic rights, they have typically been referenced separately in discussions of rights in South Africa.

13 Elite interview 118 (August 25, 2017).

14 Elite interview 178 (May 14, 2018).

actors seemed to agree on the language of the debate (oriented toward existing international human rights law), and the experts appointed to advise these political elites expressed even less variance in their views on the potential Bill of Rights.

The Final Constitution was adopted in May 1996, with the support of nearly 90 percent of the members of the Constitutional Assembly, though it was almost immediately challenged in court, and the Constitutional Court refused to certify the text. The Court instead asked the Constitutional Assembly to review and revise eight sections of the constitutional text. In December, the Court certified the revised text, which entered into force early the following year.

As described in the previous chapters with respect to the Colombian experience, the adoption or certification of a constitutional text does not mean that it will necessarily become socially or legally embedding and shape social and legal behavior. One key difference between the Colombian and South African experiences is that the South African Interim and Final Constitutions of the 1990s were really the country's first sustained forays into constitutionalism (though legalism was not a new phenomenon[15]) and judicial, rather than parliamentary, supremacy. What would become of these efforts? I now turn to the uneven embedding of the South African Final Constitution of 1996.

9.3 CONSTITUTIONAL EMBEDDING IN SOUTH AFRICA

As detailed in Chapter 2, constitutional embedding refers to the process by which constitutions come to be meaningful in social and legal life. Legal embedding occurs as judges and lawyers come to have new shared expectations about a particular constitutional vision. They make legal arguments and issue decisions on the basis of constitutional provisions, including newly recognized rights, rather than other sources of law. Social embedding, on the other hand, involves potential claimants and other societal actors coming to make rights claims and view problems in their lives as legal grievances under the new constitutional framework. Empirically, legal and social embedding can combine in different ways. Where legal embedding accompanies social embedding, these processes become mutually reinforcing, as we saw in the case of Colombia described throughout this book. As will become clear throughout

[15] See Meierhenrich (2010) on this point.

this section, in South Africa, by contrast, we see a high degree of legal embedding without concomitant social embedding.

9.3.1 Legal Embedding

I turn first to the question of legal embedding: to what extent were lawyers and judges impacted by the constitutional vision set out by the 1996 Constitution? In what follows, I offer an overview of social rights cases, which show that social constitutionalism did become legally embedded in South Africa. I then describe how legal mobilization and particular actions taken by the Constitutional Court facilitated this embedding process. This section closes with a discussion of embedding below the level of the South African Constitutional Court.

9.3.1.1 *Legal Embedding at the Constitutional Court*

I look to social rights jurisprudence to examine whether or not the legal embedding of social constitutionalism took place at all. If this kind of embedding did not occur at the level of the new Constitutional Court, we would not expect it at any level of the South African judiciary. The South African Constitutional Court has heard an average of just under three social rights cases each year (with a maximum of eight social rights cases in a given year) between 1996 and 2019, and of these cases, the majority have dealt with the right to housing. In fact, as of 2019, the Court had decided thirty-seven housing rights cases, compared to twenty-one education rights cases, eight social security cases, eight health cases, and two cases involving water. Overall, social rights cases make up about 9.5 percent of the Court's work.

The first social rights case[16] to come before the Court, *Soobramoney v. Minister of Health (Kwazulu-Natal)* (1997), involved a claim regarding the right to health advanced by a man suffering from kidney failure who was seeking access to a dialysis machine at a state-run medical facility.[17] In deciding the case, Judge President Chaskalson wrote:

> There is a high level of unemployment, inadequate social security, and many do not have access to clean water or to adequate health services. These conditions already existed when the Constitution was adopted

[16] In 1996, the Court heard a case related education, *Gauteng Provincial Legislature in re: Gauteng School Education Bill of 1995*, but did not actually reference the Section 29 constitutional right to education.

[17] The next five paragraphs, analyzing early social rights decisions, draw directly from Taylor (forthcoming).

> and a commitment to address them, and to transform our society into one in which there will be human dignity, freedom and equality, lies at the heart of our new constitutional order. For as long as these conditions continue to exist that aspiration will have a hollow ring.[18]

He noted the "constitutional commitment" to address these conditions was expressed in Sections 26 and 27, which detail the rights to have access to adequate housing, healthcare, food, water, and social security and social assistance. Ultimately, the Court decided against Mr. Soobramoney, with Judge President Chaskalson concluding: "The State has to manage its limited resources … There will be times when this requires it to adopt a holistic approach to the larger needs of society rather than to focus on the specific needs of particular individuals within society." In a concurring decision, Justice Sachs held that an acknowledgment of the dignity and equality of all citizens required the rationing of healthcare services.[19] Overall, this case challenged the Court to navigate a commitment to the realization of social rights and human dignity and a concern with balancing individual needs and collective consequences.[20]

The next substantive social rights case, *Government of the Republic of South Africa and Others* v. *Grootboom and Others*, came before the Court in 2000.[21] This case involved the attempted eviction of 900 people living in a squatter settlement near the city of Cape Town. In the decision, Justice Zak Yacoob noted the centrality of dignity in South African constitutional rights jurisprudence, and held that

[18] See the full decision here: www.saflii.org/za/cases/ZACC/1997/17.html.

[19] Specifically, he wrote: "In all the open and democratic societies based upon dignity, freedom and equality with which I am familiar, the rationing of access to life-prolonging resources is regarded as integral to, rather than incompatible with, a human rights approach to health care."

[20] The public reacted with outrage to this decision, as Mr. Soobramoney died shortly after it was handed down.

[21] Technically, the Court released two decisions on an education-related cases earlier. The first, a case known as *Premier, Province of Mpumalanga and Another* v. *Executive Committee of the Association of Governing Bodies of State Aided Schools: Eastern Transvaal* (1998), involved the right to education insofar as it dealt with schools, but the case was decided on the basis of administrative law. The second case, *Christian Education South Africa* v. *Minister of Education* (2000), centered on whether or not corporal punishment should be allowed in private religious schools. The analysis did not rely on the right to education as such (though it did engage with the right to maintain independent educational institutions), but instead on the balance between religious freedom, privacy, culture, dignity, equality, security of the person, and the rights of children.

"[s]ocio-economic rights are expressly included in the Bill of Rights; they cannot be said to exist on paper only." This move can be interpreted as an attempt to indicate that social rights are meaningful in South Africa, despite the Soobramoney decision. Yet, how exactly rights would exist beyond their inscription on paper would be defined by judicial decisions. The Soobramoney decision made clear that they would not exist, at least in the judicial sphere, at the level of the individual claimant. The Grootboom decision further clarified a focus on the "reasonableness" of policy decisions, drawing on the phrase "reasonable legislative and other measures" included in the Constitution (reasonableness was not quite defined, though the decision did indicate that clear respect for human dignity would be integral to an assessment of reasonableness).[22] Ultimately, the Court found that the state's housing policy was unreasonable and therefore unconstitutional because it neglected to provide for those in desperate need, and the decision mandated that the government develop an emergency housing policy. The justices of the Constitutional Court could have decided these cases differently, and many analysts and observers have suggested that they should have.

Social rights cases continued to make it to the Constitutional Court, numbering two or three per year through the early 2000s. Between 2000 and 2002, the Court considered three additional education-related cases, declining to hear one, deciding one on the basis of the minister of education's powers (while explicitly refraining from addressing any constitutional rights questions), and relying on an analysis of just administrative action in the third.[23] In 2001, another housing-related case came before the Court, though the case hinged on whether or not the state could build a temporary transit camp on a specific piece

[22] "It is fundamental to an evaluation of the reasonableness of state action that account be taken of the inherent dignity of human beings. The Constitution will be worth infinitely less than its paper if the reasonableness of state action concerned with housing is determined without regard to the fundamental constitutional value of human dignity. Section 26, read in the context of the Bill of Rights as a whole, must mean that the respondents have a right to reasonable action by the state in all circumstances and with particular regard to human dignity. In short, I emphasize that human beings are required to be treated as human beings" (Section 83). See the full decision here: www.saflii.org/za/cases/ZACC/2000/19.html.

[23] *Permanent Secretary of the Department of Education of the Government of the Eastern Cape Province and Another* v. *Ed-U-College* (2000), *Minister of Education* v. *Harris* (2001), and *Bel Porto School Governing Body and Others* v. *Premier of the Western Cape Province and Another* (2002), respectively.

of public land rather than on an interpretation of the meaning of the right to housing as such.[24]

The next case that resulted in a substantive development to social rights jurisprudence was *Minister of Health and Others* v. *Treatment Action Campaign and Others* (2002).[25] The Treatment Action Campaign case involved the rollout of a state-led program meant to combat mother-to-child transmission of HIV through a medication by the name of nevirapine. Initially, the state wanted to make the medication available only at certain medical facilities (two per province), arguing that it had concerns about the safety and cost of nevirapine, though then President Mbeki's AIDS denialism likely also played some role in this approach. The Treatment Action Campaign attempted to hone an argument focused on policy reasonableness (Heywood 2009), and the Court's decision in this case once again affirmed the commitment to evaluating the reasonableness of policy designs. Unlike previous cases, this decision does not rely on an explicit assessment of dignity in its evaluation of policy reasonableness. Still, the case served as an important move for the Court in challenging a prominent national policy and in considering the right to healthcare as justiciable in practice like the rights to housing and education.

The Soobramoney, Grootboom, and Treatment Action Campaign cases are typically recognized as setting out the parameters of social rights jurisprudence in South Africa. Together, they point to an approach that combined a focus on policy choices – specifically the "reasonableness" of those choices – with respect for human dignity. Whether a policy was reasonable and whether it afforded sufficient protections to the dignity of South Africans would be decided on a case-by-case basis. South African judges made clear an aversion to firmly defining the substance or content of rights, which contrasts with the declaration of the Colombian Constitutional Court in T-406/92 that "today, with the new constitution, rights are what judges say they are through tutela decisions," and contrary to the preferences of prominent civil society organizations and human rights lawyers, which favored the minimum core approach to outlining the content of social rights establishing in international law. As one former clerk and current advocate noted, "the way our Court interpreted its role made it very clear that

24 *Minister of Public Works and Others* v. *Kyalami Ridge Environmental Association and Others* (2001).

25 See the full decision here: www.saflii.org/za/cases/ZACC/2002/15.html.

it was secondary to the role of the elected representatives … I think it created a very restrained role for itself."[26] South African judges focused on policies and processes, and on the societal rather than individual effects of decisions. Thus, we see legal embedding of the constitutional vision, but in a more limited way than was the case in Colombia.

As was the case with Colombia, we see a relationship between the continued exposure of judges to particular kinds of legal claims and the problems they implicate and judicial receptivity, especially when judges interpret these claims as consonant with contemporary sociolegal values. Again, the exposure mechanism refers to the process by which continued experience with claims related to a specific grievance cumulatively inform judges about an issue, causing them to become comfortable with the issue and to identify with claimants. The process can result in an increased receptivity of judges to claims pertaining to that issue area. We see this clearly in the realm of housing, where Constitutional Court justices connected the specific issue of access to housing with the general value of human dignity and steadily expanded the understanding of the scope of the right to housing. One former clerk currently working as a litigator at a Johannesburg-based NGO described the development of the right to housing as follows:

> Under apartheid, it was illegal to be a squatter, and you could be kicked out and you could be thrown in jail … [Now] you [can] evict someone, but only with a court order, and only if it's equitable … Built into the right is if eviction is going to lead to homelessness, the state must provide you with temporary alternative accommodation. And over the past twenty years, that has been expanded. It's not just if you're flood victim the state must provide this accommodation, it's also if the state evicts you. Then the next step is when the state evicts you from private land. Then the next step, if a private owner evicts you, also you have this right. And now we're getting to the content of what that alternative accommodation looks like … So, we're seeing – and what's so lovely and unexpected – is the Court has started writing case law on this, kind of like a handbook for litigators … The jurisprudence has developed to such a level that the courts are now writing, "Judges, when they decide this issue, have to do X, Y, Z."[27]

[26] Elite interview 101 (August 3, 2017). James Fowkes, another former clerk, reiterated this view in an interview (elite interview 131, September 5, 2017) and in his 2016 book.

[27] Elite interview 119 (August 28, 2017).

Another former clerk suggested that:

> Housing cases are numerous at this point in the jurisprudence, in the High Court and the [Constitutional] Court, and I think that maybe it's just getting judges and courts comfortable in that terrain so that the more of a particular kind of case they see, the more comfortable they become with the numbers and statistics and so on … Especially in the [Johannesburg] courts they've seen it again and again and again so they're becoming more comfortable. I don't know … [but] that's something that I suspect.[28]

This view is consistent with hands-on interventions undertaken by the Court in housing cases such as *Residents of Joe Slovo Community, Western Cape* v. *Thubelisha Homes and Others* (2009), which specified "the exact time and manner and conditions" of the eviction, including precise directives about the alternative accommodation to be provided to those subject to eviction.[29] The existence of a robust support structure around housing issues and the fact that eviction orders must be granted by judges meant that judges would continue to be exposed to housing rights cases. Another former clerk pointed to this support structure and the history of land and housing issues in South Africa as being particularly influential on the judicial receptivity of these kinds of claims:

> There's a long history of land and housing litigation as kind of an anti-apartheid move … A lot of the liberal and progressive judges who went on to High Courts and the Supreme Court of Appeal and the Constitutional Court identified with these cases as sort of, as sites of progressive fighting. I think [that] is one reason. There's been incredibly organized and coordinated litigation and planning around housing rights specifically … There's this kind of feedback happening between an issue that is obviously quite dire on the ground … [and] good organization among clients, lawyers, and receptiveness on the part of judges.[30]

Yet another former clerk noted that the problem of inadequate housing was visible in such a way that judges were exposed to it, such that "even judges can see them for themselves."[31]

Still, exposure is not enough on its own to precipitate judicial receptivity. Judges must also have the sense that the kind of rights violation

[28] Elite interview 169 (March 1, 2018).
[29] Elite interview 167 (February 23, 2018).
[30] Elite interview 101 (August 3, 2017).
[31] Elite interview 110 (August 17, 2017).

in question is incompatible with contemporary sociolegal values – in this case, the value of human dignity is crucial. In early health rights cases, including *Soobramoney* and *Treatment Action Campaign*, South African judges suggested that while human dignity remained central to the post-apartheid South African legal order, the link between a difficulty with access to healthcare might not be an infringement on dignity (in *Soobramoney*) or they simply did not consider dignity as a fundamental part of the legal analysis (in *Treatment Action Campaign*).

In contrast, in early housing rights decisions, human dignity featured prominently. For example, in *Grootboom*, Justice Yacoob wrote: "The case brings home the harsh reality that the Constitution's promise of dignity and equality for all remains for many a distant dream." Here, dignity and access to adequate housing are understood as necessarily connected, and this understanding combined with exposure spurred judicial receptivity to housing claims. This receptivity involved not only hearing housing rights cases but also issuing interventionist decisions, rather than leaving the issue to be resolved by the executive or legislature (even if those same judges otherwise embrace a philosophy of judicial deference). These decisions, particularly as they detailed what one lawyer quoted earlier described as "a handbook for litigators," served as cues for potential claimants and incentivized further legal claim-making related to the right to housing, forming a positive feedback loop. By examining these social rights cases, we see evidence of legal embedding of the 1996 Constitution and its social rights provisions, particularly at the level of the Constitutional Court.

9.3.1.2 Legal Embedding beyond the Constitutional Court?

Considering that South African law changed not only in the adoption of a new constitution that set out a social vision for law, but also in the shift to constitutional supremacy in itself, we might think that the legal embedding faced an even steeper challenge among the legal community working below the level of the Constitutional Court. Here, I turn primarily to interviews with fifty current and former Constitutional Court clerks, many of whom later would go on to work as attorneys or advocates, at private firms or for NGOs, throughout the country. Their experiences both at the Constitutional Court and engaging in litigation across the lower courts offer a perspective on the broader judiciary and legal profession in South Africa.

Some clerks expressed the view that social constitutionalism has not been accepted throughout the judiciary. One former clerk and current member of the Johannesburg Bar explained that she has witnessed what she called "compassion fatigue" among judges at the high courts, especially when deciding eviction cases. She continued, "I think it's judges who are tired of what they see as people using their rights to gain unfair or untrue benefits or advantage … That's my experience and that's of course not the case of all judges but there is a definite sense that of fatigue for judges for cases brought by NGOs trying to enforce constitutional rights."[32] Here, repeated exposure to certain evictions/ housing rights claims seems to have had the opposite impact to the one we saw on justices of the Constitutional Court. In the absence of a perceived connection to contemporary sociolegal values, namely human dignity, repeated exposure in these cases may have led not to receptivity but to its opposite.

There is also the perception that some older lawyers and judges, who came of age in a time without a constitution and without social rights recognitions, do not view constitutional law as proper law. Many clerks spoke of there being something of a split bar, with "black letter lawyers" on the one hand and constitutional lawyers on the other. Where these clerks disagreed, though, was on the extent to which this divide remains. Expressing the view that the divide persists, one clerk held:

> There's been a selective trickle down. And some people have really taken it onboard and others not at all. I mean some of the ones who've not at all are just kind of old and set their ways. But there's also still I think a split about the perception that, you know, you have hard commercial law and then your wishy-washy constitutional law and I think some judges themselves probably secretly hold that belief and will avoid applying the Constitution if they can.[33]

Other former clerks, though, suggested that the legal culture has changed over time, especially around the idea of (social) constitutionalism. For instance, one explained:

> Many of those [early] High Court decisions had to be set right by the Constitutional Court because those judges weren't imbued with that sensitivity [to the Constitution] … I do think that that has changed quite fundamentally in the last fifteen years. It has filtered down. I mean, you still have renegades, but the general idea that all law must be viewed through the prism of the Bill of Rights, for example, and that it

[32] Elite interview 101 (August 3, 2017).
[33] Elite interview 120 (August 28, 2017).

> must be infused with it, is something that is generally understood and practiced … Everyone understands that it is infused in the system.[34]

Another similarly noted that years ago, constitutional law "was seen as an option [not an obligation]; 'I don't actually have to consider the Constitution,' whereas now, especially with the younger lawyers or judges, they are aware that everything starts with the Constitution."[35] Another summarized the present state neatly: "I do think that there is a willingness of judges on all levels to consider constitutional arguments, they know they have to."[36] In the view of these former clerks and current advocates, a legal embedding of the 1996 Constitution has occurred throughout the South African judiciary, though others did suggest reasons for skepticism about the extent of embedding.

Overall, then, we see that although fewer social rights cases came before the South African Constitutional Court than in Colombia, Constitutional Court justices did come to adopt the 1996 Constitution and pursue its social ends. They developed robust standards for eviction cases and institutionalized protections for folks facing evictions. Compared to the Colombian Constitutional Court, they took a more restrained approach to other social rights issues, but as James Fowkes (2016) argues, this approach signaled the justices' view that they shared the task of constitution-building and transformation with the executive and legislature. The Court did not express wholesale reluctance about or disregard for the new constitution; instead, they saw themselves as having a more limited role than their Colombian counterpart. Lower-court judges were perhaps initially hesitant to embrace social constitutionalism – or constitutionalism in any form – but over time, that hesitance appears to have given way to the application of constitutional provisions and principles.

9.3.2 Social Embedding

Legal embedding is only part of the story, however. Without social embedding, the flow of claims that come before the courts will be quite limited in both quantity and scope. So, to what extent has the vision set out by the 1996 Constitution permeated broader social life? Do everyday citizens have knowledge about the constitution, or is that limited to a select few who have close connections to NGOs? Do most

[34] Elite interview 100 (August 3, 2017).
[35] Elite interview 159 (October 17, 2017).
[36] Elite interview 124 (August 31, 2017).

citizens talk about the Constitution and their rights with familiarity? Do they believe they can make legal claims to their rights? Do they actually do so? I first consider how citizens may have been exposed to the 1996 Constitution and the work of the newly created Constitutional Court, before assessing these questions about social embedding in South Africa.

The drafting process of the post-apartheid constitution was met with both international fear and fanfare. Would South Africans be able to work within formal institutions to refound the country, or would extra-judicial violence rule the day? Of course, South Africans were intimately aware that a political transition was occurring, and most had strong feelings about the transition. Whether or not this general interest translates to specific knowledge about the constitution-drafting process or the nature of the new constitution's new rights provisions is less obvious.

I first look to the major forums through which the constitutional designers sought to include the general South African public: media campaigns, public submissions, and public meetings (also known as "the constitutional roadshow"). The Constitutional Assembly put together a weekly television show called *Constitutional Talk*, which featured a panel discussion on various issues related to the new constitution (rights, separation of powers, etc.). A newsletter by the same name featuring both articles and comic strips circulated twice per month. In addition to the television show and newsletter, the assembly also sponsored radio programs and paper advertisements across the country.

The Constitutional Assembly solicited public submissions in the form of signed petitions and written requests, which, in theory, could propel both interest in the new constitution and subsequent constitutional buy-in, if the public felt that the new constitution truly reflected their input. Paul Davis, who worked in the submissions department, explained the procedure:

> Every morning, Box 15, Cape Town, 8000, is emptied and all the letters are opened and date-stamped. Then they are taken to the submissions department where they are sorted into subject matter and placed in boxes. Those that are in languages other than English are sent for translation and all handwritten submissions are retyped.[37]

[37] According to Constitution Hill Trust.

2517

34 Corfu
1st Avenue
Lyndhurst
JOHANNESBURG
2192
18 February 1995

The Executive Director
CA
P O Box 15
CAPE TOWN
8000

THEME COMMITTEE IV (4)

Dear Sir/madam

The future South Africa without the entrenched Bill of Rights will be like tea without sugar.

The freedom of speech, the right to life, the right to information and freedom of movement must be clear and viable, cut and dry in the Bill of Rights.

Yours faithfully

KULANI HLEKANE

Gift Masedi

BILL OF RIGHTS

I am happy to get this opportunity, because I never ever get a chance to say something about pollution. I am asking that please get rid of people who pollute our land. And nowadays people are so ignorant about whats going on in our land. The people are throwing rubbish everywhere they like to throw. The industries are polluting too, trees are dying and I don't know whether you can help. We are breathing carbon dioxide coming from the industries. At Soweto there is a lot of pollution. Toilet pipes are broken and sewerage is running down the streets. Please let us keep our environment clean. At my street there is a huge place that people use for garbage. Please give a hand.

Busisiwe Mashala

May I please put a clause in the "Bill of Rights". We have a problem of pollution in our country. I mean what I say is people don't care what damage is. There are several people that are doing because of pollution.

What I would to suggest is talk to people of our country. Interview this in radio and television all over the country. For the example the farmers are frustrated about this pollution. There is a lack of water in the farm the soil is not even fertile and also the factories, there are the people whom they know that cause pollution but they know there is no other way they can do because factories are helping people a lot. But they must try to reduce their air pollution.

The government must make sure that people have the electricity in their homes and make sure that there is no sewage that is disturbing this. This will all reduce from having illness and cause of pollution.

Thanks for the attention.

Figure 9.1 Written submissions to the South African Constitutional Assembly. Source: Author's photographs of submissions held in the Constitutional Court archive.

In total, the assembly received over 1.7 million submissions (Segal and Cort 2012), though the vast majority of the submissions were individual signatures in support of petitions. Around 15,000 featured substantive written suggestions from individuals or civil society groups (Gloppen 1997). Figure 9.1 shows three of these submitted and retyped appeals. In her analysis of the substantive written submissions, Siri Gloppen (1997: 259) found that "a disproportionate share of the submissions seem[s] to come from the well-educated, the middle class, former politicians, academics, professionals and political activists."[38] While potentially a concern for matters of legitimacy and representation, this kind of distortion does not necessarily cut against the possibility

[38] She wryly notes that "people surfing the Internet and emailing the Constitutional Assembly are hardly representative of the majority of South Africans."

of social embedding. If this group came to adopt the resulting constitution as their own, spread the word about new rights and new legal tools, and push forward rights claims, then widespread social embedding could follow from this more limited beginning. After reviewing these submissions, the constitutional debates, and the resulting text, Gloppen (1997: 263) concludes, however, that "the millions of submissions from the public had little direct influence on the outcome of the constitutional-making process."

Beyond the media campaign and submissions requests, the Public Participation Program of the Constitutional Assembly sought to bring the constitution-drafting process to the people. They convened more than twenty meetings throughout the country in 1995. Attendance at each of these meetings ranged from 130 to 4,000.[39] South African History Online reports that over 20,000 people and over 700 organizations participated in these meetings.[40] Alexander Hudson (2021: 58) notes that "the Constitutional Assembly did go to great lengths to hold public meetings in very remote parts of South Africa, including the sparsely inhabited Northern Cape. The transcripts of the public meetings describe well-planned and orderly engagements between members of the public and members of the Theme Committees."

In addition, the justices of the Constitutional Court worked to publicize their decisions after the 1996 Constitution went into effect, offering another opportunity for South African citizens to learn about the Constitution and its functions. Integral to these outreach efforts were the formation of a media committee and the introduction of television cameras into the courtroom. In an interview, former Justice Goldstone recalled:

> We had seminars with senior journalists. We had annual meetings with the editors of the main newspapers and a lot of things came together from that. One of them was issuing a press summary together with judgments. The summary was drafted by the judge who wrote the lead opinion. That was very useful for the journalists … because, you know, sometimes it was a 150-page judgment.[41]

These press summaries allowed journalists to more easily engage with potentially complicated legal decisions and translate what the Court

[39] According to Constitution Hill Trust.
[40] According to South African History Online.
[41] Elite interview 92 (July 18, 2017).

was doing to the public. Further, because the South African Broadcasting Company carried court proceedings that were almost live, citizens – at least those with access to a television – could see the Court in action and learn about its work for themselves.[42] In these ways, the Court attempted to close the gap between citizens and constitutional law.

These efforts, however, were not clearly successful over the long term. In 1995, the Community Agency for Social Enquiry (CASE) and Roots Marketing were tasked with assessing the media strategy of the Constitutional Assembly. They found that 60 percent of respondents had heard of the Constitutional Assembly (and therefore the constitution-drafting process) by mid-1995. The report notes that "while three-quarters (76%) of respondents first heard of the [Constitutional Assembly] via mainstream media, 12% were first informed of it by word-of-mouth (from a friend, at work, at school and so on)." CASE concludes that the Constitutional Assembly "campaign has been able to achieve one of the key goals of a social education media campaign, namely to generate interpersonal communication, and enter popular discourse" (1995: 4). Yet, in 2015, only 10 percent of the population had read the final document put out by the Constitutional Assembly, the 1996 Constitution, or had it read to them (Fish Hodgson 2015: 191). And by 2018, only 51 percent of South Africans reported that they had *heard of* the Constitution or the Bill of Rights in 2018, up from 46 percent in 2015 (FHR Report 2018: 38). Tim Fish Hodgson (2015: 190) notes that "statements of regret about the dearth of knowledge about constitutional rights have been a constant refrain of the Constitutional Court ever since its inception." Many of the justices, clerks, and lawyers I interviewed in 2017 and 2018 echoed this concern. We might expect that knowledge and familiarity with the Constitution and the Constitutional Court would drop after the hubbub around their creation dies down. Together, these findings are indicative of a lack of exposure to the 1996 Constitution among everyday South Africans.

Further, relatively few South Africans have sought to make social rights claims, and not only because of this limited exposure to the contours of the constitution.[43] Many South African citizens do not find

[42] There was a slight delay so that in the event that any confidential information was shared, the chief justice could halt the broadcast.

[43] This is not to say that no South Africans make rights claims. Obviously, that would not be true. Some individuals, like Irene Grootboom, are named litigants, as are

this kind of claim-making "thinkable," a term that Kira Tait introduced to sociolegal studies scholarship. Even beyond traditional barriers to access to justice (e.g., precise knowledge about how to initiate a legal case, the material and time costs of litigation, and proximity to courthouses), people must be able to imagine making a legal claim. The ability to imagine making a claim can be broken down into a variety of constituent beliefs, including whether or not individuals believe they are technically able to make claims, whether or not people view the law as something that could or should work for them, whether or not they conceive of their problems as potential legal grievances, and whether or not they perceive courts as a resource they should use to address those grievances (Tait and Taylor 2022).

To explore legal claim-making perceptions and practices, I draw on an original 551-person survey fielded in South Africa in November 2017 (Taylor 2020b). The survey was available in four languages: English, Tswana, Xhosa, and Zulu.[44] Respondents were not selected on the basis of race, but survey respondents largely reflect national statistics on racial group membership.[45]

I sought to sample respondents who had prior legal system experience and respondents who did not. As such, the survey did not rely on a standard random sampling design. Instead, I used two alternative sampling procedures. First, I attempted to oversample individuals with legal system experience. With the help of a South African NGO, I identified three of what I call "claimant communities," located in

some social movement organizations, like Abahlali baseMjondolo and Treatment Action Campaign. However, these individuals and organizations stand apart from most South African citizens.

44 Potential respondents were asked which languages they were most comfortable using. If respondents did not choose one of the survey languages as their first or second most comfortable language, they were excluded from the survey. Of those individuals who indicated that they were most comfortable with a language other than one of the four survey languages, twenty spoke Afrikaans, eleven Tsonga, seven Sotho, and one Shona. Each of these respondents noted that they felt "second most comfortable" speaking one of the four survey languages, and they took the survey in that second language.

45 In the survey, respondents with the official racial category "Black" comprised 80.6 percent of the total, compared to 80.2 percent nationally; "White" respondents were slightly overrepresented at 11.2 percent of the survey, compared to 8.4 percent nationally; "Coloured" respondents were slightly underrepresented at 6.5 percent of the survey and 8.8 percent nationally; and "Asian/Indian" respondents made up 1.6 percent of those surveyed compared to 2.5 percent of the national population.

provinces across the country. These communities are the informal settlements of Ratanang, Marikana,[46] and Thusong.[47] Each community was either presently involved in housing rights litigation at the High Court level or had been involved in such litigation in the previous five years.[48] The communities (residents of *x* location) were named as litigants in these cases. Individuals living in the claimant communities may or may not have identified as claimants, but my hunch was that a larger percentage of these individuals would report having legal system experience than what we see in the general population.[49] This hunch was borne out: while about 9 percent of respondents sampled from the general identified as having legal system experience, about 31 percent of claimant community members reported such experience.[50] Second, I randomly sampled respondents from the three provinces in which the three claimant communities are located: Gauteng, North West, and Western Cape. Every respondent was randomly sampled, regardless of which sampling strategy was used. However, individuals from claimant communities were more likely to be selected than respondents living

[46] This is not the Marikana of the massacre of striking mine workers perpetrated by state police forces in North West province. Instead, this is an informal settlement located in the Philippi area of Cape Town in Western Cape.

[47] The communities were chosen because of their involvement in litigation and their relationship with the NGO. In other words, these communities are likely not representative of the whole population of "claimants" in South Africa (though due to the lack of public official records regarding litigation, that population is unknown).

[48] The choice of housing rights litigation was made for several reasons. First, housing rights litigation has emerged as the most common type of social rights litigation in South Africa, comprising about 60.8 percent of all social rights litigation in the country and 51.7 percent of social rights cases heard by the Constitutional Court. Second, housing rights litigation historically has involved communities, a feature that makes identifying and contacting a substantial number of "claimants" possible. It is feasible that claimants involved in other forms of litigation differ fundamentally from housing rights litigants. Third, an NGO focused on housing rights litigation was willing to work with me.

[49] The 2014–2015 wave of the Afrobarometer survey shows that only 246 out of 2,388 total respondents in South Africa reported having experience with the courts in the previous five years. With an N of 551, a random sampling strategy and the same rate would result in only fifty-seven respondents with experience in the courts. The South African Social Attitudes Survey of 2014 found that 16 percent of respondents had been involved in some way in a court case in the previous twenty years which with a sample size of 551 would have resulted in eighty-eight "claimants," higher than the estimate derived from Afrobarometer.

[50] See Taylor (2020b) for a more in-depth discussion of this finding.

elsewhere in the provinces. My intention is not to compare provinces or make generalizable claims about all of South Africa – both are inappropriate given my sampling strategy. What I hope to do, instead, is to conduct an initial investigation into claim-making behavior.

The survey asked about experiences with problems related to housing, water, sanitation, electricity, work, education, and health. I chose these seven social welfare goods for their connection to the basic necessities of daily life. Each of these goods can be understood in the context of the 1996 Constitution, or, stated differently, problems related to accessing these goods could be understood as rights violations. The right to adequate housing is enshrined in Section 26 of the Constitution, and this right has been referenced in cases about both sanitation and electricity. Both water and healthcare are covered by Section 27 (as is food and social security). Rights associated with access to employment and employment conditions fall within Sections 22 and 23. Finally, Section 29 lays out the right to education. Of course, not every problem related to these goods will entail a constitutional rights violation, but I wanted to err on the side of overinclusion of potential rights violations.

Roughly three-quarters of survey respondents indicated that they had problems related to each of these seven social welfare goods. I also asked how respondents reacted to the problems they faced: did they do nothing, ask friends and family for help, turn to the law (operationalized as talking to a lawyer, entering into litigation, or filing a formal complaint with the Human Rights Commission) or to public officials, or participate in protests? Unsurprisingly, most respondents noted that they "lumped" their grievances, doing nothing to resolve the problem (Galanter 1974). Even so, other respondents engaged each of the other strategies that the survey asked about. Figure 9.2 shows the responses by issue area.

The survey also asked whether or not respondents agreed with the following statement: "If my rights are violated, I should file a legal claim, because the government has the obligation to protect my rights." In the results, 183 (33.2 percent) of respondents reported strong agreement and 263 (47.7 percent) reported that they agreed with the statement. However, while about 80 percent of those surveyed said one should file legal claims in response to rights violations, only about 9 percent of respondents who faced difficulties accessing social welfare goods indicated that they had actually brought claims to the courts.

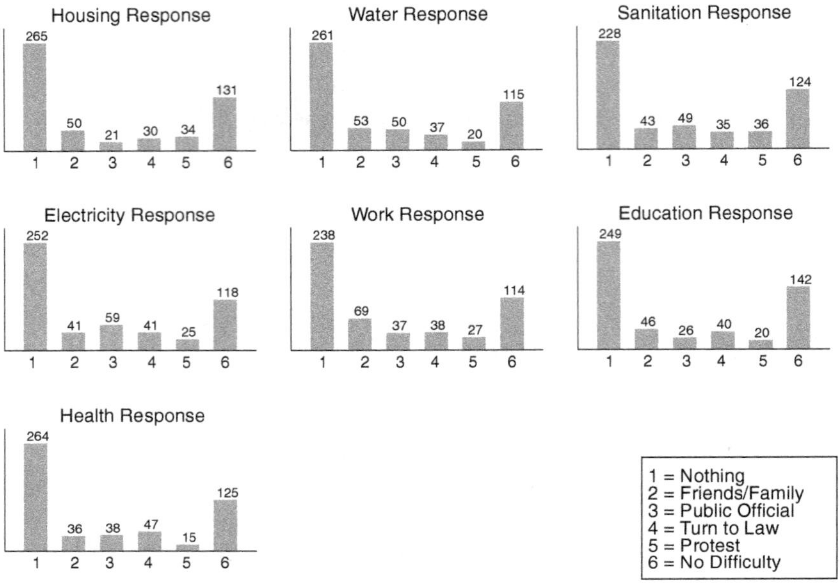

Figure 9.2 Reported response to difficulties in accessing social welfare goods.
Source: Author's original survey.

Table 9.1 breaks down these findings by issue area. Not everything that could be thought of as a rights violation will be – that is why rights consciousness and legal consciousness cannot be assumed. And there are often disconnects between what people say they would do and the things they actually do. That there is a gap between these things is not in itself surprising. We can conclude, however, that – at least with respect to certain kinds of rights claims – survey respondents do view the legal system as a venue in which claims can or should be made, but it does not appear to be "thinkable" for respondents to bring social rights claims to the courts. Tait (2022) finds similar results in her interviews with rural and peri-urban Black South Africans in KwaZulu-Natal province.

This gap in the "thinkability" of legal claim-making does not mean that there is no claim-making for constitutional rights through the courts or no rights talk.[51] Indeed, the previous section on legal

[51] In addition, this does not imply the absence of contentious politics. Indeed, service delivery and other kinds of protests are prevalent across the country (see, e.g., Booysen 2007; Alexander 2010; Zuern 2011), as is vigilantism in some areas (see, e.g., Smith 2015, 2019).

TABLE 9.1 Likelihood of turning to the law to deal with a social rights difficulty

	Reported access difficulty	Reported turning to law	Percentage with difficulty	Percentage turning to law
Housing	420	30	76.22	7.14
Water	436	37	79.13	8.49
Sanitation	427	35	77.50	8.20
Electricity	433	41	78.58	9.47
Work	437	38	79.31	8.70
Education	409	40	74.23	9.78
Health	426	47	77.31	11.03
Average			77.47	8.97

Source: Author's original survey.

embedding outlined how social rights cases have been decided over the last thirty years in South Africa. Social rights cases do come before the Constitutional Court and decisions on these cases do have significant impacts on peoples' lives. However, unlike in Colombia, these cases usually involve a collective actor rather than an individual, backed by NGOs, pro bono legal services, and/or movement organizations. Legal claim-making, therefore, is more centralized and mediated in South Africa than it is in Colombia. In Colombia, the diffuse ability of individuals to make legal claims meant that social embedding could spread rapidly, as folks across the country and across swaths of life were able to experience the power of the new constitutional promises for themselves. Legal claim-making in South Africa, under these circumstances of centralization and mediation, has not served to bolster social embedding and propel continued claim-making.

9.4 THE CONSEQUENCES OF PARTIAL EMBEDDING

Unlike in Colombia, where social and legal embedding occurred together and reinforced one another, in South Africa we see one form of partial embedding: legal embedding without social embedding. Why was this the case? There are important institutional differences between Colombia and South Africa, most notably the absence of the tutela procedure in South Africa. We might think that the relative dearth of claims and limited constitutional literacy might be a consequence of this difference. It is easy to make constitutional rights claims in Colombia and less so in South Africa. But there is a direct access mechanism in South Africa. The 1996 Constitution sets out that: "National legislation or the rules of the Constitutional Court must allow a person, when it is in the interests of justice and with leave of the Constitutional Court to bring a matter directly to the Constitutional Court." What constitutes the interests of justice is left up to interpretation. Jackie Dugard (2015: 116–17) analyzed direct access petitions to the Constitutional Court between 1995 and 2013 and concluded that the following four principles guide decisions about whether or not to accept these petitions:

- Exceptional circumstances;
- Undesirability to sit as a court of first and last instance especially where there are disputes of fact;
- Urgency/desirability of an immediate decision; and
- Reasonable prospects of success based on the substantive merits of the case.

The Court denies the vast majority of direct access petitions, usually on the grounds of more than one of these principles. Ultimately, these decisions have meant that the mechanism has a limited scope. Dugard (2015: 124) estimates that the Court accepted only eighteen direct access petitions between 1995 and 2013. Clearly, direct access petitions do not function the same way as the tutela does, and the direct access mechanism was never designed to mimic the tutela.

However, to focus only on the differences in the design of these mechanisms misses the point. Neither mechanism was meant to allow citizens to make claims to social rights. But the tutela came to serve that purpose to the extent that hundreds of thousands of such claims occur each year in Colombia, while the direct access petition is rarely used or accepted in South Africa. The starting point or institutional design does not in itself determine the future shape or scope of these mechanisms. The emergence of a particular kind of constitutional vision can prompt judges, lawyers, and societal actors to expand or contract their expectations and behaviors, pushing legal mechanisms beyond their original purview (as was the case in Colombia) or limiting them after the fact (as was the case in South Africa).

The embedding process can unfold in unexpected and uncontrolled ways. No single actor holds the reins. Even the most charismatic jurist cannot determine the extent of legal embedding or the contours of the constitutional vision that becomes embedded. The same applies to social embedding. In the messiness of social, political, and legal interaction, what emerged in South Africa is the legal embedding of social constitutionalism, undergirded by a somewhat deferential view on the relationship between the courts and the other branches of government (what Fowkes (2016) describes as a "constitution-building approach"), without social embedding, as evidenced by the combination of limited knowledge about the Constitution and skepticism about the efficacy of constitutional rights on the part of everyday South Africans. Does this mean the constitutional experiment failed? No, not at all. Instead, what I suggest is that the constitutional embedding process in South Africa is far less deep or stable than what we observe in Colombia. Legal claim-making, as a result, plays a more limited role in the pursuit of constitutional rights promises than might otherwise be the case, and most citizens, in practice, have one less mechanism available for rights redressal.

What has been the impact of the partial embedding of the 1996 Constitution? On the one hand, social constitutionalism has become embedded within the South African legal community. The South African Constitutional Court has developed a set of rules and procedures that set out the parameters of social rights protections. These rules and procedures, such as the requirement of "meaningful engagement" in eviction processes, are tangible to judges and lawyers alike. On the other hand, social embedding seems to be lagging. A "support structure" of NGOs and pro bono litigators helps to push social rights litigation, but buy-in from everyday South Africans has not followed. Thus, we see continued legal mobilization around certain issues, such as potential evictions (in part because of the requirement that evictions be preceded by a court order), but a lack of cases and demand-side pressure to fuel the kind of expansion we saw in Colombia. Legal mobilization is partially pushed forward by legal embedding, but it is not secured by social embedding.

This limited legal mobilization has yielded vitally consequential changes to the rules regarding eviction procedures, the rollout of anti-retroviral medications, and a variety of other issues (Heywood 2009; Budlender et al. 2014; Langford 2014). These are important advances that have made a real difference in the lives of South Africans. It is hard to imagine that these advances would have resulted from executive action or legislative debate in the absence of this litigation. But if the measuring stick is instead the number of folks living in inadequate housing or without access to other social goods, the picture is less rosy. As of 2015, over thirty million people lived below the poverty line, compared to about twenty-four million at the end of apartheid – in terms of the percentage of the total population, this means 55 percent in 2015 compared to 57 percent in 1996 (HSRC 2004; Statistics SA 2017). The appropriate standard is perhaps up for debate. We can confidently say, however, that the limits of legal claim-making for social rights have not been tested in South Africa, in part because the 1996 Constitution has only been partially embedded.

9.5 CONCLUSION

This chapter detailed the processes by which the 1996 South African Constitution was firmly legally embedded, particularly at the level of the Constitutional Court, but not significantly socially embedded. Justices of the Constitutional Court and their clerks, who would go on to work at prominent law firms, NGOs, and law schools, embraced social constitutionalism. They were especially receptive to housing rights cases, as they came across housing rights issues in both their daily and professional lives and viewed these issues as conflicting with their sense of contemporary sociolegal values, especially human dignity. Overall, this new constitutional vision included the courts as partners with the executive and legislative branches of government, following what Fowkes (2016) calls a "constitution-building" approach. These judges, clerks, and practicing lawyers developed a substantive set of rules of engagement with respect to social rights cases and a particularly robust jurisprudence around issues related to potential evictions.

The relative dearth of social embedding was not for lack of trying. The South African government, like the Colombian government, put together informational campaigns both before and after the new constitutions went into effect. They sought to use popular media to spread knowledge about rights and the possibility to claim rights before the courts. This knowledge did not stick or further spread in South Africa, at least not outside of NGOs and a few social movements. I argue that robust social embedding did not occur – despite substantial opportunities for exposure to the new constitution – because frequent legal mobilization did not occur. While important legal advances have been made in South Africa that have impacted policies and livelihoods, individuals have not been nearly as involved in legal claim-making as in Colombia, with hundreds of thousands of tutela claims being filed and debated every year. Without this kind of legal mobilization to reinforce early exposure to the new constitution and new rights regime, the social element of constitutional embedding lagged. Partial embedding has meant a more circumscribed role for the 1996 South African Constitution than that of the 1991 Colombian Constitution in most people's daily lives.

CHAPTER TEN

CONCLUSION

Social Constitutionalism and the Politics of Rights

Scholars have long noted how law can both enable and constrain those who wish to contest existing power relations (e.g., Scheingold 1974; Thompson 1975). While elite control of the drafting of legal rights and regulations and over the operation of legal institutions may result in the perversion of the supposedly even-handed law, this codification, this formalization, and this claim to fairness and justice at times can empower nonelites and work against those in power. Still, though "rights talk" may offer new opportunities to claimants or to movements in their myriad quests to improve the conditions of their lives, the very invocation of rights may legitimate an illegitimate state or further embed a hegemonic discourse, reifying existing power relations (see, e.g., Glendon 1993; Nonet and Selznick 2001; Silbey 2005). However, as many scholars have documented, these concerns may have been overstated as individuals and movements deftly and selectively use rights talk and legal tools in pursuit of their goals (McCann 1994; Ewick and Silbey 1998; Epp 2009; Lovell 2012; Taylor 2018).

These questions about elite machinations and counter-hegemonic possibilities can overshadow fundamental questions about lived experience. All too often, everyday discussions of law and social change (or politics writ large) are divorced from the ways in which people experience opportunities, constraints, advances, and setbacks. Yet, as Robert Cover (1986: 1601) rightly proclaimed, "legal interpretation takes place in a field of pain and death." Far from simply being parchment promises, social rights recognitions make clear that Cover was right that legal interpretations of the scope, meaning, and content of social rights have life and death consequences. For those without access to health, housing, food, water, sanitation, and other social welfare goods, life is remarkably insecure. Absent a fundamental level of access to welfare, individuals cannot participate fully in political, social, or economic life.

The Social Constitution explores how law influences lived experience, from the everyday to the exceptional, as well as the meaning of rights and the ways in which people struggle to improve their lives. In this book, I look to the constitutional codification of social promises as rights and then track how citizens work to make claims to those rights, how judicial officials respond, and the forces that work against significant rights claim-making. The widespread constitutional recognition of social rights and the empowerment of courts to hear claims to those rights came to the fore during the third wave of democratization and the height of neoliberalism; yet, it set out a new, dramatically different understanding of state obligations and the interaction of the state, markets, and citizens. Social constitutionalism creates opportunities for citizens to make new types of claims to social goods – but only to the extent that the Constitution and its vision of law become something more than words on paper; only to the extent that the Constitution becomes embedded in social and legal life.

This book details the process of constitutional embedding, or the conditions under which particular visions of law come to take root both socially and legally. The social component of constitutional embedding (the focus of Chapter 4) occurs when rights talk has entered the vernacular and does so with respect to specific rights and legal tools that can be used to claim those rights, while the legal component of constitutional embedding (the focus of Chapter 5) occurs when judges establish, alter, and expand precedent related to a particular vision of constitutional law. In short, embeddedness refers to the degree to which something is no longer unusual in social or legal life. Without embedding, law remains a parchment promise, a window dressing, or simply irrelevant. Constitutional rights or constitutional orders can be partially or unevenly embedded, and they can become dislodged or left latent in a variety of ways, including challenges related to the scope of the law, struggles over political power, and the everyday work of processing legal claims. Further, it is possible to see significant legal embedding without equivalent social embedding, or vice versa.

Chapter 6 documents how, despite evidence of significant legal and social embedding in much of Colombia, embedding has not spread to all marginalized communities. Not everyone's problems are legible to the law. When this is the case, legal mobilization cannot serve to embed a constitutional vision. Chapter 7 explores the tensions that can emerge between actors in favor of and against the new constitutional order. It also shows how continued legal mobilization can protect against powerful challenges to embedding. Chapter 8 examines how the daily work of social constitutionalism can provide challenges to constitutional embedding, and it demonstrates how changes in institutional rules and role conceptions (solidified through legal mobilization) can counteract these challenges. Chapter 9 turns to the case of South Africa to explore a case of the partial embedding of a social constitution, where the new constitutional system has been adopted by and ingrained in legal actors, as well as some NGOs, but not by society writ large.

A focus on constitutional embedding brings to light important questions and avenues for research in the study of law and society, especially legal mobilization and legal consciousness, comparative constitutionalism, and social citizenship. In what follows, I turn first to the possibilities of social incorporation and the deepening of citizenship through law. I then consider the relationship between legal mobilization and organized civil society support. Next, I examine the impact that ambivalence about the law and technically incorrect understandings about the law have on constitutional development and rights realizations. I close with a few words on the applicability of the concept of embedding across contexts, the range of possible embedding outcomes, and the mechanisms that can propel embedding.

10.1 SOCIAL INCORPORATION THROUGH LAW?

The Social Constitution uncovers how social actors can shape citizenship rights and their enactment or enforcement. It examines how social constitutionalism plays out on the ground over the long term and comes to shape claim-making and access to social welfare goods. In addition, this book demonstrates the utility of viewing legal mobilization as a form of political participation and as an important part of state–society relations, in this case allowing for an investigation of how social constitutionalism impacts access to social services and creates a new mode of social service provision. This mode hinges on the ability and willingness of citizens to make claims to constitutional rights that are universal in theory, though bounded in practice.

Studies of social incorporation or the provision of social welfare in developing societies have focused on three dominant models of state–society relations: patron-clientelism (Bratton and van de Walle 1997; Auyero 2001; Chandra 2004; Kitschelt and Wilkinson 2007; Stokes 2013), corporatism (Schmitter 1974; Collier and Collier 1979; Yashar 1999), or the market alternative (Hall and Soskice 2001; Adésínà 2009). Social constitutionalism, by contrast, opens up another path to social citizenship (Marshall 1950). In the context of social constitutionalism, all citizens can turn to claim-making in the courts to attempt to gain access to social welfare goods, regardless of whether or not they have ties to politicians and political parties or the ability to purchase those goods privately.

However, as Sandra Botero, Daniel Brinks, and Ezequiel González-Ocantos (2022: 2) note, "the promise of judicialization [or of social constitutionalism] falls short when the superstructure of judicialization remains unmoored from deeper social and political roots, and when it produces heavy demands that cannot be met by weak states and institutions." By "the superstructure of judicialization," they mean "formal institutional and elite cultural changes," such as constitutional reforms, adoption of regional and global human rights instruments, and the professional incentives within the legal sphere (2022: 13–15). Unless changes to the constitutional text are accompanied by broad social support, the possibilities of social change – whether for the individual or broader society – are severely limited and vulnerable to backlash and regression.

Similarly, Roberto Gargarella (2020) warns that twentieth-century constitutionalism in Latin America is not without its flaws. While his seven theses focus on the monsters that Latin America's "old constitutionalism" gave rise to, Latin America's new constitutionalism, which largely fits the social constitutionalist model, has not been able to outpace the monsters it creates either: unequal political and economic power endure, and the promises of full representation are, as of yet, unrealized. He attributes this to the dual character, or the "two souls," of these constitutions. On the one hand, the sections of these constitutions on rights showcase a social and democratic orientation, while the sections on the organization of the state instead privilege elite power and serve to exclude many sectors of society. The existence of these two souls has the effect of creating points of tension that threaten to limit the possibilities of substantive change through constitutional reform. *The Social Constitution* documents how constitutional embedding can occur, how the judicialization of politics can become moored firmly in a particular sociopolitical context, and how points of tension within a constitutional model can be smoothed over.

Turning now to the Colombian case, what are the material consequences of social constitutionalism for everyday Colombians? The most visible consequence has come in the form of the Colombian Constitutional Court fundamentally reshaping healthcare policy and the healthcare system. The *acción de tutela* – a legal mechanism introduced by the 1991 Constitution that allows individuals and groups to easily make claims to their constitutional rights – was central to this outcome. In 2008, the Constitutional Court grouped together twenty-two tutela claims and issued a structural decision (T-760/08). That decision called for a restructuring of the benefits plan that would outline which medicines and services had to be covered by the *entidades promotoras de salud* (which are akin to insurance companies), regulate transfers of administrative costs to patients, and solidify the freedom to choose among healthcare providers. In addition, the decision called for the adoption of deliberate measures to realize universal coverage. The Court has required concrete changes to the healthcare system in other cases as well.[1]

When evaluating the impacts of individual health tutela decisions, however, we must ask whether people are turning to the tutela to demand coverage for procedures and services that are not included in the national healthcare plan, thus expanding spending on health, or whether, on the other hand, they are turning to the tutela to enforce the system as designed and to reduce the incidence of arbitrary and corrupt denial of services. The answer is, "some of both," though the trend appears to be more of the latter as time goes on. In the early 2000s, when the Defensoría del Pueblo began to collect and publish data on the topic, just under half of all claims were attempts to expand coverage, while half were efforts to obtain access to covered medicines and services. Figure 10.1 shows the percentage of tutelas claiming covered goods by healthcare regime, contributory versus subsidized. Over time, however, the percentage of claims having to do with goods or services officially covered by the national health benefits plan increased to over 85 percent. That is true for both the contributory and the subsidized health systems.

[1] For an assessment of these cases, see Yamin and Parra-Vera (2009). See also Uprimny and Durán (2014).

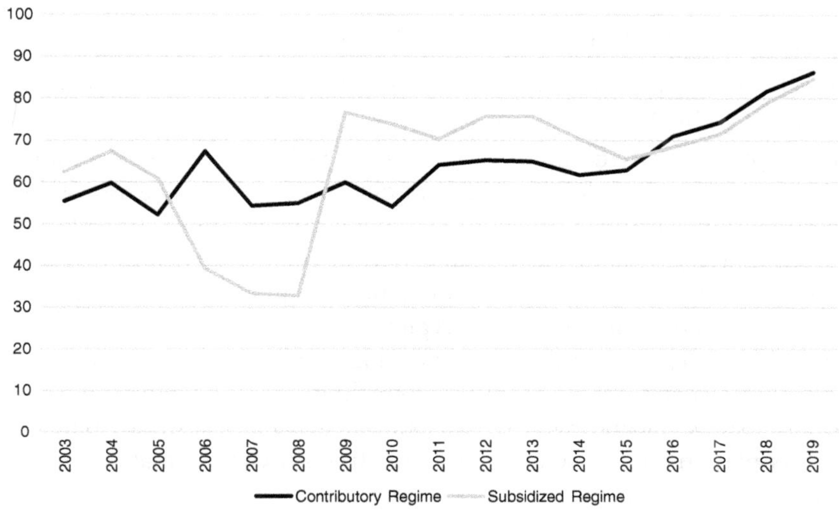

Figure 10.1 Percentage of tutelas for covered goods and services by healthcare regime. Source: Author's elaboration using data from the Defensoría del Pueblo.

Between 2009 and 2019 (the years for which disaggregated data are available), Colombians filed 1,576,627 tutelas that invoked the right to health. On average, judges found in favor of these applicants 82.1 percent of the time (ranging from a low of 79.7 percent in 2010 to a high of 85.6 percent in 2017). To date, there has only been one study on compliance with tutela orders, which was conducted by Ryan Carlin et al. (2022) on tutela claims filed in 2014. The study found a compliance rate of 72 percent. If we assume that the compliance rate has held steady over time (an assumption that should be empirically verified in future studies), then we can conclude that more than 930,000 claimants gained access to medications, appointments, and procedures that otherwise would have remained out of reach.

Even if compliance with tutela orders is less than perfect – again the Carlin et al. (2022) study found noncompliance 28 percent of the time – at least some of the time social constitutionalism, when activated by claim-making with the tutela procedure, results in tangible gains in access to the goods and services promised to every Colombian citizen. In other words, social incorporation expands. Additional comparative research, however, is needed to fully probe the promise and limits of social incorporation through social constitutionalism.

10.2 LEGAL MOBILIZATION WITHOUT SUPPORT?

Much scholarship on legal mobilization has focused on either when and how individuals or movements decide to make claims in the formal legal sphere or when and how judges offer rights-protective decisions. Yet, these processes do not occur in isolation and should be assessed in conjunction with one another. This book demonstrates the value in examining legal claim-making and judicial behavior together, considering how claimants or potential claimants; intermediaries, including lawyers, activists, and actors not typically associated with the legal system, like insurance companies; and judges affect the process of legal mobilization and potential for the embedding of social constitutionalism. Only by expanding our understanding of the roles that different actors play in the process of legal mobilization can we make sense of the complex, recursive dynamics at work.

The book further underscores the need to revisit our understanding of what a "support structure" is (Epp 1998), moving beyond shrewd cause lawyers (Scheingold 1974), resources, and elite connections. In his seminal work, Charles Epp explores the utility of the support structure concept, demonstrating that receptive judges, a strong bill of rights, and a robust rights consciousness alone are not always enough to surmount challenges in accessing the courts and spurring a rights revolution. Subsequent scholarship examined how social movement actors could serve to facilitate the development of a support structure (Cichowski 2007; Vanhala 2010).

The Colombian case, however, shows that other sets of actors, including corporations (specifically insurance companies) and even ordinary citizens are also part of the story. Where the "legal opportunity structure" is open and cost of filing legal claims is low, changes in social understandings about formal access mechanisms, like the tutela procedure, can lead to changes in the rules regulating those mechanisms, which in turn can reshape opportunities for claim-making, even in the absence of formal resource support. With the tutela, an individual can initiate a legal claim against a public or private actor without having to pay any fees whatsoever, as the claim can be delivered verbally and does not require the use of a lawyer. Importantly, the claimant does not technically need to articulate a legal argument about their rights; the judge of first instance is tasked with making sense of the situation described by the claimant and determining whether or not a constitutional rights violation occurred. Further, insurance companies and other healthcare providers actively encouraged the use of the tutela and helped to inform citizens about how to make health rights claims. The formal rules regarding the tutela – particularly those on standing, procedure, and costs – enable legal mobilization without the need for a support structure.

Future research should also examine in greater detail the ways in which different features of legal opportunity combine, where the existence of certain features might mitigate the need for others. Are tools such as the tutela necessary or merely permissive for legal mobilization in the absence of a support structure? Under what conditions can claimants self-fund their efforts at legal mobilization and when must they turn to external sources of support? How does the source of support impact the kind of claim made or the likelihood of success?

10.3 EVERYDAY CONSTITUTIONAL STRUGGLES AND THE POLITICS OF RIGHTS

The Social Constitution highlights the importance of assessing how people understand the conditions of their own lives as well as the lives of their fellow citizens, the rights to which they can legitimately lay claim, and how those understandings shape whether, when, and how constitutions come to be embedded. It drills down to where grand documents, like constitutions, meet the people who interpret them and fight for what they could mean. These struggles over the meaning of rights have profound material and symbolic consequences. They provide the tools for people to not only live, but live well – and to imagine a better life.

As such, the book takes up Stuart Scheingold's (2004 [1974]) suggestion to consider both the myth and the politics of rights together and Michael McCann's (1994: 9) call to view the law's role in political struggle as "expansive, subtle, and complex." The myth of rights necessarily connects rights and rights claim-making with social change – simply, the myth creates the understanding that rights realizations follow rights litigation. The politics of rights, however, encourages us to think of rights not as "accomplished social facts or as moral imperatives," but instead "as authoritatively articulated goals of public policy and, on the other, as political resources of unknown value in the hands of those who want to alter the course of public policy" (Scheingold 2004 [1974]: 7). Rights can serve as resources not just to challenge public policy, but also to make and remake the conditions of individuals' everyday lives. The embedding of social constitutionalism – a process that occurs through the repeated interaction of individuals, movements, judges, lawyers, activists, and even actors we do not normally associate with the formal legal sphere, like health insurance companies – helps to realize a politics of rights, creating toeholds for those who wish to make claims and seek access to social goods. There is no guarantee of success, but there is a chance.

The Colombian case also indicates that the macro-level politics of rights may be informed by a variety of micro-level features, in addition to and beyond strategic considerations regarding when and how to make rights claims. These include deep institutional knowledge without rights consciousness, inaccurate beliefs about both claim-making procedures and the content of rights, and ambivalence about legal claim-making. Chapters 4 and 6 show how residents of the marginal community of Agua Blanca hold detailed knowledge about the tutela and the Victims' Law of 2011. They referred to specific provisions and procedures, even when suggesting that these legal tools did not work for people like them. Even under the limited circumstances in which they did work, folks described these tools more as bureaucratic hoops to jump through rather than anything to do with rights.

These understandings can be mobilizing or demobilizing, regardless of their accuracy. Take, for instance, the example from Chapter 4 of the domestic worker who wanted to file a tutela claim to gain access to state benefits for having been displaced. She had not been displaced, and yet, she talked to a judge about filing such a claim. This is evidence that inaccurate beliefs can be mobilizing. Such inaccurate beliefs can even become self-fulfilling prophecies, as social facts reshape institutional rules over time. Many people I spoke with suggested that the tutela could only be used to claim the right to health. There may have been an implied "with any hope of success" at the end of that sentence, but some folks may have firmly believed that the tutela is for health rights claims and nothing else. Either way, something that is not technically true shapes the possibility of claim-making. Future research should further examine the relationship between legal consciousness, legal mobilization, and knowledge, whether accurate or inaccurate.

Further, this book demonstrates that mobilization can be an ambivalent process that is still deeply ingrained and embedded in expectations about how the world works, but neither reflective of buy-in to the myth of rights nor hope in the politics of rights. This ambivalence presents a challenge for how we understand the relationship between legal consciousness and legal mobilization. There is more to it than legal hegemony and unthinking deference on one end of the spectrum and counter-hegemonic discourse and legal alienation on the other (Ewick and Silbey 1998; Hertogh 2018; Halliday 2019). Ambivalence, the perception that there is no alternative (Taylor 2018), and misunderstandings can prompt the turn to law in everyday life. Questions remain, though, about how long these dynamics can remain stable. If folks only see incremental and uneven changes in their lives and they have not bought into a dominant discourse about how law works, will they continue to turn to legal claim-making (and continue to facilitate the process of constitutional embedding)? Can incremental and uneven gains from legal mobilization in one issue area spill over into others? How do potential claimants' expectations change over time? When might legal alienation emerge from conditions that had been defined by ambivalence, either as an expression of counter-hegemonic discourses or apathy and a turning away from law?

10.4 CONSTITUTIONAL EMBEDDING, A CHANGING RIGHTS TERRAIN, AND A DEFENSE OF CONSTITUTIONALISM

Around the world, and particularly in the Global South, the 1990s and 2000s brought with them an expanding rights terrain – at times formalized in constitutional rights protections, at times implicated in directive principles, and at times found instead in ordinary legislation. This growth in rights recognitions on paper makes the question of when and how rights become "real" or matter for people's everyday lives all the more important. Now, thirty years later, we can start to assess the consequences of this expansion.

As Janice Gallagher, Gabrielle Kruks-Wisner and I (forthcoming) document elsewhere, claim-making as a form of political participation has come to be increasingly salient during this period. In the absence of programmatic policies and strong political parties, citizens turn to claim-making in both judicial and administrative forums to try to attain access to needed goods and services. Claim-making, under certain conditions, can have both material and political consequences: not only changing who gets what when, but also reshaping how citizens relate to the state and creating new kinds of institutional spaces available to citizens. The "embeddedness" of law and policy helps us to understand when and how claim-making has these tangible impacts on peoples' lives.

I hold that under conditions of both social and legal embedding, we see the most significant rights protections. As this book demonstrates, legal mobilization is one mechanism that can initiate feedback processes that result in constitutional embedding. However, legal mobilization is not the only such mechanism. Future studies should focus attention on other ways that different audiences come to learn about rights provisions, find them meaningful, and work to incorporate them into everyday life.

Examples of partial embedding – whether defined by social or legal embedding, but not both, or unevenness in subnational embedding – abound. For example, Chapter 9 explores the case of South Africa, documenting the substantial development of legal embedding without the accompanying social embedding. While some community-based organizations and many lawyer-driven NGOs have turned to constitutional rights claim-making, everyday South Africans have not come to view the Constitution or legal claim-making as central to their lives. Kira Tait (2022) provides a robust account of why social embedding has not occurred, pointing particularly to the "thinkability" (or lack thereof) of legal mobilization among Black South Africans in the province of KwaZulu-Natal. It is not that formal access to courts does not exist, though it is limited, or that the constitutional rights infrastructure is lacking. Instead, people's "perceptions from their lived experiences or the retelling of others' experiences encountering the law, its actors, and the broader state," ranging from allegations of corruption to witchcraft to institutional inefficiencies, inhibit the ability of potential claimants from even imagining the possibility of turning to the formal legal sphere to deal with certain kinds of problems (Tait 2022: 3).

In contrast, Janice Gallagher (2022) skillfully details how rights protections related to disappearances have become socially embedded in Mexico, while substantive (as opposed to rhetorical) legal embedding has lagged. Those whose loved ones were disappeared have developed a robust knowledge of rights, rules, and procedures and have innovatively used repeated claim-making to try to attain information about what happened and ideally justice and accountability for the disappearances, but the legal sphere has not been receptive to these claims. Social embedding, at least for certain communities, endures despite this disconnect with the formal legal system. Gallagher (2022) attributes this to the nature of the grievance: a loved one being disappeared is fundamentally reorienting, and experiences that might otherwise dissuade one from continuing to make claims pale in comparison to that life-shaking event.

Turning to China presents another window into how legal embedding can develop independently of and even at times undercut social embedding. The Chinese state both developed a set of workplace legal protections and actively disseminated information about these new laws to the public. In fact, it attempted to actively use the media to construct the legal consciousness of citizens across the country and across issue areas (Whiting 2017). Workers, in particular, adeptly took up the task of turning to law to protect themselves from rights violations, simultaneously developing a greater sense of internal efficacy and "disenchantment" with the legal and administrative institutions associated with workplace legal protections (Gallagher 2006, 2017). Chinese citizens also began to engage in "open government information" litigation with frequency, continuing even when their claim-making efforts did not have material consequences. However, judges also attempted to stymie the efforts of the most litigious claimants by creating new legal categories to divert claims away from the legal system (Kim et al. 2021). Unlike the case of health rights in Colombia, judicial receptivity did not develop in conjunction with social understandings of the law. Instead, judges maintained their own understandings of the law, ones that prompted a sense of alienation and a widening disconnect with social actors. Here, we see how the experience of mobilizing law can undermine the creation of a social understanding that these rights are meaningful in themselves. Future research should further explore the subnational terrain of constitutional embedding and the consequences of the various combinations of partial constitutional embedding across contexts.

Today, a wide variety of countries, including Armenia, Belarus, Dominican Republic, El Salvador, Gambia, Sri Lanka, Taiwan, Turkey, and Uzbekistan, are currently considering the drafting of new constitutions or the adoption of significant constitutional reforms (ConstitutionNet 2021). Perhaps most notably, in May 2022, the Chilean Constitutional Convention introduced a new draft constitution that recognizes a range of social rights, which is a substantial change from the Pinochet-era constitution being replaced. While Chilean voters rejected this draft constitution via a referendum in September 2022, the debate about the new constitution continues. Following the eventual promulgation of whatever version of the constitution is approved, a pressing question will be: to what extent are the actors in favor of and against the constitutional order (whether new or old) able to embed their visions of constitutional law?

At the same time as these constitutional reforms are being drafted, academics have begun to debate with renewed vigor the merits of constitutionalism itself, regardless of modifiers. To some extent, these arguments revive early critiques of powerful constitutions and powerful courts. For example, traditional accounts of judicial politics highlighted the ways in which courts have protected elite interests rather than the needs of the poor or politically marginalized (Galanter 1974; Scheingold 1974; Rosenberg 1991; Nonet and Selznick 2001). Others pointed to the dangers of "counter-majoritarianism" (Bickel 1962), or the possibility that special interest groups representing the preferences of the few win out in the courts at the expense of the interests of the general population. The extent to which social constitutionalism contributes to the deepening of democracy or, in fact, thwarts democratic processes is an open empirical question that is contingent on whether and how social constitutionalism becomes embedded.

These more recent critiques of constitutionalism express skepticism about the value of judicial review, especially in its strong form (Gyorfi 2016), and the potential erasure of the lines between national and international bodies and between the power of the judge and elected representatives (Loughlin 2022). Tamas Gyorfi proposes a theory of weak judicial review, which would allow a role for judges in the specification of rights, but only under the umbrella of an approach that is largely deferential to the legislature would this be acceptable. This kind of review would allow courts to assess whether or not legislation corresponded to structural-organizational norms, rather than a bill of rights. For Gyorfi (2016: 257), "the speculative and marginal improvement in human rights protection [brought about by strong constitutional courts] does not justify the direct, imminent and systematic exclusion of the citizenry from some of the most important political decisions of the community." As Gyorfi acknowledges elsewhere in his provocation, however, the extent to which either legislatures and courts adequately – or even partially – represent citizens' interests varies substantially across contexts.

Martin Loughlin (2022: 195) laments the demise of a form of constitutionalism that endorses limited government and the emergence of a constitutionalism that would encompass all of social life, "provid[ing] a comprehensive scheme of society" and serving as the "symbolic representation of collective political identity." That a constitution exists perhaps means that it will provide such a scheme, but it will be impactful only to the extent that it is embedded socially and legally. The embedding process seems to be what Loughlin takes issue with, though arguably embedding is just as democratic (and as anti-democratic) as most other political processes currently up for debate. Embedding occurs not by a formal vote but through "voting with one's feet," by citizen action and interaction, sometimes consciously and sometimes subconsciously. All members of the polity can participate, though their ability to participate equally will by heavily mediated by their power and resources (which, of course, are largely determined by socially constructed categories of difference, including race, class, and gender), as is the case with electoral politics.

The implicit alternative to social constitutionalism – with its justiciable individual rights and courts with strong review powers – is the construction of participatory institutions and a strong, representative legislature (which would ostensibly allow for politics to be conducted through ordinary legislation rather than constitutional law). First, these institutions are not necessarily mutually exclusive with social constitutionalism, and second, they are not immune to power differentials or vested interests. Traditional legislatures certainly cannot always be counted on to receive broad public support, avoid elite capture, or operate without dysfunction. Loughlin (2022: 197) suggests that "legislatures are now losing authority to governments, regulatory officials, and courts," which "erodes the principle of popular authorization, simultaneously weakening legislatures and political parties." However, in many places, including Colombia, the failures of legislatures and parties long preceded the creation of constitutional courts or the move from liberal or limited constitutionalism to the more robust form of social constitutionalism. The rise of the strong courts was not the source of the erosion of public support for the legislature or the failure of legislatures to govern effectively through ordinary legislation. In theory, strong courts and strong legislatures serve as checks on one another, moderating one another. Thus, in some ways, these critiques of constitutionalism are more concerned with how constitutionalism has been embedded in specific places than with constitutionalism itself.

The claim that constitutionalism "has been widely perceived as a positive phenomenon largely because it has never been closely analyzed" is perhaps a fair one (Loughlin 2022: 22). This book has endeavored to carry out such an analysis. I do not conclude that constitutionalism is an unqualified good. But neither is constitutionalism necessarily at fault for the ills currently plaguing global politics. Constitutions set out rules of the game, but, as this book shows, those rules both reflect and respond to politics on the ground. An embedded constitution can offer citizens a forum through which to pursue their needs, and viable alternatives are often few and far between. The experiment with social constitutionalism will not inhibit the possibility of more radical experiments in the future, but it does provide vulnerable citizens with one more tool – however blunt or ill-formed – with which they can push for changes to the conditions of their lives.

Further, as we see trends toward rights retrenchment elsewhere in the world, from the United States to countries in Africa, eastern Europe, and South Asia, we might well ask, "when and how can societies push against that?" One answer is to ensure that rights – whether codified in constitutional law, directive principles, or legislation – are embedded both socially and legally. When those rights are embedded and routinely claimed through legal mobilization, as the Colombian case demonstrates, they can withstand challenges from those who would wish to unravel them and those who feel no sense of obligation.

APPENDIX: INTERVIEWEES

In the following table, white entries are from Colombia, gray entries are from South Africa.

Name	Position(s)	Location of interview
F. Adeleke	Government (SA Human Rights Commission)	Johannesburg
N. Álvarez	Civil society	Bogotá
S. Ansari	Constitutional Court clerk	Skype
R. Arango	Constitutional Court and Council of State clerk, alternate Constitutional Court), academic, Justice in the Special Jurisdiction for Peace	Bogotá
V. Arango	Government (Personería)	Medellín
C. Avidon	Constitutional Court clerk, lawyer	Johannesburg
B. Barua	Constitutional Court clerk, lawyer	Johannesburg
H. Barnes	Lawyer, Acting High Court, Labor Court, and Land Claims Court judge	Johannesburg
N. Barrera	Lawyer (Constitutional Court and Council of State)	Bogotá
A. Barreto	Constitutional Court clerk, academic	Bogotá
A. Barrios	Civil society	Bogotá
J. Berger	Constitutional Court clerk, lawyer	Johannesburg
V. Bernal	Judge	Cali
S. Bernal	Government (TV producer)	Zoom
M. Bishop	Constitutional Court clerk, lawyer	Cape Town

Name	Position(s)	Location of interview
J. Bonivento	Supreme Court and Council of State justice, lawyer	Bogotá
J. Braulio	Judge	Medellín
S. Brener	Constitutional Court clerk, civil society	Johannesburg
J. Brickhill	Constitutional Court clerk, academic, civil society	Skype
G. Budlender	Lawyer, civil society, government	Cape Town
C. Cabezas	Judge	Cali
M. Cajas	Academic	Skype
J. Cardenas	Academic	Bogotá
M. Cardona	Judge	Cali
C. Carvajal	Constitutional Court clerk	Bogotá
E. Castellanos	Constitutional Court clerk, academic	Bogotá
F. Cepeda	Government, academic	Bogotá
M. Cepeda	Constitutional Court justice, government, academic	Bogotá
L. Chamberlain	Constitutional Court clerk, civil society, academic	Johannesburg
M. Chaskalson	Lawyer, civil society	Johannesburg
A. Chetuan	Government, lawyer	Bogotá
E. Cifuentes	Constitutional Court justice, government, academic	Bogotá
S. Coronado	Civil society, academic	Bogotá
M. Correa	Constitutional Court clerk, academic	Bogotá
H. Correa	Constitutional Court clerk, academic, Constitutional Court justice	Bogotá
S. Cowen	Constitutional Court clerk, lawyer	Johannesburg
I. de Vos	Constitutional Court clerk, civil society	Skype
P. Dela	Constitutional Court clerk, lawyer	Johannesburg
A. Dodson	Lawyer	Johannesburg
L. du Plessis	Civil society	Pretoria
P. du Rand	Government	Pretoria
P. Dube	Civil society	Skype
O. Dueñas	Constitutional Court clerk, lawyer, academic	Bogotá
John Dugard	Lawyer, academic, UN	Skype
J. Elkin Mejía	Government (Defensoría del Pueblo)	Medellín
C. Escobar	Constitutional Court clerk	Bogotá
J. Esguerra	Government, lawyer, Minister of Justice, Minister of Defense, academic	Bogotá
D. Fajardo	Constitutional Court clerk, government, Constitutional Court justice	Bogotá

Name	Position(s)	Location of interview
N. Ferreira	Constitutional Court clerk, lawyer	Johannesburg
M. Finn	Constitutional Court clerk, lawyer	Johannesburg
A. Fitzgerald	Constitutional Court clerk	Johannesburg
J. Fowkes	Constitutional Court clerk, academic, lawyer	Skype
A. Friedman	Constitutional Court clerk, lawyer	Johannesburg
J. Froneman	Constitutional Court justice	Johannesburg
G. Gallón	Civil society	Bogotá
M. García	Constitutional Court clerk, civil society	Bogotá
A. Gaviria	Government, Minister of Health, Minister of Education, academic	Bogotá
A. Goetz	Constitutional Court clerk, lawyer	Johannesburg
R. Goldstone	Constitutional Court justice	Johannesburg
Al. Gómez	Constitutional Court clerk, academic	Medellín
An. Gómez	Academic, board game designer	Zoom
J. Gómez	Civil society	Cali
J. González	Academic	Bogotá
C. González	Civil society	Medellín
S. González	Lawyer	Cali
I. Goodman	Constitutional Court clerk, lawyer	Johannesburg
K. Govender	Government (SA Human Rights Commission)	Durban
L. Granville	Constitutional Court clerk, lawyer	Skype
P. Gregoriou	Government (SA Human Rights Commission)	Johannesburg
A. Gutiérrez	Academic	Bogotá
M. Hathorn	Lawyer	Johannesburg
J. Henao	Constitutional Court justice, academic	Bogotá
D. Hernández	Judge	Bogotá
H. Herrera	Government, academic, civil society, Alternate Council of State and Superior Council of the Judiciary justice	Skype
F. Hobden	Constitutional Court clerk, lawyer	Johannesburg
K. Hofmeyr	Constitutional Court clerk, lawyer	Johannesburg
M. Hunter	Constitutional Court clerk, civil society	Johannesburg
A. Ismail	Civil society	Cape Town
F. Ismail	Government, academic, civil society	Cape Town
M. Jain	Constitutional court clerk, lawyer	Cape Town
I. Jaramillo	Academic, Alternate Constitutional Court and Council of State justice	Bogotá
"Judge"	Judge	Cauca

Name	Position(s)	Location of interview
"Judge"	Judge	Palmira
U. Jugroop	Constitutional Court clerk, civil society	Johannesburg
S. Kalmanovitz	Government, academic	Bogotá
S. Kazee	Constitutional Court clerk, lawyer	Johannesburg
P. Kruger	Lawyer, judge, civil society	Johannesburg
M. Krynauw	Constitutional Court clerk, government	Cape Town
E. Lamprea	Constitutional Court clerk, academic	Bogotá
L. Laverde	Government	Bogotá
"Lawyer"	Lawyer	Medellín
J. Lemaitre	Academic, justice in the Special Jurisdiction for Peace	Bogotá
C. Lewis	Supreme Court justice	Johannesburg
S. Liebenberg	Lawyer, academic, civil society	Skype
G. Lopera	Lawyer, academic, Constitutional Court clerk, Alternate Constitutional Court justice	Skype
A. López	Judge	Cali
D. López	Academic, lawyer, civil society, Alternate Constitutional Court justice	Bogotá
J. Love	Civil society	Johannesburg
A. Marín	Judge	Palmira
C. Martínez	Civil society, lawyer, UN	Bogotá
T. Matthews	Government (SA Human Rights Commission)	Johannesburg
M. Mbikiwa	Constitutional Court clerk, lawyer	Johannesburg
S. McGibbon	Constitutional Court clerk, lawyer	Johannesburg
S. McKenzie	Constitutional Court clerk, lawyer	Johannesburg
N. Memese	Constitutional Court clerk, civil society	Johannesburg
L. Mogollón	Government, lawyer (Constitutional Court, and Special Jurisdiction for Peace)	Bogotá
C. Molina	Academic, alternate Superior Council of the Judiciary justice	Bogotá
J. Montes	Judge, lawyer	Cali
S. Morelli	Government, lawyer	Bogotá
M. Moreno	Government (Defensoría del Pueblo)	Bogotá
K. Moshikaro	Constitutional Court clerk, academic	Cape Town
T. Mugunyani	Civil society	Pretoria
N. Muvangua	Constitutional Court clerk, lawyer	Skype
E. Naidu	Civil society	Durban
A. Nase	Civil society	Johannesburg
A. Navarro	Government, Minister of Health	Bogotá

Name	Position(s)	Location of interview
C. Neira	Lawyer (Constitutional Court), academic	Bogotá
T. Nichols	Lawyer	Durban
K. O'Regan	Constitutional Court justice, academic	Skype
H. Olano	Academic, lawyer (Constitutional Court)	Bogotá
L. Oliveros	Civil society, lawyer	Bogotá
A. Orjuela	Government (Defensoría del Pueblo)	Bogotá
J. Ortiz	Supreme Court and Superior Council of the Judiciary justice, Constitutional Court clerk, lawyer	Bogotá
N. Osuna	Academic, Superior Council of the Judiciary justice, alternate Constitutional Court justice, Minister of Justice	Bogotá
H. Pardo	Government (Defensoría del Pueblo)	Bogotá
J. Parsonage	Constitutional Court Clerk	Johannesburg
K. Paterson	Constitutional Court clerk, civil society	Johannesburg
"Patrick"	Civil society	Durban
A. Peters	Civil society	Cape Town
S. Plana	Civil society	Bogotá
A. Potter	Civil society	Johannesburg
N. Poveda	Civil society, lawyer	Bogotá
P. Puertas	Civil society	Bogotá
M. Quinche Ramírez	Constitutional Court clerk, academic	Bogotá
F. Quintana	Civil society	Skype
J. Raizon	Constitutional Court clerk, lawyer	Johannesburg
A. Ramelli	Constitutional Court and Council of State clerk, justice in the Special Jurisdiction for Peace	Bogotá
G. Ramírez	Constitutional Court clerk, academic	Bogotá
A. Raw	Constitutional Court clerk, civil society	Johannesburg
C. Reales	Constitutional Court clerk, civil society, academic	Bogotá
G. Recalde	Lawyer, academic	Cali
C. Rodríguez	Judge	Cali
J. Rodríguez	Academic	Bogotá
G. Roldán	Judge	Medellín
G. Rome	Lawyer, acting High Court judge	Johannesburg
C. Romero	Civil society	Bogotá
M. Rubio	Academic	Bogotá
P. Rueda	Constitutional Court clerk, academic, lawyer	Bogotá

Name	Position(s)	Location of interview
A. Sachs	Constitutional Court justice	Skype
C. Sánchez	Academic	Bogotá
Y. Sánchez	Government	Bogotá
T. Scott	Constitutional Court clerk, lawyer	Johannesburg
"Sergio"	Government (Defensoría del Pueblo)	Medellín
C. Shahim	Constitutional Court clerk, lawyer	Johannesburg
"Sifiso"	Civil society	Durban
D. Simonsz	Constitutional Court clerk, academic	Cape Town
A. Singh	Constitutional Court clerk, lawyer, civil society	Johannesburg
P. Singh	Constitutional Court clerk, lawyer	Johannesburg
L. Sisilana	Constitutional Court clerk, lawyer	Johannesburg
L. Siyo	Lawyer, civil society	Johannesburg
N. Stein	Constitutional Court clerk, civil society	Johannesburg
Z. Sujee	Civil society	Johannesburg
J. Tamayo	Supreme Court justice, lawyer	Skype
L. Theron	Constitutional Court justice	Skype
T. Thipanyane	Government (SA Human Rights Commission)	Johannesburg
J. Tisnés	Judge	Medellín
W. Trengove	Lawyer, civil society	Johannesburg
M. Trespalacios	Civil society	Bogotá
Y. Van Leeve	Constitutional Court clerk, lawyer	Johannesburg
L. Van Zyl	Constitutional Court clerk, lawyer	Skype
J. Vera	Lawyer	Bogotá
N. Vera	Civil society	Bogotá
P. Wayburne	Constitutional Court clerk, academic	Skype
E. Webber	Constitutional Court clerk, lawyer	Johannesburg
J. Wilké	Constitutional Court clerk, academic	Cape Town
B. Winks	Constitutional Court clerk, lawyer	Johannesburg
L. Xaso	Constitutional Court clerk, lawyer	Johannesburg
M. Zamora	Constitutional Court and Supreme Court clerk, prosecutor, Superior Council of the Judiciary justice, UN, Special Jurisdiction for Peace	Skype
J. Zapata	Government (Defensoría del Pueblo)	Medellín
"Zoleta"	Civil society	Cape Town

REFERENCES

Abdulai, Abdul-Gafaru, and Sam Hickey. 2016. "The Politics of Development under Competitive Clientelism: Insights from Ghana's Education Sector." *African Affairs* 115(458): 44–72.

Abel, Richard. 1995. *Politics by Other Means: Law in the Struggle against Apartheid, 1980–1994*. New York: Routledge.

Acemoglu, Daron, and James Robinson. 2006. *Economic Origins of Dictatorship and Democracy*. New York, NY: Cambridge University Press.

Adésínà, Jìmí O. 2009. "Social Policy in Sub-Saharan Africa: A Glance in the Rear-View Mirror." *International Journal of Social Welfare* 18 (1): 37–51.

Afrobarometer Data, available at www.afrobarometer.org.

Albarracín, Juan, Laura Gamboa, and Scott Mainwaring. 2018. "Deinstitutionalization without Collapse: Colombia's Party System." In *Party Systems in Latin America: Institutionalization, Decay, and Collapse*, ed. Scott Mainwaring. New York, NY: Cambridge University Press, 227–54.

Alexander, Michelle. 2012. *The New Jim Crow: Mass Incarceration in the Age of Colorblindness*. New York: The New Press.

Alexander, Peter. 2010. "Rebellion of the Poor: South Africa's Service Delivery Protests: A Preliminary Analysis." *Review of African Political Economy* 37 (123): 25–40.

Alter, Karen J. 2014. *The New Terrain of International Law*. Princeton, NJ: Princeton University Press.

Amat, Yamid. 2003. "LONDOÑO QUIERE UN ESTADO MONÁRQUICO Y SIN CONTROLES." El Tiempo. www.eltiempo.com/archivo/documento/MAM-1038668.

Angel-Cabo, Natalia, and Domingo Lovera. 2014. "Latin American Social Constitutionalism: Courts and Popular Participation." In *Social and Economic Rights in Theory and Practice: Critical Inquiries*, ed. Helena García, Karl E. Klare, and Lucy A. Williams. New York: Routledge.

Auyero, Javier. 2001. *Poor People's Politics: Peronist Survival Networks and the Legacy of Evita*. Durham, NC: Duke University Press.

Baird, Vanessa A. 2007. *Answering the Call of the Court: How Justices and Litigants Set the Supreme Court Agenda*. Charlottesville, VA: University of Virginia Press.

Banco de la República. n.d. "Miembros de La Asamblea Nacional Constituyente de 1991 - Enciclopedia | Banrepcultural." Accessed February 14, 2019.

http://enciclopedia.banrepcultural.org/index.php?title=Miembros_de_la_Asamblea_Nacional_Constituyente_de_1991.

Barreto, Antonio. 2011. *La generación del estado de sitio*. Bogotá, Colombia: Universidad de los Andes.

Bermeo, Nancy. 2016. "On Democratic Backsliding." *Journal of Democracy* 27 (1): 5–19.

Bermudez Maya, Luz Estella, and Julio Cesar Gomez Mejia. 2016. "Procedencia de la Acción de Tutela Por Vía de Hecho." Trabajo de grado para optar al título de Especialista en Derecho Procesal Contemporáneo, Universidad de Medellín, on file with the author.

Bickel, Alexander M. 1962. *The Least Dangerous Branch: The Supreme Court at the Bar of Politics*. New Haven, CT: Yale University Press.

Boesten, Jan. 2016. "Between Democratic Security and Democratic Legality: Discursive Institutionalism and Colombia's Constitutional Court." Ph.D. diss., Department of Political Science, University of British Columbia, on file with the author.

Bonilla, Daniel. 2013. *Constitucionalismo del Sur Global*. Bogotá: Siglo del Hombre Editores.

Booysen, Susan. 2007. "With the Ballot and the Brick: The Politics of Attaining Service Delivery." *Progress in Development Studies* 7 (1): 21–32.

Botero, Sandra, Daniel M. Brinks, and Ezequiel A. Gonzalez-Ocantos, eds. 2022. *The Limits of Judicialization: From Progress to Backlash in Latin America*. Cambridge, UK: Cambridge University Press.

Bratton, Michael, and Nicholas van de Walle. 1997. *Democratic Experiments in Africa: Regime Transitions in Comparative Perspective*. Cambridge, UK: Cambridge University Press.

Brewer-Carías, Allan R. 2009. *Constitutional Protection of Human Rights in Latin America: A Comparative Study of Amparo Proceedings*. Cambridge, UK: Cambridge University Press.

Brinks, Daniel M., and William Forbath. 2014. "The Role of Courts and Constitutions in the New Politics of Welfare in Latin America." In *Law and Development of Middle Income Countries*. Randall Peerenboom and Tom Ginsburg, eds. Cambridge, UK: Cambridge University Press.

Brinks, Daniel M., Varun Gauri, and Kyle Shen. 2015. "Social Rights Constitutionalism: Negotiating the Tension between the Universal and the Particular." *Annual Review of Law and Social Science* 11: 289–308.

Budlender, Steven, Gilbert Marcus, and Nick Ferreira. 2014. "Public Interest Litigation and Social Change in South Africa:" Atlantic Philanthropies.

Burstein, Paul. 1991. "Legal Mobilization as a Social Movement Tactic: The Struggle for Equal Employment Opportunity." *American Journal of Sociology* 96 (5): 1201–25.

Cammett, Melani Claire, and Lauren M. MacLean, eds. 2014. *The Politics of Non-State Social Welfare*. Ithaca, NY: Cornell University Press.

Carey, John M. 2000. "Parchment, Equilibria, and Institutions." *Comparative Political Studies* 33 (6–7): 735–61.

Carlin, Ryan, Mariana Castrellón, Varun Gauri, Jaramillo Sierra, Isabel Cristina, and Jeffrey Staton. 2022. Public Reactions to Noncompliance with Judicial Orders. *American Political Science Review*, 116 (1): 265–82.

Carpenter, R. Charli. 2007. "Studying Issue (Non)-Adoption in Transnational Advocacy Networks." *International Organization* 61 (3): 643–67.

Casper, Gerhard, and Richard Posner. 1974. "A Study of the Supreme Court's Caseload." *The Journal of Legal Studies* 3 (2): 339–75.

Cepeda, Manuel José. 2004. "Judicial Activism in a Violent Context: Origin, Role, and Impact of the Colombian Constitutional Court." *Washington University Global Studies Law Review* 3: 529–700.

Chandra, Kanchan. 2004. *Why Ethnic Parties Succeed: Patronage and Ethnic Head Counts in India*. Cambridge, UK: Cambridge University Press.

Chua, Lynette J., and David M. Engel. 2019. "Legal Consciousness Reconsidered." *Annual Review of Law and Social Science* 15 (1): 335–53. https://doi.org/10.1146/annurev-lawsocsci-101518-042717.

Cichowski, Rachel A. 2007. *The European Court and Civil Society: Litigation, Mobilization and Governance*. New York: Cambridge University Press.

Collier, Ruth Berins, and David Collier. 1979. "Inducements versus Constraints: Disaggregating 'Corporatism.'" *American Political Science Review* 73 (4): 967–86.

Community Agency for Social Enquiry (CASE). 1995. Report. On file with author.

Consejo Superior de la Judicatura. 2001. *Informe al Congreso de La República 2001–2002*. www.ramajudicial.gov.co/web/publicaciones/informe-al-congreso-de-la-republica/2001-2002

2016. *Informe al Congreso de La República: Gestión de La Administración de Justicia 2016*. www.ramajudicial.gov.co/web/publicaciones/2016-2017

2017. *Informe al Congreso de La República 2017*. www.ramajudicial.gov.co/web/publicaciones/129

2021. *Informe de Gestión de La Rama Judicial al Congreso de La República 2021*. www.ramajudicial.gov.co/web/publicaciones/2021-2022

Constitution Hill Trust. "The People Have Their Say." Our Constitution. https://ourconstitution.constitutionhill.org.za/south-africas-constitution/writing-one-law-for-one-nation/people-have-their-say/

ConstitutionNet. 2021. "In the World of Constitution Building in 2021." ConstitutionNet. https://constitutionnet.org/news/world-constitution-building-2021.

Corporación Excelencia en la Justicia. 2018. "Tasa de Jueces Por Habitantes En Colombia y El Mundo." *Corporación Excelencia en la Justicia*. https://cej.org.co/sala-de-prensa/justiciometro/tasa-de-jueces-por-habitantes-en-colombia-y-el-mundo/

2022. "Índice de Congestión de La Justicia Ordinaria En Colombia." https://cej.org.co/indicadores-de-justicia/efectividad/indice-de-congestion-de-la-justicia-ordinaria-en-colombia/

Cosoy, Natalio. 2015. "A 30 años de las '28 horas de terror': así fue la toma del Palacio de Justicia en Colombia." Accessible at: www.bbc.com/mundo/noticias/2015/11/151030_colombia_30_aniversario_toma_palacio_de_justicia_nc

Council of Europe. 2002. European Judicial Systems CEPEJ Evaluation Report. https://rm.coe.int/cepej-report-2020-22-e-web/1680a86279

Cover, Robert M. 1986. "Violence and the Word." *The Yale Law Journal* 95 (8): 1601.

Cronin-Furman, Kate, and Roxani Krystalli. 2021. "The Things They Carry: Victims' Documentation of Forced Disappearance in Colombia and Sri Lanka." *European Journal of International Relations* 27 (1): 79–101.

Cross, John Christopher. 1998. *Informal Politics: Street Vendors and the State in Mexico City*. Stanford, CA: Stanford University Press.

Cruz Rodríguez, Edwin. 2013. "¿Fin de la Tutela?" Palabras Al Margen (blog). December 15, 2013. http://palabrasalmargen.com/edicion-23/fin-de-la-tutela/.

Defensoría del Pueblo. 2003. "La Tutela y el derecho a la salud, 1999–2003." On file with the author.

2005. "La Tutela y el Derecho a la Salud, 2003–2005." On file with the author.

2008. "La Tutela y el Derecho a la Salud, Periódo 2006–2008." On file with the author.

2009. "La Tutela y el Derecho a la Salud, 2009." On file with the author.

2010. "La Tutela y el Derecho a la Salud, 2010." On file with the author.

2011. "La Tutela y el derecho a la salud, 2011." On file with the author.

2012. "La Tutela y el derecho a la salud, 2012." On file with the author.

2013. "La Tutela y los derecho a la salud y a la seguridad social, 2013." On file with the author.

2014. "LA TUTELA Y LOS DERECHO A LA SALUD Y A LA SEGURIDAD SOCIAL, 2014." On file with the author.

2015. "LA TUTELA Y LOS DERECHO A LA SALUD Y A LA SEGURIDAD SOCIAL, 2015." On file with the author.

2016. "La Tutela y el derecho a la salud, 2016." On file with the author.

2017. "La Tutela: Los Derecho a la Salud y a la Seguridad Social, 2017." On file with the author.

2018. "La Tutela y los derecho a la salud y a la seguridad social, 2018." On file with the author.

2019. "La Tutela y los derecho a la salud y a la seguridad social, 2019." On file with the author.

2020. "La Tutela y los derecho a la salud y a la seguridad social, 2019." On file with the author.

Dixon, Rosalind, and Ginsburg, Tom. 2017. The Forms and Limits of Constitutions as Political Insurance. *International Journal of Constitutional Law*, 15 (4), 988–1012.

Dugas, John C. 2001a. "Drugs, Lies, and Audiotape: The Samper Crisis in Colombia" *Latin American Research Review* 36 (2): 157–74.

2001b. "The Origin, Impact and Demise of the 1989–1990 Colombian Student Movement: Insights from Social Movement Theory." *Journal of Latin American Studies* 33 (4): 807–37.

Dugard, Jackie. 2015. "Closing the Doors of Justice: An Examination of the Constitutional Court's Approach to Direct Access, 1995–2013." *South African Journal on Human Rights* 31 (1): 112–35.

Dueñas Ruiz, Oscar José. 1997. *Control constitucional: análisis de un siglo de jurisprudencia*. Bogotá: Ediciones Librería del Profesional.

El Espectador. 2012. "Fiscalía capturó a cinco directivos de EPS por fraude a la salud." December 17. www.elespectador.com/noticias/judicial/fiscalia-capturo-cinco-directivos-de-eps-fraude-salud-articulo-392896.

El Tiempo. 1994. "Mayulay: Jugando, Jugando… Voy Entutelando." *El Tiempo*. October 8, 1994. Accessed June 4, 2021. www.eltiempo.com/archivo/documento/MAM-229122.

1995. "La Tutela Cumplió Su Ciclo." *El Tiempo*. February 2, 1995. www.eltiempo.com/archivo/documento/MAM-298725.

2012. "Aseguradas siete personas por el caso del desfalco al Fosyga." May 4. www.eltiempo.com/archivo/documento/CMS-11719964.

Elkins, Zachary, Tom Ginsburg, and Beth Simmons. 2013. "Getting to Rights: Treaty Ratification, Constitutional Convergence, and Human Rights Practice." *Harvard International Law Journal* 54: 37.

Elkins, Zachary and Tom Ginsburg. 2021 "Characteristics of National Constitutions, Version 3.0." Comparative Constitutions Project. Last modified: May 20, 2021. Available at comparativeconstitutionsproject.org.

Elkins, Zachary, Tom Ginsburg, and James Melton. 2009. *The Endurance of National Constitutions*. New York: Cambridge University Press.

Epp, Charles R. 1998. *The Rights Revolution: Lawyers, Activists, and Supreme Courts in Comparative Perspective*. Chicago: University of Chicago Press.

2009. *Making Rights Real: Activists, Bureaucrats, and the Creation of the Legalistic State*. Chicago: University of Chicago Press.

Esping-Andersen, Gøsta. 1990. *The Three Worlds of Welfare Capitalism*. Princeton, NJ: Princeton University Press.

Ewick, Patricia, and Susan S. Silbey. 1998. *The Common Place of Law: Stories from Everyday Life*. Chicago: University of Chicago Press.

Feeley, Malcolm M., and Edward L. Rubin. 1998. *Judicial Policy Making and the Modern State: How the Courts Reformed America's Prisons*. Cambridge, UK: Cambridge University Press.

Felstiner, William L. F., Richard L. Abel, and Austin Sarat. 1980. "The Emergence and Transformation of Disputes: Naming, Blaming, Claiming..." *Law & Society Review*: 631–54.

Ferguson, James. 2015. *Give a Man a Fish: Reflections on the New Politics of Distribution*. Durham: Duke University Press.

Ferraz, Motta and Octavio Luiz. 2011. "Harming the Poor through Social Rights Litigation: Lessons from Brazil." *Texas Law Review* 89: 1643–68.

Fish Hodgson, Tim. 2015. "Bridging the Gap between People and the Law: Transformative Constitutionalism and the Right to Constitutional Literacy." *Acta Juridica* 2015 (1): 189–212.

Fiszbein, Ariel, Norbert Rüdiger Schady, and Francisco H. G. Ferreira. 2009. *Conditional Cash Transfers: Reducing Present and Future Poverty*. A World Bank Policy Research Report. Washington, DC: World Bank.

Fowkes, James. 2016. *Building the Constitution: The Practice of Constitutional Interpretation in Post-Apartheid South Africa*. Cambridge, UK: Cambridge University Press.

France, Anatole. 1910. *The Red Lily*. London and New York: J. Lane Company.

Freedom House. 2011. *Countries at the Crossroads 2011: Colombia*. www.refworld.org/docid/4ecba650c.html.

Galanter, Marc. 1974. "Why the 'Haves' Come Out Ahead: Speculations on the Limits of Legal Change." *Law & Society Review* 9(1): 95.

Gallagher, Janice. 2022. *Bootstrap Justice: The Search for Mexico's Disappeared*. Oxford and New York: Oxford University Press.

Gallagher, Janice, Gabrielle Kruks-Wiser, and Whitney K. Taylor. Forthcoming. *Beyond Ballots and Barricades: The Practice and Consequences of Everyday Claim-Making*. Cambridge, UK: Cambridge University Press.

Gallagher, Mary E. 2006. "Mobilizing the Law in China: 'Informed Disenchantment' and the Development of Legal Consciousness." *Law & Society Review* 40(4): 783–816.

2017. *Authoritarian Legality in China: Law, Workers, and the State*. Cambridge, UK: Cambridge University Press.

Gallagher, Mary, and Yujeong Yang. 2017. "Getting Schooled: Legal Mobilization as an Educative Process." *Law & Social Inquiry* 42(1): 163–94.

Garay, Candelaria. 2016. *Social Policy Expansion in Latin America*. New York, NY: Cambridge University Press.

García Villegas, Mauricio. 2001. "Constitucionalismo perverso. Normalidad y anormalidad constitucional en Colombia: 1957–1997," in Santos, Boaventura de Sousa y García Villegas, Mauricio (eds.). *El caleidoscopio de las justicias en Colombia. Análisis socio-jurídico*. Santafé de Bogotá: Siglo del Hombre: 317–70.

Gargarella, Roberto. 2020. *La derrota del derecho en América Latina: Siete tesis*. Ciudad Autónoma de Buenos Aires: Siglo XXI Editores.

Gauri, Varun, and Daniel M. Brinks. 2008. *Courting Social Justice: Judicial Enforcement of Social and Economic Rights in the Developing World*. Cambridge and New York: Cambridge University Press.

Gaviria, César. 1993. "Palabras del señor presidente de la republica, César Gaviria Trujillo, en la presentación del juego 'Tutea y Juega.'" On file with the author.

Genn, Hazel. 1999. *Paths to Justice: What People Do and Think about Going to Law*. Oxford: Hart.

Ginsburg, Tom. 2003. *Judicial Review in New Democracies: Constitutional Courts in Asian Cases*. Cambridge, UK: Cambridge University Press.

Ginsburg, Tom, Aziz Z. Huq, and Mila Versteeg. 2018. "The Coming Demise of Liberal Constitutionalism?" *The University of Chicago Law Review*: 17.

Glendon, Mary Ann. 1993. *Rights Talk: The Impoverishment of Political Discourse*. New York, NY: Free Press.

Gloppen, Siri. 1997. *South Africa: The Battle Over the Constitutional Court*. Farnham, UK: Ashgate.

González-Ocantos, Ezequiel. 2014. Persuade Them or Oust Them: Crafting Judicial Change and Transitional Justice in Argentina. *Comparative Politics*, 46 (4), 479–98.

2016. *Shifting Legal Visions: Judicial Change and Human Rights Trials in Latin America*. Cambridge, UK: Cambridge University Press.

Gough, Ian, Geof Wood, Armando Barrientos, Philippa Bevan, Peter Davis, and Graham Room. 2004. *Insecurity and Welfare Regimes in Asia, Africa and Latin America: Social Policy in Development Contexts*. Cambridge, UK: Cambridge University Press.

Graaff, David. 2012. "¿Se volverá conservadora la Corte Constitucional?" La Silla Vacía, August 18, 2012. https://lasillavacia.com/historia/se-volvera-conservadora-la-corte-constitucional-35546.

Gutierrez, John. 1997. "CONGRESO NO DIO LA TALLA EN REFORMA DE TUTELA." *El Tiempo*. www.eltiempo.com/archivo/documento/MAM-680262.

Gyorfi, Tamas. 2016. *Against the New Constitutionalism*. Northampton, MA: Edward Elgar Publishing.

Haggard, Stephan, and Robert R. Kaufman. 2008. *Development, Democracy, and Welfare States: Latin America, East Asia, and Eastern Europe*. Princeton: Princeton University Press.

Hall, Peter A., and David Soskice. 2001. *Varieties of Capitalism: The Institutional Foundations of Comparative Advantage*. Oxford: Oxford University Press.

Halliday, Simon. 2019. "After Hegemony: The Varieties of Legal Consciousness Research." *Social & Legal Studies* 28 (6): 859–78.

Hammergren, Linn. 2006. "Latin American Experience with Rule of Law Reforms and Applicability of Nation Building Efforts." *Case Western Reserve Journal of International Law* 38: 33.

Helfer, L. R. 2008. "Redesigning the European Court of Human Rights: Embeddedness as a Deep Structural Principle of the European Human Rights Regime." *European Journal of International Law* 19(1): 125–59. https://doi.org/10.1093/ejil/chn004.

Heller, Patrick. 2013. *Challenges and Opportunities: Civil Society in a Globalizing World*. New York: United Nations Development Programme.

Henao, Juan Carlos. 2013. "El ideario de la Constitución de 1863 no ha muerto." Accessible at: www.eltiempo.com/archivo/documento/CMS-12785475.

Hertogh, Marc. 2018. *Nobody's Law*. London: Palgrave Macmillan UK. https://doi.org/10.1057/978-1-137-60397-5.

Heywood, M. 2009. "South Africa's Treatment Action Campaign: Combining Law and Social Mobilization to Realize the Right to Health." *Journal of Human Rights Practice* 1 (1): 14–36.

Hilbink, Lisa. 2007. *Judges beyond Politics in Democracy and Dictatorship: Lessons from Chile*. Cambridge, UK: Cambridge University Press.

2008. "Assessing the New Constitutionalism." *Comparative Politics* 40(2): 227–45.

2014. "Location, Location, Location: On Judicial Attitudes and Transitional Justice in Spain and Chile." https://papers.ssrn.com/abstract=2712003.

Hilson, Chris. 2010. "Climate Change Litigation: An Explanatory Approach (Or Bringing Grievance Back In)." In *Climate Change: La Riposta Del Diritto*, edited by Fabrizio Fracchia and Massimo Occhiena, 421–36. Naples, Italy: Editoriale Scientifica.

Hirschl, Ran. 2004. "The Political Origins of the New Constitutionalism." *Indiana Journal of Global Legal Studies* 11(1): 71–108.

2008. "The Judicialization of Politics." *The Oxford Handbook of Law and Politics*.

Holland, Alisha C. 2017. *Forbearance as Redistribution: The Politics of Informal Welfare in Latin America*. Cambridge, UK: Cambridge University Press.

Holland, Alisha C., and Ben Ross Schneider. 2017. "Easy and Hard Redistribution: The Political Economy of Welfare States in Latin America." *Perspectives on Politics* 15 (04): 988–1006.

Hollis-Brusky, Amanda. 2015. *Ideas with Consequences: The Federalist Society and the Conservative Counterrevolution*. Studies in Postwar American Political Development. Oxford: Oxford University Press.

Huber, Evelyne, and John D. Stephens. 2012. *Democracy and the Left: Social Policy and Inequality in Latin America*. Chicago: University of Chicago Press.

Hudson, Alexander. 2021. *The Veil of Participation: Citizens and Political Parties in Constitution-Making Processes*. New York: Cambridge University Press.

Human Sciences Research Council (HSRC). 2004. Fact Sheet: Poverty in South Africa. On file with author.

Iversen, Torben. 2005. *Capitalism, Democracy, and Welfare*. Cambridge, UK: Cambridge University Press.

Keohane, Robert, Andrew Moravcsik, and Anne-Marie Slaughter. 2003. "Legalized Dispute Resolution: Interstate and Transnational." *International Organization* 54.

Kim, Jieun, Rachel E. Stern, Benjamin L. Liebman, and Xiaohan Wu. 2021. "Closing Open Government: Grassroots Policy Conversion of China's Open Government Information Regulation and Its Aftermath." *Comparative Political Studies* 1–29.

Kitschelt, Herbert, and Steven Wilkinson, eds. 2007. *Patrons, Clients, and Policies: Patterns of Democratic Accountability and Political Competition*. Cambridge, UK: Cambridge University Press.

Klare, Karl E. 1998. "Legal Culture and Transformative Constitutionalism." *South African Journal on Human Rights* 14 (1): 146–88.

Klug, Heinz. 2000. *Constituting Democracy: Law, Globalism and South Africa's Political Reconstruction*. Cambridge, UK: Cambridge University Press.

Kruks-Wisner, Gabrielle. 2018. *Claiming the State: Active Citizenship and Social Welfare in Rural India*. Cambridge, UK: Cambridge University Press.

2021. "Great Expectations, Great Grievances: The Politics of Citizens' Complaints in India." *Comparative Politics* 54 (1): 27–64.

Kurtz, Marcus J. 2004. "The Dilemmas of Democracy in the Open Economy: Lessons from Latin America." *World Politics* 56 (2): 262–302.

La tutela factor humano episode, n.d. Accessible at: www.youtube.com/watch?v=3G5PxCkM5ws (also on file with author).

Lamprea, Everaldo. 2015. *Derechos en la práctica: Jueces, litigantes y operadores de políticas de salud en Colombia*. Bogotá, Colombia: Universidad de los Andes.

Lamprea, Everaldo, and Johnattan García. 2016. "Closing the Gap between Formal and Material Health Care Coverage in Colombia." *Health and Human Rights Journal* 18 (2): 49–65.

Landau, David. 2012. The Reality of Social Rights Enforcement. *Harvard International Law Journal*, 53, 60.

2014. "Beyond Judicial Independence: The Construction of Judicial Power in Colombia." Ph.D. diss. Department of Government, Harvard University, on file with the author.

Langford, Malcolm. 2014. "Introduction: Civil Society and Socio-Economic Rights." In *Socio-Economic Rights in South Africa: Symbols or Substance?*, edited by Malcolm Langford, Ben Cousins, Jackie Dugard, and Tshepo Madlingozi, 1–32. Cambridge, UK: Cambridge University Press.

Lasswell, Harold D. 1936. *Politics: Who Gets What, When, How*. New York: Whittlesey House.

"Latinobarómetro: Online Analysis." www.latinobarometro.org/latOnline.jsp.

Lehoucq, Emilio, and Whitney K. Taylor. 2020. "Conceptualizing Legal Mobilization: How Should We Understand the Deployment of Legal Strategies?" *Law & Social Inquiry* 45 (1): 166–93.

Lemaitre, Julieta. 2009. *El derecho como conjuro: Fetichismo legal, violencia y movimientos sociales*. Bogotá: Grupo IDEAS (Investigación, Derecho y Acción Social) Facultad de Derecho Universidad de los Andes.

2019. El Estado siempre llega tarde. Siglo Veintiuno Editores Argentina S.A. y Universidad de los Andes.

Lempert, Richard. 1976. "Mobilizing Private Law: An Introductory Essay." *Law & Society Review* 11 (2): 173.

Levinson, Sanford. 1990. "Veneration and Constitutional Change: James Madison Confronts the Possibility of Constitutional Amendment. The Federalist Symposium." *Texas Tech Law Review* 21 (4): 2443–62.

Levitsky, Steven, and Maria Victoria Murillo. 2013. Building Institutions on Weak Foundations: Lessons from Latin America. In D. Brinks, M. Leiras, & S. Mainwaring (Eds.), *Reflections on Uneven Democracies: The Legacy of Guillermo O'Donnell* (pp. 189–213). Baltimore, MD: JHU Press.

Levitsky, Steven, and Daniel Ziblatt. 2018. *How Democracies Die*. New York: Crown.

Loaiza Henao, Claudia Janneth. 2014. *La acción de tutela contra providencias judiciales y el debido proceso. Estudio de la jurisprudencia de la Corte Constitutional de Colombia*. Artículo elaborado para optar el título de Especialista en Derecho Procesal de la Universidad de Antioquia, on file with the author.

Loughlin, Professor Martin. 2022. *Against Constitutionalism*. Cambridge, MA: Harvard University Press.

Lovell, George I. 2012. *This Is Not Civil Rights: Discovering Rights Talk in 1939 America*. Chicago: University of Chicago Press.

Lynch, Julia. 2006. *Age in the Welfare State: The Origins of Social Spending on Pensioners, Workers, and Children*. Cambridge, UK: Cambridge University Press.

Mainwaring, Scott. 2006. "The Crisis of Representation in the Andes." *Journal of Democracy* 17 (3): 13–27.

Malagón Pinzón, Miguel. 2012. *Los modelos de control administrativo en colombia (1811–2011)*. Bogotá: Universidad de los Andes.

Mandela, Nelson. 1995. *Long Walk to Freedom: The Autobiography of Nelson Mandela*. Boston: Back Bay Books.

Mares, Isabela. 2003. *The Politics of Social Risk: Business and Welfare State Development*. Cambridge, UK: Cambridge University Press.

Mares, Isabela, and Matthew E. Carnes. 2009. "Social Policy in Developing Countries." *Annual Review of Political Science* 12 (1): 93–113.

Marshall, Anna-Maria. 1998. "Closing the Gaps: Plaintiffs in Pivotal Sexual Harassment Cases." *Law & Social Inquiry* 23 (4): 761–93.

Marshall, T.H. 1950. *Citizenship and Social Class*. Cambridge, UK: Cambridge University Press.

Martínez Cortés, Paula. 2013. "The Victims and Land Restitution Law in Colombia in Context." *Forschungs- und Dokumentationszentrum Chile-Lateinamerika (FDCL), Transnational Institute (TNI) Report*.

Martínez Franzoni, Juliana. 2008. "Welfare Regimes in Latin America: Capturing Constellations of Markets, Families, and Policies." *Latin American Politics and Society* 50 (2): 67–100.

Martz, John. 1997. *The Politics of Clientelism: Democracy and the State in Colombia*. New Brunswick, NJ: Transaction Publishers.

McCann, Michael W. 1994. *Rights at Work: Pay Equity Reform and the Politics of Legal Mobilization*. Chicago: University of Chicago Press.

McCann, Michael, and Filiz Kahraman. 2021. "On the Interdependence of Liberal and Illiberal/Authoritarian Legal Forms in Racial Capitalist Regimes …The Case of the United States." *Annual Review of Law and Social Science* 17 (1): 483–503.

McCann, Michael W., and George I. Lovell. 2020. *Union by Law: Filipino American Labor Activists, Rights Radicalism, and Racial Capitalism*. Chicago: University of Chicago Press.

McCarthy, John D., and Mayer N. Zald. 1977. "Resource Mobilization and Social Movements: A Partial Theory." *American Journal of Sociology* 82 (6): 1212–41.

Meierhenrich, Jens. 2010. *The Legacies of Law: Long-Run Consequences of Legal Development in South Africa, 1652–2000*. Cambridge, UK: Cambridge University Press.

Merry, Sally Engle. 1985. "Concepts of Law and Justice among Working-Class Americans: Ideology as Culture." *Legal Studies Forum* 9: 59.

1990. *Getting Justice and Getting Even: Legal Consciousness among Working-Class Americans*. Chicago: University of Chicago Press.

2003. "Rights Talk and the Experience of Law: Implementing Women's Human Rights to Protection from Violence." *Human Rights Quarterly* 25 (2): 343–81.

Miller, Richard E., and Austin Sarat. 1980. "Grievances, Claims, and Disputes: Assessing the Adversary Culture." *Law & Society Review* 15 (3/4): 525–66.

Mnookin, Robert H., and Lewis Kornhauser. 1979. "Bargaining in the Shadow of the Law: The Case of Divorce." *The Yale Law Journal* 88 (5): 950.

Morgan, Jana. 2013. *Bankrupt Representation and Party System Collapse*. University Park: Penn State University Press.

National Center for Historical Memory. 2013. *¡Basta ya! Colombia: memorias de guerra y dignidad*. Accessible at: www.centrodememoriahistorica.gov.co/micrositios/informeGeneral/descargas.html

Nattrass, Nicoli, and Jeremy Seekings. 2011. "The Economy and Poverty in the Twentieth Century." In *The Cambridge History of South Africa*, eds. Robert Ross, Anne Kelk Mager, and Bill Nasson. Cambridge, UK: Cambridge University Press, 518–72.

Negretto, Gabriel, and Jaiver Couso. 2018. "Constitution-Building Processes in Latin America." International IDEA Discussion Paper 3/2018.

Nonet, Philippe, and Philip Selznick. 2001. *Law and Society in Transition: Toward Responsive Law*. London, UK, and New York, NY: Routledge.

North, Douglass, and Barry Weingast. 1989. "Constituents and Commitment: The Evolution of Institutions Governing Public Choice in Seventeenth-Century England" *The Journal of Economic History* 49 (4): 802–32.

Nunes, Rodrigo. 2010a. *Ideal Justice in Latin America: Interests, Ideas, and the Political Origins of Judicial Activism in Brazil and Colombia* [PhD Dissertation]. University of Texas at Austin.

2010b. "Ideational Origins of Progressive Judicial Activism: The Colombian Constitutional Court and the Right to Health." *Latin American Politics and Society*, 52 (3), 67–97.

O'Donnell, Guillermo. 1993. "On the State, Democratization and Some Conceptual Problems: A Latin American View with Glances at Some Postcommunist Countries." *World Development* 21 (8): 1355–69.

Ortiz, Jaime. 1991. "Proyecto de Acto Reformatorio de la Constitución Política de Colombia No. 10." *Gaceta Constitucional* 9: 21.

Páez, Angela M., and Catalina Vallejo Piedrahíta. 2021. "Channeling Water Conflicts through the Legislative Branch in Colombia." *Water* 13 (9): 1214.

Palacios, Marco. 2006. *Between Legitimacy and Violence: A History of Colombia, 1875–2002*. Translated by Richard Stoller. Durham: Duke University Press Books.

Pavone, Tommaso. 2022. *The Ghostwriters: Lawyers and the Politics behind the Judicial Construction of Europe*. Cambridge, UK: Cambridge University Press.

Pedriana, Nicholas. 2006. "From Protective to Equal Treatment: Legal Framing Processes and Transformation of the Women's Movement in the 1960s." *American Journal of Sociology* 111 (6): 1718–61.

Petrova, Dimitrina. 2018. Strategic human rights litigation in tough times. OpenGlobalRights. www.openglobalrights.org/strategic-human-rights-litigation-in-tough-times/

Pham, Phuong, Patrick Vinck, Bridget Marchesi, Doug Johnson, Peter Dixon, and Kathryn Sikkink. 2016. "Evaluating Transitional Justice: The Role of Multi-Level Mixed Methods Datasets and the Colombia Reparation Program for War Victims." *Transitional Justice Review* 1 (4). https://ir.lib.uwo.ca/tjreview/vol1/iss4/3.

Piven, Frances Fox, and Richard Cloward. 1977. *Poor People's Movements: Why They Succeed, How They Fail*. New York, NY: Knopf Doubleday Publishing Group.

Polanyi, Karl. 1944. *The Great Transformation: The Political and Economic Origins of Our Time*. Boston, MA: Beacon Press.

Pou Giménez, Francisca. 2018. "The Rights of Rivers and Forests and Apex Court Dynamics in Colombia: On Natural and Institutional Environments." *I-CONnect*. www.iconnectblog.com/2018/06/the-rights-of-rivers-and-forests-and-apex-court-dynamics-in-colombia-on-natural-and-institutional-environments-i-connect-column/.

Powell, Martin. 2002. "The Hidden History of Social Citizenship" *Citizenship Studies* 6 (3): 229–44.

Powell, Martin, and Armando Barrientos. 2004. "Welfare Regimes and the Welfare Mix." *European Journal of Political Research* 43 (1): 83–105.

Pribble, Jennifer. 2011. "Worlds Apart: Social Policy Regimes in Latin America." *Studies in Comparative International Development* 46 (2): 191–216.

Quinche Ramírez, Manuel Fernando. 2007. *Vías de hecho: acción de tutela contra providencias*. 3rd ed. Bogotá, Colombia: Universidad del Rosario.

2020. *Vías de hecho: acción de tutela contra providencias*. 9th ed. Bogotá, Colombia: Temis.

Revelo-Rebolledo, Javier. 2008. "La independencia judicial en tiempos de Uribe." *Papel Político* 13 (1): 42.

Restrepo Piedrahita, Carlos. 1993. *Primeras constituciones de Colombia y Venezuela, 1811–1830*. Bogotá, Colombia: Universidad Externado de Colombia.

Restrepo-Yepes, Olga Cecilia, Mauricio Bocanument-Arbeláez, and Milton Andrés Rojas-Betancur. 2014. *Voces de la Asamblea Nacional Constituyente de 1991*. Medellín, Colombia: UNIVERSIDAD DE MEDELLIN.

Ríos-Figueroa, Julio. 2016. *Constitutional Courts as Mediators: Armed Conflict, Civil-Military Relations, and the Rule of Law in Latin America*. Cambridge, UK: Cambridge University Press.

Rodríguez-Raga, Juan Carlos. 2011. "Strategic Deference in the Colombian Constitutional Court, 1992–2006." In *Courts in Latin America*, eds. Gretchen Helmke and Julio Ríos-Figueroa, 81–98. Cambridge, UK: Cambridge University Press.

Roberts, Kenneth M. 1998. *Deepening Democracy? The Modern Left and Social Movements in Chile and Peru*. Palo Alto, CA: Stanford University Press.

2002. "Social Inequalities without Class Cleavages in Latin America's Neoliberal Era." *Studies in Comparative International Development* 36 (4): 3–33.

Rodríguez Garavito, César A. 2009. *Más allá del desplazamiento. Políticas, derechos y superación del desplazamiento forzado en Colombia*. Bogotá, Colombia: Universidad de Los Andes.

2011. "Beyond the Courtroom: The Impact of Judicial Activism on Socioeconomic Rights in Latin America." *Texas Law Review* 89: 1669–98.

Rosenberg, Gerald N. 1991. *The Hollow Hope: Can Courts Bring about Social Change?* Chicago: University of Chicago Press.

Rothstein, Richard. 2017. *The Color of Law: A Forgotten History of How Our Government Segregated America.* New York and London: Liveright.

Rudra, Nita. 2008. *Globalization and the Race to the Bottom in Developing Countries: Who Really Gets Hurt?* Cambridge, UK: Cambridge University Press.

Rueda, Pablo. 2010. "Legal Language and Social Change during Colombia's Economic Crisis." In *Cultures of Legality*, edited by Javier Couso, Alexandra Huneeus, and Rachel Sieder, 25–50. Cambridge, UK: Cambridge University Press.

Ruggie, John Gerard. 1982. "International Regimes, Transactions, and Change: Embedded Liberalism in the Postwar Economic Order." *International Organization* 36 (2): 379–415.

Santos, Alvaro. 2006. "The World Bank's Uses of the 'Rule of Law' Promise in Economic Development." In *The New Law and Economic Development*, edited by David M. Trubek and Alvaro Santos, 253–300. Cambridge, UK: Cambridge University Press.

Scheingold, Stuart A. 1974. *The Politics of Rights: Lawyers, Public Policy, and Political Change.* Ann Arbor: University of Michigan Press.

Schmitter, Philippe C. 1974. "Still the Century of Corporatism?" *The Review of Politics* 36 (1): 85–131.

Scott, James C. 1985. *Weapons of the Weak: Everyday Forms of Peasant Resistance.* New Haven, CT: Yale University Press.

Segal, Lauren, and Sharon Cort. 2012. *One Law, One Nation: The Making of the South African Constitution.* Auckland Park: Jacana Media.

Sieder, Rachel, L. Schjolden, and A. Angell, eds. 2011. *The Judicialization of Politics in Latin America.* 2005th edition. New York, NY: Palgrave Macmillan.

Silbey, Susan. 2005. "After Legal Consciousness." *Annual Review of Law and Social Science* 1 (1): 323–68.

Simmons, Erica S. 2014. "Grievances Do Matter in Mobilization." *Theory and Society* 43 (5): 513–46.

2016. *Meaningful Resistance: Market Reforms and the Roots of Social Protest in Latin America.* Cambridge, UK: Cambridge University Press.

Singh, Prerna. 2017. *How Solidarity Works for Welfare: Subnationalism and Social Development in India.* Cambridge, UK: Cambridge University Press.

Singh Grewal, David, and Jedediah Purdy. 2014. "Introduction: Law and Neoliberalism." *Law and Contemporary Problems* 77 (4): 1–23.

Smith, Nicholas Rush. 2015. "Rejecting Rights: Vigilantism and Violence in Post-Apartheid South Africa." *African Affairs* 114 (456): 341–60.

2019. *Contradictions of Democracy: Vigilantism and Rights in Post-Apartheid South Africa.* New York: Oxford University Press.

Soss, Joe, and Vesla Weaver. 2017. "Police Are Our Government: Politics, Political Science, and the Policing of Race-Class Subjugated Communities." *Annual Review of Political Science* 20: 565–91.

South African History Online. "Chapter 13 - The Public Participation Process." www.sahistory.org.za/archive/chapter-13-public-participation-process

Sparks, Allister. 1995. *Tomorrow Is Another Country: The Inside Story of South Africa's Road to Change*. Chicago: University of Chicago Press.

Statistics South Africa. 2017. "Poverty Trends in South Africa: An Examination of Absolute Poverty Between 2006 and 2015." *Report No. 03–10–06*. On file with author.

Stokes, Susan Carol. 2013. *Brokers, Voters, and Clientelism: The Puzzle of Distributive Politics*. Cambridge, UK: Cambridge University Press.

Sutorius, Mies, and Sonia Rodríguez. 2015. "La fundamentalidad del derecho al agua en Colombia." *Revista Derecho del Estado* (35): 243.

Swenson, Peter A. 2002. *Capitalists against Markets: The Making of Labor Markets and Welfare States in the United States and Sweden*. Oxford: Oxford University Press.

Tait, Kira. 2022. "The Power of Perspectives: Thinkability as an Approach to Understanding Legal Mobilization." Unpublished manuscript. On file with author.

Tait, Kira, and Whitney K. Taylor. 2022. "The Possibility of Rights Claim-Making in Court: Looking Back on Twenty-Five Years of Social Rights Constitutionalism in South Africa." *Law & Social Inquiry*.

Tate, Winifred. 2007. *Counting the Dead: The Culture and Politics of Human Rights Activism in Colombia*. Berkeley, CA: University of California Press.

Taylor, Whitney K. 2018. "Ambivalent Legal Mobilization: Perceptions of Justice and the Use of the Tutela in Colombia." *Law & Society Review* 52 (2), 337–67.

2020a. "On the Social Construction of Legal Grievances: Evidence from Colombia and South Africa." *Comparative Political Studies* 53 (8), 1326–56.

2020b. "Constitutional Rights and Social Welfare: Exploring Claims-Making Practices in Post-Apartheid South Africa." *Comparative Politics* 53 (1): 25–48.

Forthcoming. "Judicial Agency and the Adjudication of Social Rights." *Human Rights Quarterly*.

Thompson, E. P. 1975. *Whigs and Hunters*. London: Breviary Stuff Publications.

Tilly, Charles. 1990. *Coercion, Capital, and European States, AD 990–1990*. Hoboken, NJ: Wiley.

Uprimny, Rodrigo. 2005. *LA JUSTICIA COLOMBIANA EN LA ENCRUCIJADA*. www.dejusticia.org/en/the-crossroads-of-justice/.

2007. "Judicialization of Politics in Colombia." *Sur - International Journal on Human Rights* (6). https://sur.conectas.org/en/judicialization XE "judicialization" -politics-colombia/.

2011. *COUNTRIES AT THE CROSSROADS*. https://freedomhouse.org/sites/default/files/inline_images/COLOMBIAFINAL.pdf.

Uprimny, Rodrigo, and Juanita Durán. 2014. "Equidad y protección judicial del derecho a la salud en Colombia," 197 *CEPAL – Serie Políticas Sociales*.

UN-Habitat. 2013. *Prosperity of Cities: The State of the World's Cities*. New York: Routledge.

Valencia Lomelí, Enrique. 2008. "Conditional Cash Transfers as Social Policy in Latin America: An Assessment of Their Contributions and Limitations." *Annual Review of Sociology* 34 (1): 475–99.

Van Cott, Donna. 2000. *The Friendly Liquidation of the Past: The Politics of Diversity in Latin America*. Pittsburgh: University of Pittsburgh Press.

Vanhala, Lisa. 2010. *Making Rights a Reality?: Disability Rights Activists and Legal Mobilization*. Cambridge, UK: Cambridge University Press.

2011. "Legal Mobilization." www.oxfordbibliographies.com/display/id/obo-9780199756223-0031.

2016. "Legal Mobilization under Neo-Corporatist Governance: Environmental NGOs before the Conseil d'Etat in France, 1975–2010." *Journal of Law and Courts* 4 (1): 103–30.

2018a. "Shaping the Structure of Legal Opportunities: Environmental NGOs Bringing International Environmental Procedural Rights Back Home: Shaping the Structure of Legal Opportunities." *Law & Policy* 40 (1): 110–27.

2018b. "Is Legal Mobilization for the Birds? Legal Opportunity Structures and Environmental Nongovernmental Organizations in the United Kingdom, France, Finland, and Italy." *Comparative Political Studies* 51 (3): 380–412.

Versteeg, Mila, and Emily Zackin. 2016. "Constitutions Unentrenched: Toward an Alternative Theory of Constitutional Design." *American Political Science Review* 110 (4): 657–74.

Voytas, Elsa, and Benjamin Crisman. (forthcoming). "State Violence and Participation in Transitional Justice: Evidence from Colombia." *Journal of Peace Research* https://drive.google.com/file/d/1MTSsICqDdYqAV-7Vbre-3az4xDHNNeEX/view

Weyland, Kurt. 1996. *Democracy without Equity: Failures of Reform in Brazil*. Pittsburgh: University of Pittsburgh Press.

Whiting, Susan H. 2017. "Authoritarian 'Rule of Law' and Regime Legitimacy." *Comparative Political Studies* 50 (14): 1907–40.

Forthcoming. *Illiberal Law and Development: Property Rights and Conflict over Land in China*.

Wilfahrt, Martha. 2018. "Precolonial Legacies and Institutional Congruence in Public Goods Delivery." *World Politics* 70 (2): 239–74.

Williamson, John. 2004. "A Short History of the Washington Consensus." Paper commissioned by Fundación CIDOB for a conference "From the

Washington Consensus towards a new Global Governance," Barcelona, September 24–25, 2004.

Wilson, Bruce M. 2009. "Institutional Reform and Rights Revolutions in Latin America: The Cases of Costa Rica and Colombia." *Journal of Politics in Latin America* 1 (2): 59–85.

Wilson, Bruce M., and Camila Gianella-Malca. 2019. "Overcoming the Limits of Legal Opportunity Structures: LGBT Rights' Divergent Paths in Costa Rica and Colombia." *Latin American Politics and Society* 61 (2): 138–63.

Wood, Geof, and Ian Gough. 2006. "A Comparative Welfare Regime Approach to Global Social Policy." *World Development* 34 (10): 1696–712.

Yamin, Alicia Ely, and Oscar Parra-Vera. 2009. "How Do Courts Set Health Policy? The Case of the Colombian Constitutional Court." *PLoS Medicine* 6 (2).

Yashar, Deborah J. 1999. "Democracy, Indigenous Movements, and Postliberal Challenge in Latin America." *World Politics* 52 (1): 76–104.

2005. *Contesting Citizenship in Latin America: The Rise of Indigenous Movements and the Postliberal Challenge*. Cambridge, UK: Cambridge University Press.

Zemans, Frances Kahn. 1983. "Legal Mobilization: The Neglected Role of the Law in the Political System." *American Political Science Review* 77 (3): 690–703.

Zuern, Elke. 2011. *The Politics of Necessity: Community Organizing and Democracy in South Africa*. Madison, WI: University of Wisconsin Press.

INDEX

CAMBRIDGE STUDIES IN LAW AND SOCIETY

Books in the Series

Diseases of the Will: Alcohol and the Dilemmas of Freedom
Mariana Valverde

The Politics of Truth and Reconciliation in South Africa: Legitimizing the Post-Apartheid State
Richard A. Wilson

Modernism and the Grounds of Law
Peter Fitzpatrick

Unemployment and Government: Genealogies of the Social
William Walters

Autonomy and Ethnicity: Negotiating Competing Claims in Multi-Ethnic States
Yash Ghai

Constituting Democracy: Law, Globalism and South Africa's Political Reconstruction
Heinz Klug

The Ritual of Rights in Japan: Law, Society, and Health Policy
Eric A. Feldman

Governing Morals: A Social History of Moral Regulation
Alan Hunt

The Colonies of Law: Colonialism, Zionism and Law in Early Mandate Palestine
Ronen Shamir

Law and Nature
David Delaney

Social Citizenship and Workfare in the United States and Western Europe: The Paradox of Inclusion
Joel F. Handler

Law, Anthropology, and the Constitution of the Social: Making Persons and Things
Edited by Alain Pottage and Martha Mundy

Judicial Review and Bureaucratic Impact: International and Interdisciplinary Perspectives
Edited by Marc Hertogh and Simon Halliday

Immigrants at the Margins: Law, Race, and Exclusion in Southern Europe
Kitty Calavita

Lawyers and Regulation: The Politics of the Administrative Process
Patrick Schmidt

Law and Globalization from Below: Towards a Cosmopolitan Legality
Edited by Boaventura de Sousa Santos and César A. Rodríguez-Garavito

Public Accountability: Designs, Dilemmas and Experiences
Edited by Michael W. Dowdle

Law, Violence and Sovereignty among West Bank Palestinians
Tobias Kelly

Legal Reform and Administrative Detention Powers in China
Sarah Biddulph

The Practice of Human Rights: Tracking Law between the Global and the Local
Edited by Mark Goodale and Sally Engle Merry

Judges beyond Politics in Democracy and Dictatorship: Lessons from Chile
Lisa Hilbink

Paths to International Justice: Social and Legal Perspectives
Edited by Marie-Bénédicte Dembour and Tobias Kelly

Law and Society in Vietnam: The Transition from Socialism in Comparative Perspective
Mark Sidel

Constitutionalizing Economic Globalization: Investment Rules and Democracy's Promise
David Schneiderman

The New World Trade Organization Knowledge Agreements: Second Edition
Christopher Arup

Justice and Reconciliation in Post-Apartheid South Africa
Edited by François du Bois and Antje du Bois-Pedain

Militarization and Violence against Women in Conflict Zones in the Middle East: A Palestinian Case-Study
Nadera Shalhoub-Kevorkian

Child Pornography and Sexual Grooming: Legal and Societal Responses
Suzanne Ost

Darfur and the Crime of Genocide
John Hagan and Wenona Rymond-Richmond

Fictions of Justice: The International Criminal Court and the Challenge of Legal Pluralism in Sub-Saharan Africa
Kamari Maxine Clarke

Conducting Law and Society Research: Reflections on Methods and Practices
Simon Halliday and Patrick Schmidt

Planted Flags: Trees, Land, and Law in Israel/Palestine
Irus Braverman

Culture under Cross-Examination: International Justice and the Special Court for Sierra Leone
Tim Kelsall

Cultures of Legality: Judicialization and Political Activism in Latin America
Javier Couso, Alexandra Huneeus, and Rachel Sieder

Courting Democracy in Bosnia and Herzegovina: The Hague Tribunal's Impact in a Postwar State
Lara J. Nettelfield

The Gacaca Courts, Post-Genocide Justice and Reconciliation in Rwanda: Justice without Lawyers
Phil Clark

Law, Society, and History: Themes in the Legal Sociology and Legal History of Lawrence M. Friedman
Edited by Robert W. Gordon and Morton J. Horwitz

After Abu Ghraib: Exploring Human Rights in America and the Middle East
Shadi Mokhtari

Adjudication in Religious Family Laws: Cultural Accommodation, Legal Pluralism, and Gender Equality in India
Gopika Solanki

Water on Tap: Rights and Regulation in the Transnational Governance of Urban Water Services
Bronwen Morgan

Elements of Moral Cognition: Rawls' Linguistic Analogy and the Cognitive Science of Moral and Legal Judgment
John Mikhail

Mitigation and Aggravation at Sentencing
Edited by Julian V. Roberts

Institutional Inequality and the Mobilization of the Family and Medical Leave Act: Rights on Leave
Catherine R. Albiston

Authoritarian Rule of Law: Legislation, Discourse and Legitimacy in Singapore
Jothie Rajah

Law and Development and the Global Discourses of Legal Transfers
Edited by John Gillespie and Pip Nicholson

Law against the State: Ethnographic Forays into Law's Transformations
Edited by Julia Eckert, Brian Donahoe, Christian Strümpell and Zerrin Özlem Biner

Transnational Legal Ordering and State Change
Edited by Gregory C. Shaffer

Legal Mobilization under Authoritarianism: The Case of Post-Colonial Hong Kong
Waikeung Tam

Complementarity in the Line of Fire: The Catalysing Effect of the International Criminal Court in Uganda and Sudan
Sarah M. H. Nouwen

Political and Legal Transformations of an Indonesian Polity: The Nagari from Colonisation to Decentralisation
Franz von Benda-Beckmann and Keebet von Benda-Beckmann

Pakistan's Experience with Formal Law: An Alien Justice
Osama Siddique

Human Rights under State-Enforced Religious Family Laws in Israel, Egypt, and India
Yüksel Sezgin

Why Prison?
Edited by David Scott

Law's Fragile State: Colonial, Authoritarian, and Humanitarian Legacies in Sudan
Mark Fathi Massoud

Rights for Others: The Slow Home-Coming of Human Rights in the Netherlands
Barbara Oomen

European States and Their Muslim Citizens: The Impact of Institutions on Perceptions and Boundaries
Edited by John R. Bowen, Christophe Bertossi, Jan Willem Duyvendak, and Mona Lena Krook

Environmental Litigation in China: A Study in Political Ambivalence
Rachel E. Stern

Indigeneity and Legal Pluralism in India: Claims, Histories, Meanings
Pooja Parmar

Paper Tiger: Law, Bureaucracy and the Developmental State in Himalayan India
Nayanika Mathur

Religion, Law and Society
Russell Sandberg

The Experiences of Face Veil Wearers in Europe and the Law
Edited by Eva Brems

The Contentious History of the International Bill of Human Rights
Christopher N. J. Roberts

Transnational Legal Orders
Edited by Terence C. Halliday and Gregory Shaffer

Lost in China? Law, Culture and Society in Post-1997 Hong Kong
Carol A. G. Jones

Security Theology, Surveillance and the Politics of Fear
Nadera Shalhoub-Kevorkian

Opposing the Rule of Law: How Myanmar's Courts Make Law and Order
Nick Cheesman

Ironies of Colonial Governance: Law, Custom and Justice in Colonial India
James Jaffe

The Clinic and the Court: Law, Medicine and Anthropology
Edited by Ian Harper, Tobias Kelly, and Akshay Khanna

The World of Indicators: The Making of Government Knowledge through Quantification
Edited by Richard Rottenburg, Sally E. Merry, Sung-Joon Park, and Johanna Mugler

Contesting Immigration Policy in Court: Legal Activism and Its Radiating Effects in the United States and France
Leila Kawar

The Quiet Power of Indicators: Measuring Governance, Corruption, and Rule of Law
Edited by Sally Engle Merry, Kevin E. Davis, and Benedict Kingsbury

Investing in Authoritarian Rule: Punishment and Patronage in Rwanda's Gacaca Courts for Genocide Crimes
Anuradha Chakravarty

Contractual Knowledge: One Hundred Years of Legal Experimentation in Global Markets
Edited by Grégoire Mallard and Jérôme Sgard

Iraq and the Crimes of Aggressive War: The Legal Cynicism of Criminal Militarism
John Hagan, Joshua Kaiser, and Anna Hanson

Culture in the Domains of Law
Edited by René Provost

China and Islam: The Prophet, the Party, and Law
Matthew S. Erie

Diversity in Practice: Race, Gender, and Class in Legal and Professional Careers
Edited by Spencer Headworth, Robert L. Nelson, Ronit Dinovitzer, and David B. Wilkins

A Sociology of Constitutions: Constitutions and State Legitimacy in Historical-Sociological Perspective
Chris Thornhill

A Sociology of Transnational Constitutions: Social Foundations of the Post-National Legal Structure
Chris Thornhill

Genocide Never Sleeps: Living Law at the International Criminal Tribunal for Rwanda
Nigel Eltringham

Shifting Legal Visions: Judicial Change and Human Rights Trials in Latin America
Ezequiel A. González-Ocantos

The Demographic Transformations of Citizenship
Heli Askola

Criminal Defense in China: The Politics of Lawyers at Work
Sida Liu and Terence C. Halliday

Contesting Economic and Social Rights in Ireland: Constitution, State and Society, 1848–2016
Thomas Murray

Buried in the Heart: Women, Complex Victimhood and the War in Northern Uganda
Erin Baines

Palaces of Hope: The Anthropology of Global Organizations
Edited by Ronald Niezen and Maria Sapignoli

The Politics of Bureaucratic Corruption in Post-Transitional Eastern Europe
Marina Zaloznaya

Revisiting the Law and Governance of Trafficking, Forced Labor and Modern Slavery
Edited by Prabha Kotiswaran

Incitement on Trial: Prosecuting International Speech Crimes
Richard Ashby Wilson

Criminalizing Children: Welfare and the State in Australia
David McCallum

Global Lawmakers: International Organizations in the Crafting of World Markets
Susan Block-Lieb and Terence C. Halliday

Duties to Care: Dementia, Relationality and Law
Rosie Harding

Insiders, Outsiders, Injuries, and Law: Revisiting "The Oven Bird's Song"
Edited by Mary Nell Trautner

Hunting Justice: Displacement, Law, and Activism in the Kalahari
Maria Sapignoli

Injury and Injustice: The Cultural Politics of Harm and Redress
Edited by Anne Bloom, David M. Engel, and Michael McCann

Ruling Before the Law: The Politics of Legal Regimes in China and Indonesia
William Hurst

The Powers of Law: A Comparative Analysis of Sociopolitical Legal Studies
Mauricio García-Villegas

A Sociology of Justice in Russia
Edited by Marina Kurkchiyan and Agnieszka Kubal

Constituting Religion: Islam, Liberal Rights, and the Malaysian State
Tamir Moustafa

The Invention of the Passport: Surveillance, Citizenship and the State, Second Edition
John C. Torpey

Law's Trials: The Performance of Legal Institutions in the US "War on Terror"
Richard L. Abel

Law's Wars: The Fate of the Rule of Law in the US "War on Terror"
Richard L. Abel

Transforming Gender Citizenship: The Irresistible Rise of Gender Quotas in Europe
Edited by Eléonore Lépinard and Ruth Rubio-Marín

Muslim Women's Quest for Justice: Gender, Law and Activism in India
Mengia Hong Tschalaer

Children as 'Risk': Sexual Exploitation and Abuse by Children and Young People
Anne-Marie McAlinden

The Legal Process and the Promise of Justice: Studies Inspired by the Work of Malcolm Feeley
Jonathan Simon, Rosann Greenspan, Hadar Aviram

Gift Exchanges: The Transnational History of a Political Idea
Grégoire Mallard

Measuring Justice: Quantitative Accountability and the National Prosecuting Authority in South Africa
Johanna Mugler

Negotiating the Power of NGOs: Women's Legal Rights in South Africa
Reem Wael

Indigenous Water Rights in Law and Regulation: Lessons from Comparative Experience
Elizabeth Jane Macpherson

The Edge of Law: Legal Geographies of a War Crimes Court
Alex Jeffrey

Everyday Justice: Law, Ethnography, and Injustice
Sandra Brunnegger

The Uncounted: Politics of Data in Global Health
Sara L. M. Davis

Transnational Legal Ordering of Criminal Justice
Gregory Shaffer and Ely Aaronson

Five Republics and One Tradition
Pablo Ruiz-Tagle

The Law Multiple: Judgment and Knowledge in Practice
Irene van Oorschot

Health as a Human Right: The Politics and Judicialisation of Health in Brazil
Octávio Luiz Motta Ferraz

Shari'a, Inshallah: Finding God in Somali Legal Politics
Mark Fathi Massoud

Policing for Peace: Institutions, Expectations, and Security in Divided Societies
Matthew Nanes

Rule of Law Intermediaries: Brokering Influence in Myanmar
Kristina Simion

Lactation at Work: Expressed Milk, Expressing Beliefs, and the Expressive Value of Law
Elizabeth A. Hoffmann

The Archival Politics of International Courts
Henry Redwood

Global Pro Bono: Causes, Context, and Contestation
Edited by Scott L. Cummings, Fabio de Sa e Silva and Louise G. Trubek

The Practice and Problems of Transnational Counter-Terrorism
Fiona de Londras

Decoupling: Gender Injustice in China's Divorce Courts
Ethan Michelson

Anti-Constitutional Populism
Martin Krygier, Adam Czarnota and Wojciech Sadurski

The Ghostwriters: Lawyers and the Politics behind the Judicial Construction of Europe
Tommaso Pavone

The Sentimental Court: The Affective Life of International Criminal Justice
Jonas Bens

Practices of Reparations in International Criminal Justice
Christoph Sperfeldt

Seeking Supremacy: The Pursuit of Judicial Power in Pakistan
Yasser Kureshi

The Power of the Jury: Transforming Citizens into Jurors
Nancy S. Marder

Undue Process: Persecution and Punishment in Autocratic Courts
Fiona Feiang Shen-Bayh

Discounting Life: Necropolitical Law, Culture, and the Long War on Terror
Jothie Rajah

Clean Air at What Cost? The Rise of Blunt Force Regulation in China
Denise Sienli van der Kamp

Law and Precarity: Legal Consciousness and Daily Survival in Vietnam
Tu Phuong Nguyen

Prosecutors, Voters and The Criminalization of Corruption in Latin America: The Case of Lava Jato
Ezequiel A. Gonzalez-Ocantos and Paula Muñoz Chirinos

Entangled Domains: Empire, Law and Religion in Northern Nigeria
Rabiat Akande

Printed in the USA
CPSIA information can be obtained
at www.ICGtesting.com
CBHW051746040924
14056CB00004B/103

9 781009 367769